teach
yourself

Dreamweaver CS3
iain tench

Launched in 1938, the **teach yourself** series grew rapidly in response to the world's wartime needs. Loved and trusted by over 50 million readers, the series has continued to respond to society's changing interests and passions and now, 70 years on, includes over 500 titles, from Arabic and Beekeeping to Yoga and Zulu. What would you like to learn?

Be where you want to be with **teach yourself**

For UK order enquiries: please contact Bookpoint Ltd, 130 Milton Park, Abingdon, Oxon OX14 4SB. Telephone: +44 (0)1235 827720. Fax: +44 (0)1235 400454. Lines are open 09.00–17.00, Monday to Saturday, with a 24-hour message answering service. Details about our titles and how to order are available at www.teachyourself.co.uk.

For USA order enquiries: please contact McGraw-Hill Customer Services, PO Box 545, Blacklick, OH 43004-0545, USA. Telephone: 1-800-722-4726. Fax: 1-614-755-5645.

For Canada order enquiries: please contact McGraw-Hill Ryerson Ltd, 300 Water St, Whitby, Ontario L1N 9B6, Canada. Telephone: 905 430 5000. Fax: 905 430 5020.

Long renowned as the authoritative source for self-guided learning – with more than 50 million copies sold worldwide – the **teach yourself** series includes over 500 titles in the fields of languages, crafts, hobbies, business, computing and education.

British Library Cataloguing in Publication Data: a catalogue record for this title is available from The British Library.

Library of Congress Catalog Card Number: on file.

First published in UK 2008 by Hodder Education, part of Hachette Livre UK, 338 Euston Road, London NW1 3BH.

First published in USA 2008 by The McGraw-Hill Companies Inc.

The **teach yourself** name is a registered trademark of Hodder Headline.

Computer hardware and software brand names mentioned in this book are protected by their respective trademarks and are acknowledged.

The publisher has used its best endeavours to ensure that the URLs for external websites referred to in this book are correct and active at the time of going to press. However, the publisher has no responsibility for the websites and can give no guarantee that a site will remain live or that the content is or will remain appropriate.

Typeset by Mac Bride, Southampton

Printed in Great Britain for Hodder Education, an Hachette Livre UK Company, 338 Euston Road, London NW1 3BH, by CPI Cox & Wyman, Reading, Berkshire RG1 8EX.

Hachette Livre UK's policy is to use papers that are natural, renewable and recyclable products and made from wood grown in sustainable forests. The logging and manufacturing processes are expected to conform to the environmental regulations of the country of origin.

Impression number   10 9 8 7 6 5 4 3 2 1

Year   2011 2010 2009 2008

iii

contents

preface   vii

01 introduction   1
What is Dreamweaver?   2
What else might I need?   6
Navigation in Dreamweaver   8
The Dreamweaver workspace   10
Help   17
Rulers, page sizes and general preferences   19
The Status bar   19

02 building your first site   **22**
What is a site?   23
What do I need and from where?   26
Page content and site plan   27
Creating a site   27
Creating pages   31
Standard toolbar   35
Remembering where you left off   37
Page title   38
Adding content   38
Importing text into Dreamweaver   39
Displaying pages in a browser   40
Browser usage   42

03 HTML   **44**
Introduction   45
HTML – the language   45
What is XHTML?   48
Dreamweaver and (X)HTML   49
Tags and attributes   50
Fonts   51

04 **text and images**   **57**
An overview of the Properties panel   58
Page Properties   60
Choosing a font   63
Fonts   64
Changing the font properties   66
Lists   70
Using special characters   71
Colour and Dreamweaver   72
Images   74
Adding images to the page   75
Positioning and configuring images   81
Image editing   83
Integration with Photoshop   87
Create a Web photo album   88
Image placeholders   90
Adding other media   91
Undo, redo and the history panel   96

05 **links**   **100**
What is a hyperlink?   101
Standard link   101
Dreamweaver's navigation bar   106
External site links   107
Anchor links   108
Email links   111
Attaching links to images   112
Flash buttons   113
Flash text   116
Hotspots   118
Site map   120

06 **tables**   **122**
Should I be using tables?   123
Terminology   124
Table usage   124
Table sizing   124
Adding a table   125
Other table format options   130
Nesting tables   135
Deleting rows and columns   136
Practical application   136
Adding to the table   142
Layout mode   143

07	CSS	150
	Introduction	151
	CSS – an overview	151
	The syntax of CSS	153
	Methods of applying CSS	159
	Applying CSS	161
	Style sheets – creating and attaching	166
	Class and advanced rules	168
	CSS properties in Dreamweaver	180
	Box	185
	Style sheets for different media	190
	Predefined CSS	193
	Creating your own CSS layout	200
08	**forms**	**208**
	The purpose of forms	209
	What does a form contain?	209
	Creating a form	211
	Formatting a form	221
	Form validation	222
	Making your form more user-friendly	233
09	**behaviors**	**235**
	Introduction	236
	What is a behavior?	236
	Why use behaviors?	237
	Adding a behavior	237
	Popup message	239
	Rollover images	240
	Disjointed rollover	241
	Disjointed rollover – a variation	243
	Show-hide elements	245
	AP Div and a standard <div> tag	246
	Overlapping AP Elements	250
	Draggable elements	253
	Animation	256
	Controlling the animation	259
	Open new browser window	262
	Status bar message	264
	Text field text	265
	Spry effects	265
10	**templates**	**269**
	Introduction	270
	Template components	270
	Creating a template	270

	Editable regions	273
	CSS	274
	Creating pages from a template	275
	Changing a template	276
	Changing an attribute	278
	Other template features	279
	Detaching pages from templates	284
	Attaching pages to templates	284
	Library items	284
	Removing a library item from a page	286
11	**spry**	**289**
	Introduction	290
	Spry widgets	290
	Spry panels	290
	Spry validation	295
	Spry Menu Bar	304
	Displaying data	306
12	**going live**	**319**
	Preparing your site	320
	Checking spelling	320
	Broken links	321
	Browser compatibility	322
	Accessibility	323
	Amending the site definition	324
	Uploading the site	327
	Checking the uploaded site	328
	Retrieving files	330
	Synchronizing folders	331
	appendices	**337**
	A: Useful resources	337
	B: What next?	340
	C: Answers to exercises	341
	index	**355**

preface

Is this book for you?

The target audience for this book is those who have not used Dreamweaver before or have used it but in a slightly unstructured fashion. Intermediate users familiar with earlier versions should find much to read in this book, as there are some features of Dreamweaver CS3 which you will not have encountered in earlier versions, principally Spry.

What is in this book?

The focus of this book is on the practicalities of using Dreamweaver from your initial idea for a website through to its implementation on the Web. The chapters are not intended to represent mandatory steps in the creation of a web page or a site. The idea is to give you an overall feel for the major functionality of Dreamweaver, with examples as we progress. As far as possible, there are screenshots covering all actions.

There is also a background theme, aimed at getting a sample site up and running. The theme is 'your company' and is based on the assumption that you wish to set up a site selling/marketing your services. At several points, we will look at specific areas of the site in conjunction with new topics so that you may develop your site as you progress with the book, if you wish.

What is not in this book

As this book is aimed principally at novice users, the content focuses on getting you up and running with the creation of basic sites. The most obvious feature which is not covered in this book is the creation of database-driven sites. This is too advanced a topic to cover here, requiring as it does a good knowledge of database technologies as well as a solid understanding of the fundamentals of Dreamweaver.

What skills and knowledge do you need?

You obviously have a strong desire to develop websites, or even a single site, using professional software (Dreamweaver). You are not deterred by working largely on your own using this book and the various Help facilities described in later chapters. Of course you need to be keen to learn and, as with any new subject, willing to accept that at times you will encounter what may seem like insurmountable problems which, and you will have to take my word for this, will almost always have a solution – either one you work out for yourself (using the book and Dreamweaver's Help) or one you find via Internet help, colleagues, etc.

It is helpful to have an appreciation of the Web and perhaps some notions, or opinions, about web design. As a web user, you are bound to have opinions about which sites you prefer and why – this will be a useful guide when you develop your own. I am not suggesting that you copy someone else's design but we are all influenced to some extent by other designs, particularly as to what works and what does not.

01

introduction

In this chapter you will learn:

- what Dreamweaver is and how it can help you
- whether it is suitable for you
- what type of computer you need
- what else you need and what else you need to know
- about the Dreamweaver workspace

What is Dreamweaver?

Dreamweaver is a program that will help you to create, develop and manage websites, from the simple to the complex. It is extremely feature-rich and continues to evolve with each release to incorporate the latest features beneficial to web designers and developers. Originally produced by Macromedia, it is now an Adobe product (**http://www.adobe.com/products/dreamweaver**) alongside other well-known software such as Photoshop, Flash and Illustrator. The official term for the collected Adobe products is the Adobe Creative Suite (hence the CS in CS3 which stands for Creative Suite).

Through its extensive functionality, Dreamweaver provides you with the means of creating websites without the need to know underlying technologies such as HTML (Hyper Text Markup Language, which is the building block of web pages); Dreamweaver produces HTML for you, based on program options you select. As HTML is of such fundamental importance in building web pages, we will consider later in this chapter whether you need to know HTML when using Dreamweaver.

What does Dreamweaver CS3 provide?

This book is about Dreamweaver CS3. Previous versions that you might have encountered include MX, MX 2004 and 8. CS3 is the latest version of this highly popular software program and includes a number of valuable new features, such as:

- Integration with other Adobe software such as Photoshop

- Improved CSS (Cascading Style Sheets) support

- Enhanced interactivity using Spry.

With these latest enhancements Dreamweaver continues to justify its leading role in the web developer's armoury.

Where do I get it?

You might be an existing Dreamweaver user or you may not have used the software before. In either case, it makes sense to 'try before you buy'. Adobe offers a downloadable 30-day trial version of CS3 – however, it is 285MB for a Windows machine or 613MB for a Mac so you will need a pretty fast Internet connection. You may be lucky and manage to obtain an evaluation edition from a computer magazine's cover CD.

As an alternative, and to save download time, you might consider purchasing the trial versions on DVD; the DVD editions also include other Adobe trial versions – see **http://www.adobe.com/ products/creativesuite/web/trial/** for more details. At the time of writing, trial packages incorporating CS3 (Web Premium and Web Standard) may be purchased for $9.99 (around £5).

Once you have evaluated the software and determined that it is what you want, there are different purchase options available. These depend on a number of factors, e.g. whether you are a student, whether you want to buy just Dreamweaver or an Adobe package and whether you are buying a brand new licence or upgrading from a previous version.

One difficult question is whether it is worth upgrading from an earlier version. The answer to this would depend on the version you currently use, how much use you make of Dreamweaver, the reason/s you are considering upgrading and your available budget. Generally speaking in the world of software, older versions are eventually 'matured' by a supplier – this means they no longer provide support. Certainly there is a case for keeping in step with the latest releases but this is not a strong reason for paying hundreds of pounds to do so.

You may already be aware that Dreamweaver is not cheap, nor are the Adobe packages that incorporate it. However, balanced against the cost are the potential increases in productivity in using software which takes a lot of the effort out of many aspects of website creation – I say 'many' because there is no software that will do everything. Therefore, you need to be clear that you do need the software. The list of benefits that follow might help to make up, or focus, your mind (this is a selective list and not by any means definitive), though ultimately you need to construct your own business case for raiding your financial coffers:

- Speeds up development by avoiding the need to write HTML or CSS.

- Allows the use of templates which simplify the creation and maintenance of your sites.

◆ Helps to make your site accessible to all users.

◆ Contains a vast range of functions enabling you to progress from simple, static sites to complex, dynamic ones.

◆ Provides extensive Help.

◆ Makes the process of publishing your site on the Web straight-forward.

Who uses Dreamweaver?

In short, anyone who wants to create a website. Websites can be extremely simple (comprising text and images only) or extremely complex (e-commerce using databases) and all points between; Dreamweaver can be used for the whole range of web development and is as suitable for beginners as it is for the more advanced user.

As a result of its continuing evolution over the years, Dreamweaver remains the software of choice for web professionals.

Is Dreamweaver for me?

If you want to develop a website of any size or complexity quickly, avoid the need to write any code (HTML, Javascript, etc.) and publish your site on the Web, then the answer is yes. Naturally, you will need to be able to afford to buy Dreamweaver CS3, so a fairly sizeable budget will be required depending on the version you go for. However, as with everything else in life, you get what you pay for.

Is there any comparable software?

Microsoft's Expression Web (**http://www.microsoft.com/expression/products/Overview.aspx?key=web**) partially supersedes their old warhorse FrontPage which was discontinued in 2008. Expression Web is aimed at professional web designers and is thus a direct competitor to Dreamweaver. Unlike Dreamweaver, though, it is available only for the Windows platform. A downloadable trial version is available, though at 350MB+ it is not for those with 56K dial-up modems!

There are other options such as the free, open source Nvu (**http://www.nvudev.com/**) but, in the main, the alternatives do not have anything like the breadth of Dreamweaver's functionality. In addition, Nvu does not appear to have been updated in the last 3 years; over the same period, Dreamweaver has introduced significant new functionality. The Nvu download is only around 6.5MB for Windows, so it does not cost much in time or bandwidth used to evaluate this package.

You could of course write the web page code (using languages such as HTML, CSS, Javascript, PHP, etc.) yourself with a text editor such as TextPad (**http://www.textpad.com/**), but this requires knowledge of the languages plus a great deal of additional time – the click of a Dreamweaver button can in many cases easily replace several lines of HTML, and many, many lines of Javascript.

Can I use it on a Macintosh?

There are versions of CS3 for Windows and Mac platforms.

Is my computer suitable?

Adobe sets these system requirements for Dreamweaver. Note the need for a DVD drive.

Windows

- Intel® Pentium® 4, Intel Centrino®, Intel Xeon®, or Intel Core™ Duo (or compatible) processor

- Microsoft® Windows® XP with Service Pack 2 or Windows Vista™ Home Premium, Business, Ultimate, or Enterprise (certified for 32-bit editions)

- 512MB of RAM

- 1GB of available hard-disk space (additional free space required during installation)

- 1024 ×768 monitor resolution with 16-bit video card

- DVD-ROM drive

- Internet or phone connection required for product activation

- Broadband Internet connection required for Adobe Stock Photos and other services.

Macintosh

- PowerPC® G4 or G5 or multicore Intel® processor

- Mac OS X v10.4.8–10.5 (Leopard)

- 512MB of RAM

- 1.4GB of available hard-disk space (additional free space required during installation)

- 1024 × 768 monitor resolution with 16-bit video card

- DVD-ROM drive

- Internet or phone connection required for product activation

- Broadband Internet connection required for Adobe Stock Photos and other services

How do I install the software?

Installation is very straightforward and even if you have no prior experience of software installation, you should have no problems. If you download a trial copy from Adobe's site, simply double-click the downloaded file and follow the on-screen instructions; there is no need to do anything other than click **Yes** or **OK**, unless you have more expertise and wish to customize the setup. If you then decide to purchase a licence, you need to do nothing more other than to insert your licence key when prompted to do so.

If installing the full software, you do need a DVD-ROM drive. Again, installation is straightforward but it may take considerable time to complete if you have purchased one of Adobe's packages.

What else might I need?

Initially, all you will need in addition to Dreamweaver are browsers. I say browsers (plural) because you should use more than one to test your site. Why do you need to do this? Because each browser has slightly different ideas of how to render (or display) a web page. Generally speaking this is not too much of an issue with HTML, but when CSS enters the equation it can become very significant.

For testing web pages on a Windows platform, I use Firefox, various versions of Internet Explorer (as there have been significant rendering variations in them), Opera and Safari. Each of these browsers has Windows and Mac versions.

The important point to make is that testing with one browser only is unwise. What happens if you test with, Internet Explorer only, and after going live you are made aware that Firefox users are having difficulty reading your pages? Irrespective of the quality and content of your site, the answer is you will probably alienate these visitors and lose them, perhaps forever.

Internet Explorer (IE) remains the most used, followed by Firefox. In the last few years, from a dominance indicated by 95%+ usage, IE has declined to around 70–80%. This reiterates the need to use more than just IE for your testing. Firefox usage continues to increase, with a current usage figure of around 15–20%.

Here are the addresses for download of those four browsers. There are others available – just type 'browsers' into Google.

Internet Explorer: **http://www.microsoft.com/windows/products/winfamily/ie/**

Mozilla Firefox: **http://www.mozilla.org/products/firefox/**

Opera: **http://www.opera.com/**

Safari: **http://www.apple.com/safari/**

You will find when you start looking into different browser versions that there have been some significant differences between versions of IE, particularly with regards to CSS support. Therefore, testing with versions of IE would be a good idea but this means you have to install separate versions – this can be done easily with the Multiple IE installer from Tredosoft's site; find the download link at the bottom of the page **http://tredosoft.com/Multiple_IE**. Note that this software is designed to run under Windows XP. Once installed, you can test with IE 5, 5.5 and 6 directly from Dreamweaver.

Browsershots (**http://browsershots.org/**) allows you to test a web page against a wide variety of browsers and versions running on Linux, Windows and Mac operating systems. Use is free but you do have to upload your page to the web first in order to use it.

What else do I need to know to use Dreamweaver?

I have often been asked whether it is important to know any HTML if Dreamweaver can generate it at the click of a menu selection. My answer is 'yes', for the very good reason that it may do things to your page that you had not expected and you want to look into what it has done and why. Though it is a highly evolved product, Dreamweaver is not immune from doing the unexpected – I hesitate to call them 'mistakes' because it is often in the eye of the beholder.

Although not a prerequisite to using Dreamweaver, you will find that a knowledge of HTML will help you. An excellent tutorial is available at W3 Schools **http://www.w3schools.com/html/**. I will cover some of the essentials of the language in Chapter 3.

Spelling

HTML uses US spellings for attributes e.g. color, center, behavior. Dreamweaver, being the product of a US company, does likewise. Please bear this in mind when you encounter any terms which have a UK and US spelling. The rule is always to use US spellings when working with HTML.

Navigation in Dreamweaver

There are different methods used to access Dreamweaver's functionality. These may be categorized as follows:

*   **Menu bar** – in common with many applications, Dreamweaver has a menu bar near the top of the page. In the book any references to the menu bar are shown in this way:

    Insert > Image Objects > Image Placeholder

    Where the > sign indicates the hierarchy, with **Insert** the first selection in the menu bar, followed by **Image Objects** and then **Image Placeholder**.

*   **Keystrokes** – in this book, they are shown in square brackets, e.g. **[Shift]** refers to the Shift key, **[T]** to the letter 'T' key.

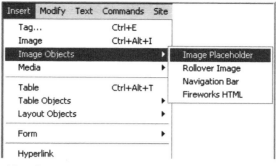

Figure 1.1 Menu bar example

◆ **Icons** – many of the actions that may be taken using the menu bar are possible using an icon in the Insert bar. Where there may be any doubt, references to icons are shown like this:

In the **Common** section of the **Insert** bar, click the **Image** icon ![icon].

Note that some icons also act as drop-down menus – in the above case, to more selections related to images. Click the icon to take the specified action or use the menu to select an alternative. The last option selected will be displayed for ease of use, so if, for example, you regularly use Image Placeholder, this icon will be displayed by default.

◆ **Button** – Dreamweaver uses buttons mainly as a means of confirming choices made in dialog boxes. A screenshot of the dialog box will be displayed where relevant. An example of a reference to button usage is shown like this:

After entering suitable **Text** and a relevant **E-Mail** address, click the **OK** button to save the link.

The Dreamweaver workspace

Dreamweaver is a complex software application which takes time to assimilate. It is not difficult, just that there is a great deal to it. On the assumption that you now have a copy of Dreamweaver and have installed it, let us have a look at the workspace to see what is available.

When you start Dreamweaver, you will see this screen:

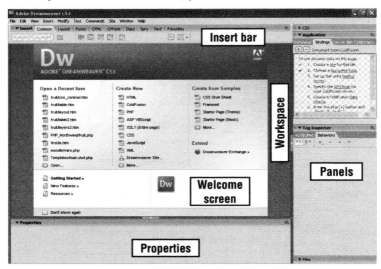

Figure 1.2 Dreamweaver start-up screen

We will take each segment of the screen in turn and look at the individual elements.

Insert bar

There are always at least three ways to carry out the same action in Dreamweaver! It would be impossible to cover every variation but generally speaking you have a choice of using the Insert bar, the menu bar, keyboard shortcuts or menus within individual panels. The starting point for most actions should be the Insert bar as it presents, in graphical format, a wide range of functions.

The Insert bar gives access to a selection of tabbed menus containing groups of commonly-used functions. For example, **Common**, as the name implies, covers many of the functions you will use most often such as inserting images, creating hyperlinks and inserting tables.

You will note that on hovering over an icon in the Insert bar you will see a popup which indicates its purpose. For example, hovering over the table icon shows the text **Table** (it might be better if it said 'Insert Table', but you will quickly come to recognise the purpose of icons without needing the text).

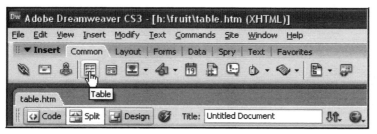

Figure 1.3   Example of popup text for toolbar icons

All of the functions you may use here may be replicated using the menu bar above the Insert bar. As an example, to insert a table, click **Insert** in the menu bar and then **Table** (or the third alternative is to use the displayed keyboard shortcut, in this case [Ctrl]+[Alt]+[T]).

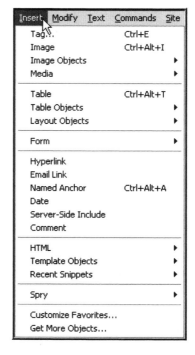

Figure 1.4   Replicating Insert bar action with the menu bar

Panels

The panels provide distinct areas for carrying out specific tasks, e.g. creating database connections, adding and updating CSS, working with site assets such as files and templates. The most important panel initially is the one labelled **Files**, which we will look at in detail later in this chapter.

The panels may be opened or closed by clicking the arrow to the left of the panel name.

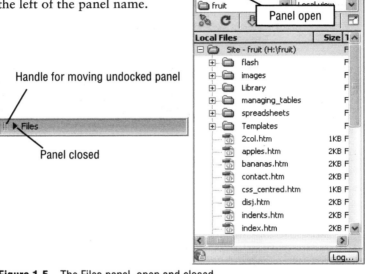

Handle for moving undocked panel

Panel closed

Figure 1.5 The Files panel, open and closed

Not all panels are automatically displayed, so if you need a particular panel, such as **Databases**, because you want to create a database connection, then go to the menu bar and click **Window** – click on the panel you want to see displayed and it will open.

If you need more space when working with panels, they may be un-docked by moving the mouse over the area next to the panel open/close arrow; when you see the cursor change to ⊕, you can then drag the panel anywhere you like on the page. Once undocked, you may resize the panel by dragging the borders until you have a workspace large enough for your needs. To redock, move the panel over the panel area and release the mouse – Dreamweaver will reposition the panel for you.

Docking and undocking

By default, everything is docked – that is, if you resize the Dreamweaver window on your computer, all workspace elements will also resize. Undocking means that you take one of the elements, such as a panel, and move it outside the unified workspace; it may then be resized individually and moved anywhere on your Desktop.

Welcome screen

This is a means, but not the only one, of starting to work with Dreamweaver. The Welcome screen will only appear when you start Dreamweaver.

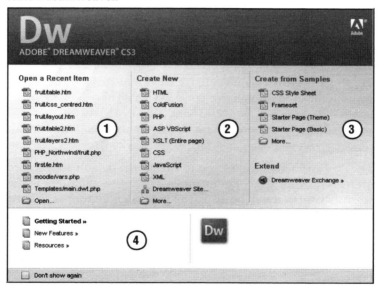

Figure 1.6 Welcome screen

1 Files you have worked with recently; click a name to re-open.

2 Create a new file with one of the specified types; HTML is best while you are still getting to grips with Dreamweaver.

3 Dreamweaver provides a number of ready-prepared template pages, which you may select here (we will look at templates in Chapter 10).

4 Links to further Help (this is also available from other places within Dreamweaver).

Workspace

This is referred to in Dreamweaver documentation as the document window. I prefer to refer to it as the workspace because this area is where you design your pages – there are different options available which we look at in 'Creating pages' on page 31.

To increase the available workspace, press [F4] which will remove everything except the workspace and menu bar; press [F4] again to restore the page to its original state.

 If you want to increase the workspace but retain everything except the panels on the right, click this pointer which is found between the workspace and panels.

Properties

The Properties area allows you to change how items are displayed without the need for you to change HTML. Though blank in the screenshot, you will notice as you use Dreamweaver that this area will change depending on what you are doing, and which elements you may have selected, in the workspace.

The Properties area allows you to change the default appearance of items on your page. For example, when you enter text in the workspace area it will be displayed in the default font as defined in the Fonts area of Preferences (it is defined as the proportional font). This is not necessarily the font that will be used when your page displays in a browser. To set the font you wish to use when the page displays, use the Properties dialog box to set your preference.

Workspace options

There are three options for the overall layout of Dreamweaver. These are accessible and changeable via **Window > Workspace Layout**. The three options are **Coder, Designer** and **Dual Screen**.

Coder and Designer look fairly similar, with the exception of the location of the panels – the emphasis, as the names suggest, is on user interfaces for those who are likely to be spending much of their time coding (Coder) or spending much of the time working with Dreamweaver's built-in functions (Designer). This book will be based on the Designer workspace, as this is the default as well as being the environment most suitable for your requirements as a new user.

Dual Screen is a much less structured interface, where panels are effectively floating. This is a hangover from older versions of Dreamweaver and is only likely to be of interest if you are used to working in this way and do not want to change. For new users, it is not recommended.

The following three screenshots show the same HTML page displayed using each of the workspace options – decide which one suits you best.

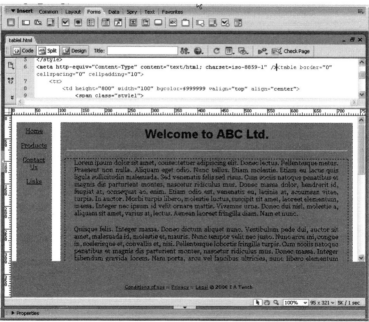

Figure 1.7   Coder layout

Figure 1.8　Designer layout (recommended)

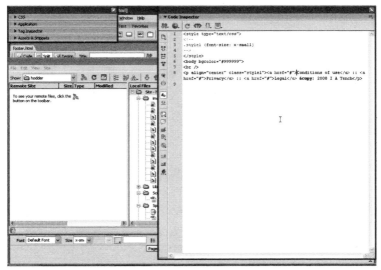

Figure 1.9　Dual Screen layout

Help

It is reassuring to know that there is extensive Help available with Dreamweaver, both within the product itself and on the Adobe website. As well as Help when you do not understand something, these resources also offer you access to tutorials, details of available training and free (as well as commercial) add-ons to increase further Dreamweaver's already extensive functionality.

Initially, Help may be accessed by pressing the function key [**F1**] or by clicking **Help** on the menu bar and selecting the type of Help you need. Note that the complete Dreamweaver Help file is available in PDF format from the Adobe site. If you want to print it, be aware that it is over 700 pages!

Context-sensitive Help is also available when you carry out many functions. For example, if you wish to add a table, as part of the table creation you will see this dialog box – click **Help** and you will be able to access more information specific to adding tables.

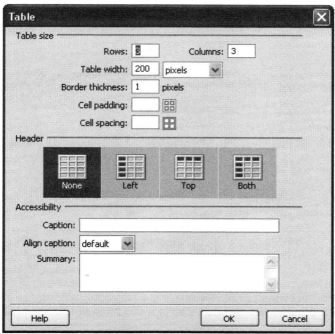

Figure 1.10   Insert table dialog box showing Help button at bottom left

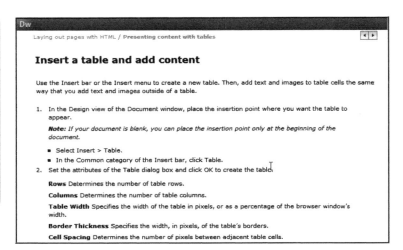

Figure 1.11 Information displayed after clicking Help

Help is also available in the form of reference documents. These may be accessed by selecting **Window > Reference** and then choosing the relevant book. It is possible to drill down further as in the following example.

Figure 1.12 Example showing HTML as the selected book

In this example, I wanted information about the HTML tag <strong>, which was selected from the Tag drop-down menu.

If all else fails...

On occasions, you will not be able to make any sense of what Dreamweaver is doing or of its error messages. If that is the case, I restart Dreamweaver. It is a very complex program so it does sometimes get itself in a twist. Restarting will often cure seemingly impossible-to-understand actions.

Rulers, page sizes and general preferences

Rulers are extremely helpful when you require precision with the contents of your page or if you simply need to see how much space elements occupy on the page. By default, rulers are turned off – to turn them on, click **View** in the menu bar followed by **Rulers** then **Show**. You can choose the measurement to be used, pixels being the default.

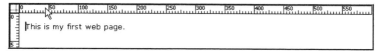

Figure 1.13   Rulers displayed in Design view

To turn rulers off, use **View > Rulers > Show**.

The Status bar

At the bottom of the Design panel is the Status bar. The first thing you notice is that an HTML tag or tags will appear at the left – in this case <body> indicates that this is the tag with focus in Design view. If you were to click <body>, Dreamweaver would select in Code and Design views all of the contents of the <body> tag. This is a useful means of identifying and selecting contents relevant to a particular tag.

The three icons for the **Select, Hand** and **Zoom** tools (see Figure 1.14) enable different actions within Design view. Select is the default, enabling selection of contents with the mouse. The Hand tool enables viewing of the page without scrolling – hold down the left mouse button and move the cursor up, down, left or right. The Zoom tool does what you think it might do – click the page in Design view and the size increases.

The drop-down menu alongside the Zoom tool, which shows a default page size of 100%, may be used to increase or decrease the visible page size. There is an indication alongside of the size, in this case 745 × 186 (pixels). To the far right, '1K / 1 sec' represents the page size in bytes followed by an estimated download time (i.e. the time taken between visitors requesting the page and the full page being displayed in their browser). A lot of information and functionality for such a small area of the workspace!

Select   Hand   Zoom

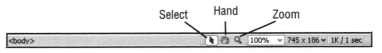

Figure 1.14   Design view footer

You will notice that if you click the drop-down menu holding the page size, all options are greyed out except **Edit Sizes...** which enables you to alter Dreamweaver's window size settings (if you really need to, which you probably do not). To demonstrate how we can view our page based on different screen sizes, what we need to do is first of all to 'undock' the workspace – to do this, click the Resize button in the header (to the far right of the tab containing the page name, not the Dreamweaver Resize button).

Figure 1.15   Design view header

You should now be 'undocked'. The intention is to simulate a page viewed on different monitors. Make sure you are working in Design view by selecting that option (i.e. switch from Split view). Press **[F4]** to remove panel displays. You can now try the drop-down again – select different options, e.g. 760 × 420 to see how your page will appear. Under no circumstances should your page include horizontal scrolling – if it does, you need to consider seriously changing your content; scrolling up and down is accepted but from side to side is not!

To return to Dreamweaver, press **[F4]** again to restore the panels and click the resize button to maximize the page – you should now be fully 'docked' again.

How to tell if you are docked or undocked

When docked, the whole Dreamweaver space is integrated – there are no floating panels, for example. When the workspace header is grey, this indicates docked status. If the workspace header changes to blue, this indicates undocked status.

Summary

Dreamweaver is a powerful program which gives you access to a wealth of functionality to create, release and maintain websites. Though not cheap, it has over the years proved its essential nature by remaining such a popular tool.

Throughout the rest of the book we will explore some of the major functions – exploring every facet of Dreamweaver's extensive functionality would require a book several times larger than this one!

Exercises

Before progressing, I strongly recommend that you ensure that you have successfully installed Dreamweaver CS3, together with (at least) two browsers – Firefox and Internet Explorer as a minimum.

To determine whether an application has been installed correctly, you need to be able to start and stop it.

To start Dreamweaver, click the Windows **Start** button and then select **All Programs**. Depending on which Adobe package you have installed determines what will be displayed – in my case, I select **Adobe Design Premium CS3** and then **Adobe Dreamweaver CS3**. Dreamweaver should now start – it will take a short while to do so, so be patient.

Stop Dreamweaver as you would any other Windows application.

Make sure your installed browsers are working by trying to access a website you commonly use.

02

building your first site

In this chapter you will learn:

- how to create sites
- the basics of site management
- how to create HTML pages
- how to test your pages in differing sizes of windows

What is a site?

Website (or site) is a commonly used word but we need to be precise as to its meaning within Dreamweaver as this is the starting point before any pages are created.

'Site' covers all of the assets (web pages, images, templates, spreadsheets, library items, scripts and movies) which together make up the website you are creating. Now of course at first you will not have scripts, movies, etc. in your site, but at some point in the future you undoubtedly will.

A Dreamweaver site has a unique name which has an internal meaning only; it has no relevance to how your site is referenced when live on the Web. For example, if you call your site 'My first site' in Dreamweaver, this name will not be used or referenced anywhere else. Unlike many other examples in the world of computing, feel free to use any characters and spaces to name your site – as long as it is unique on the computer you are using.

When you define your site, you assign to it a unique location on your computer – this is where you will be saving your web pages. (How the site is loaded to the Internet is dealt with in Chapter 12.) When I say 'your computer', I mean any accessible storage resource connected to, or part of, your computer, e.g. hard disk, writable CD, writable DVD, Flash drive, etc.

You will need to define a location (or separate folder) on your computer for each and every site you create, even if you are sharing assets such as images between sites. The main site folder is also referred to as the root folder. An example from Dreamweaver of the organization of a site folder is shown in Figure 2.1. This shows the file structure of a site called *fruit*. You will see that it has its own folder, *H:\fruit*, the name of which appears in brackets after the site name.

What should the folder be called? To some extent, you can choose whatever name you like providing it conforms to the naming conventions of your computer's operating system. A sensible idea is to give it a meaningful name which reflects the purpose or content of the site. As a rule, I would suggest that it does not contain any spaces, e.g. *ABC_International* would be OK but not *ABC International*.

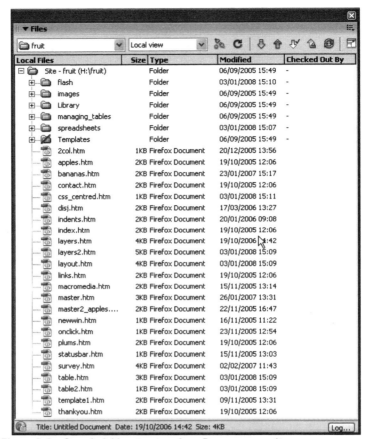

Figure 2.1 Sample folder structure for a Dreamweaver site

Let's assume we are in a browser and we want to access the site for the fictitious company AtoZ Ltd at the web address (or URL) **http://www.atoz.co.uk**. Every site has a home page which is always located in the root folder; the file is often, but not always, called *index.html*. When the user types in the URL, by default the server which is running the AtoZ site will, because no other page has been requested, find and return *index.html*.

Now let's assume the user types in **http://www.atoz.co.uk/contact. html**. In this case, a specific page has been requested – *contact. html*. This page will also be stored in the root folder because we have not specified any additional folder names in the URL.

In our third example, the user requests **http://www.atoz.co.uk/offices/europe.html**. This URL indicates that, within the root folder there is another folder named *offices*, and within that folder is a file called *europe.html*.

The AtoZ site file structure would therefore look like this in Dreamweaver:

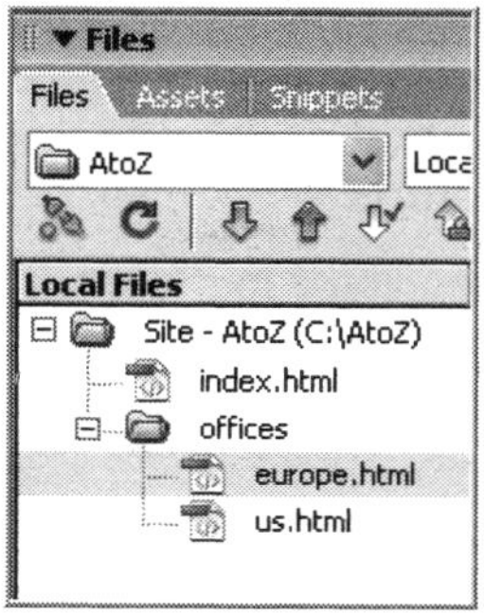

Figure 2.2 Simple example of a site's structure shown in Dreamweaver.

The root folder, which is stored at C:\AtoZ, contains the file index.html and the folder offices. The folder offices contains two files, europe.html and us.html.

Going back to Figure 2.1, we see that, within *H:\fruit*, there are a number of folders such as *flash*, *images*, *Library*, etc. The folder *images* will hold all of the images you use in the site. What is the purpose of putting assets into separate folders? For simplification – if you always use an images folder that's where you will always find them. As you develop larger sites, trying to keep track of assets is made significantly easier by adopting this approach. Your site would still work if every asset were in the root folder but think of the maintenance headache when you have hundreds or even thousands of assets.

At this stage the important points to note are that you should always have a separate folder for each site and separate subfolders for each of the asset types within the site.

As this is a vital topic which causes many learners to take a wrong turn, let's also look at a Windows directory to see how the structure might look.

Figure 2.3 Part of a sample Windows folder structure for all sites. Of course, you will not have so many sites to begin with but eventually you will appreciate the benefits of organization along these lines.

Again to make life easier, we have a folder here called *sites*, in which every site we create will store its files under its own root folder. This helps because we know automatically that any site files will be found in the *sites* folder. This is not mandatory but it does mean that rather than trawling through the contents of our chosen storage medium for Dreamweaver site files, we can quickly find them all under one folder.

As you can see, within sites, each individual site (e.g. *fruit*) has its own folder. The folders are themselves then further divided into the separate asset folders we saw in the earlier Dreamweaver screenshot.

What do I need and from where?

You can of course develop a site which contains nothing but text and does not use any assets over and above web pages created with HTML. The guru of web usability, Jakob Nielsen, has done just that (see **http://www.useit.com**) albeit with a few images. His rationale? – to improve download times and also because he admits that he is not a graphic designer. Whilst not advocating this very sparse approach, which you may well consider rather too extreme, it does demonstrate that a working website can be produced with a minimalist philosophy.

Most web designers will, particularly if working for a client, not wish, or be able, to follow the lead of Mr Nielsen. At the very least, you will want to add images which may come from a number of sources:

* The client

* Created by you or a graphic designer

* Purchased from a commercial site such as Corbis (**http://www.corbis.com**).

Some of the other assets you may consider, for example, spreadsheets and templates, may be developed in Dreamweaver, while movies can be imported from Flash and custom images from Photoshop or Fireworks. The possibilities are almost limitless and Dreamweaver provides you with the power to bring everything together into a single entity.

Page content and site plan

Before you start to develop your pages, you do of course need to have an idea why you want to create a new site. As long as you have a clear idea of what your site is for, that is a good start.

Consider the likely audience. Who is the site aimed at and why will anyone want to visit it? Your site might be unique, which may mean a limited audience, or you may be competing with other sites, in which case what is its unique selling point?

Once you have determined the likely user base, how will you ensure they will return to your site on a regular basis? Normally, this requires regular changes to the content – if there are no changes at all, why would anyone want to return to see the same thing all over again?

If you know your potential users and why they will visit, this will help when you design the page content. Each page should have a purpose, e.g. home page, contact page, links to related sites. The precise content will depend on the subject of the site, but do make sure that anything on a page is relevant and related. You would not put a contact form on your home page for example, nor would you have team photographs on your products page.

Before creating the site, then, you should have a clear idea of how many pages you need, what information each should contain and what additional assets such as images you need for each. This provides a good starting point for looking at Dreamweaver for the first time, as the information you have collated will make your initial usage more relevant and focused.

Creating a site

First, we need a name for our site to reflect its purpose. This could be 'first', 'judo club', 'books for sale' – in fact anything at all which makes it identifiable to you. Remember that only Dreamweaver knows, or cares about, the site name.

Next you need to decide where you are going to save your files. While you are still working on your site and before you publish it on the Web, the site files will typically be stored somewhere on the hard drive of your computer.

Finally, and you should have a reasonable idea of how many web pages you are going to create and what they will contain (in terms of text, images and so on).

1 You have two options when creating a site. If you select **Site** then **New Site…** you will see the Site Definition panel shown in step 3 below. The alternative, which we will look at because it provides a means of accessing information for all sites quickly is to use the **Manage Sites** dialog box – click **Site** then **Manage Sites…** No site names appear because at this stage you have not created any.

Figure 2.4 Manage Sites dialog box. No site names will appear until at least one has been created.

2 Click the **New…** button and this menu will appear immediately below the button; click **Site**.

Figure 2.5 Create new site definition from Manage Sites dialog box

3 You will now see the **Site Definition** dialog box (Figure 2.6).

Note that you have a choice of Basic or Advanced – we will use Advanced as I feel it gives more control.

In reality, there are only two boxes which need to be completed at this stage to create a valid site definition but we will look at each in turn. All fields are optional unless otherwise stated:

Site name (mandatory) – the name you give to your site. Dreamweaver will create an entry of Unnamed Site followed by a number. DO NOT leave the site name set as 'Unnamed Site *n*'.

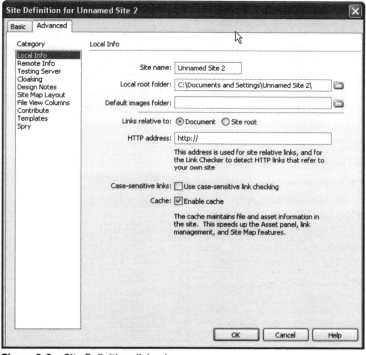

Figure 2.6   Site Definition dialog box

Local root folder (mandatory) – the folder on your computer where you will store all of the files and other assets which make up this site. If you have created a folder in advance, you can either type in the full location or use the Browse button to the right and navigate to your folder. If you type in a folder name which does not yet exist, Dreamweaver will create it for you. DO NOT leave the folder name set as 'Unnamed Site *n*'.

Default images folder – where images will be held in your site. (I have never used this setting – though intended to be a way of saving images which you have copied into your working page but have not already saved in your images folder, I have had no success in getting it to work.)

Links relative to – determines hyperlink addressing; leave this set to **Document**.

HTTP address – for link checking.

Case-sensitive links – though unchecked by default, this is well worth checking. In short, it will pick up any instances where a page name of your site and its hyperlink contain different case letters, e.g. red.html and Red.html. Whilst Windows-type systems have no problems with this incompatibility, UNIX-type systems (which run the majority of hosted websites) do. Well worth checking to avoid significant later problems.

Cache – leave enabled so as not to interfere with any of Dreamweaver's operations.

When you have completed all of the necessary fields, click **OK** and you will see again the **Manage Sites** dialog box including the name of your new site (in this case 'first').

Figure 2.7 Site 'first' has now been created

You can now carry out a range of functions which you could not before as you did not have a site. Click **Edit...** to change any of the definitions (e.g. local root folder) or **Remove** to delete the site (this action will not remove the files that make up your site). **Export...** allows you to save your site definition outside Dreamweaver (this can be useful insurance in case the definition becomes deleted or corrupted – unlikely, but anything can happen!), while **Import...** restores the definition. Site definition files always have a suffix of .ste.

When you are happy, and have finished making changes, click **Done**.

Look at the Files panel now (on the right-hand side of the workspace) to see your named site and its local root folder displayed. Also displayed in a drop-down menu is the name of the site. When you have more sites defined, this menu will allow you, to switch from working with one site to another. Another menu displays the text 'Local view' which means that the Files panel is showing your local files.

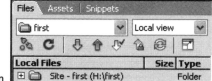

Figure 2.8 Files panel shows your created site and file location

Creating pages

We saw with the Welcome Screen earlier that there are a number of types of files or pages which can be created within Dreamweaver. Now is a good time to make a clear distinction between two main types of web pages – static and dynamic pages.

Static pages do not change. Whenever anyone accesses that page, no matter where from or when, they will always see the same content. This might take the form of a contact page, for example, which would list email and physical addresses, along with telephone numbers. This type of page is created using HTML (Hyper Text Markup Language).

Dynamic pages do change. A typical example might be an online store which, in its product page, as well as displaying product information, also displays the number of products in stock. Therefore, we might view a page for a particular product today and again tomorrow and note that the number in stock had either increased or decreased depending on whether items had been sold or restocked. This type of page is linked to a database and may be any one of a number of Dreamweaver-supported files types – this is where we encounter a whole range of acronyms such as PHP, JSP and ASP.

At this stage we do not need to delve into these acronyms as we will be producing only static pages, which will be created by Dreamweaver using HTML. There are two recognized suffixes for HTML files, .htm and .html, which you may have seen before when browsing sites on the Web. As a default, Dreamweaver will create files with .html as the suffix. (This can be changed though I see no practical need for you to do so.) It is worth mentioning that HTML as a language has been 'improved' and in this newer form it is known as XHTML – the X stands for Extensible.

Computer languages, like human languages, have rules which are also referred to as syntax rules. XHTML's syntax rules are stricter than those of HTML. It is intended that XHTML will replace HTML but when/whether this will happen is open to debate. This is a huge subject which it would not be appropriate to address here – go to the World Wide Web Consortium's (W3C) site at **http://www.w4.org/MarkUp/** for more detail; W3C is a leading developer of web standards and guidelines.

The reason for this apparent digression into XHTML is to highlight the fact that when creating an HTML page it is recommended that you create it in XHTML format, which Dreamweaver allows you to do. By doing this you are future-proofing the pages of your site – if XHTML becomes a rigorously enforced standard, you will not have to do any re-engineering of your site as a result.

1 Click **File** then **New…** in the menu bar to see the **New Document** dialog box.

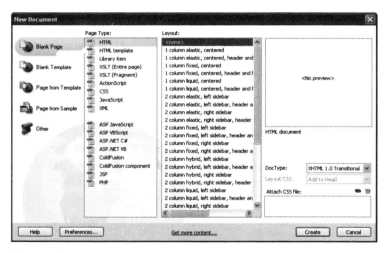

Figure 2.9 New document dialog box

2 Select **Blank Page** from the left-hand column, **HTML** from the **Page Type** column and **<none>** from the **Layout** column. This indicates that you wish to create a new HTML page with no predefined structure to which you will be adding content.

Note in the bottom-right that there is a drop-down menu labelled **Doc Type** which shows **XHTML 1.0 Transitional** by default. Do not change it. We will create our page with this default setting.

You will also note that there is a huge variety of choices that can be made from this dialog box – too many to cover here. However, by all means experiment to see what is on offer – with **HTML** still selected as the **Page Type**, select a **Layout** (e.g. 2 column fixed, left sidebar) to see a preview in the large right-hand window of how the page will look in outline.

You might also select **Page from Sample** on the left-hand side which gives you access to a number of predefined pages which you may find useful either to get you started or to see how a page is constructed using HTML and CSS (Cascading Style Sheets).

Ready-made pages

Dreamweaver provides a number of themed pages which, depending on the nature of the site you are developing, may be of interest. You can find them through **File > New...** then **Page from Sample and Starter Page (Theme)**.

3 With the settings as in Figure 2.9, click **Create** and Dreamweaver will open a new HTML page in the workspace.

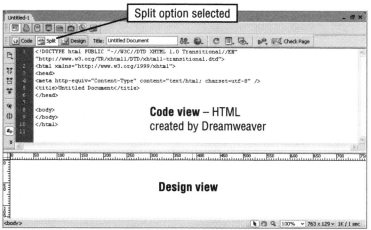

Figure 2.10 Split view – the recommended set up

There are several ways to view a page: Code, Split and Design.

◆ **Code** displays only the code, in this case HTML (you can also see the code in a floating panel by selecting **Window > Code Inspector** or clicking **[F10]**);

◆ **Split** displays a combination of Code and Design views;

◆ **Design** displays just the working area.

For beginners, I recommend using Split mainly because it will enable you to see how the code changes as you add to, or alter, your page using Dreamweaver functions.

At this stage the page has not been saved so it is called *Untitled-2*. Whenever you create a page, Dreamweaver will call it *Untitled-n* until you save it and give it a meaningful name. Though we have not yet added anything to the page, we will save it; use **File > Save** then name the file and decide where to store it. In this case, it must be saved in the folder that we created for this site, i.e. *first*.

Figure 2.11 Save files to your site folder

In the **File name** box enter *index* – you do not need to add the suffix .html as Dreamweaver will do this. Click **Save** and you will be returned to the workspace – this time the tab at the top will show the file name as being *index.html* rather than *Untitled-n*.

Why name the file index?

All sites have a home page which by is called 'index'. The server that processes requests for your pages will expect that index is your home page. Visitors do not need to type **www. yoursite.co.uk/index.html** – but simply **www.yoursite.co.uk** and the web server knows they want the home page.

If we look at the Files panel after saving *index.html*, we will see this new file now under the site name, as in this example.

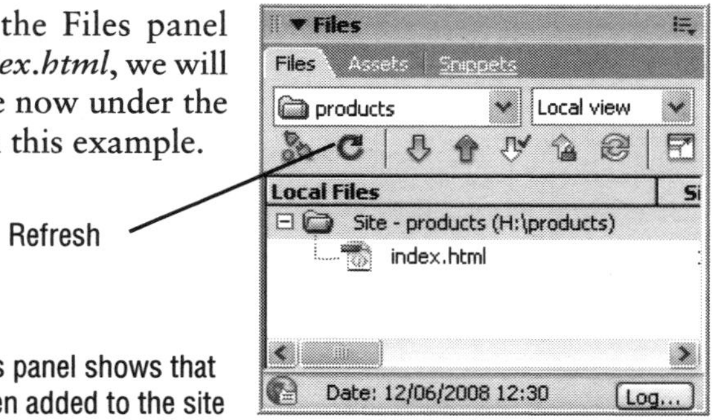

Refresh

Figure 2.12 Files panel shows that index.html has been added to the site

Hover over any of the icons in the Files panel to see text explaining their purpose. The one that is of interest is the Refresh icon. If you copy files to your site folder in Windows Explorer and then return to Dreamweaver, you will find that these files do not automatically appear in the Files panel. The Files panel does not refresh itself; you have to activate the refresh. Click the **Refresh** icon and you will now see an updated files list.

Standard toolbar

If you prefer, you may use the standard toolbar for file-related actions such as **Save** and **Save all**.

The toolbar will be displayed at the top of the page, immediately below the name of the file.

If it is not visible, then select **View > Toolbars > Standard**.

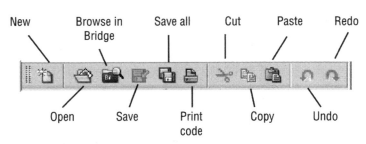

New   Browse in   Save all   Cut   Paste   Redo
        Bridge

Open   Save   Print   Copy   Undo
                  code

Figure 2.13   Standard toolbar

New and **Open** refer to documents or pages. New will display the New document dialog box (Figure 2.9). Open will display a **File Open** dialog box for the current folder, similar to Figure 2.11.

Browse in Bridge is a new feature of Dreamweaver CS3 and clicking this will start the Bridge application. Bridge is a file manager which allows you to manage all your assets; it is accessible from all CS3 components. Like Windows Explorer, Bridge gives you access to all files on your local computer but it offers a great deal more as well – for example, access to the Adobe Stock Photos library and access from Bridge Home to Adobe news and information. As an application in its own right, Bridge is outside our scope.

Save and **Save All** are self-explanatory; documents with unsaved changes will be saved to disk.

Print Code will print just the underlying page code (HTML and any other inserted code such as Javascript).

Cut, Copy and **Paste** work in the same way as in other applications. With Dreamweaver you may work with either code from Code view or elements in Design view. If there is specific code you wish to copy, you may copy it from Code view and then paste it into the relevant area of another document's code in Code view. The same principle applies with Design view. You cannot copy from Code view and paste into Design view or vice versa – well, actually you can, but the results would not necessarily be to your liking!

Undo and **Redo** will either reverse or repeat your previous action respectively.

Remembering where you left off

Before closing down Dreamweaver you should make sure that you have saved all of your open files. In a perfect world we would always make sure we had completed everything we had intended to do before closing down, but life is not like that; we may also be having technical problems which cannot be immediately resolved. In these cases, a means of recording the status of a page would be useful. Dreamweaver provides this in the form of Design Notes. These relate to an individual page and are never visible on the Internet. The quickest way to add them is to right-click in Design view and select **Design Notes for Page...** You will see the dialog box shown in Figure 2.14 – select a **Status** and add to **Notes**.

When checked, **Show when file is opened** will ensure that you see the notes the next time you open the page.

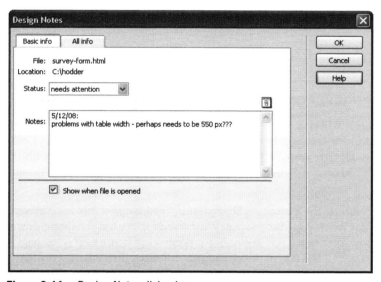

Figure 2.14 Design Notes dialog box

Click the calendar icon to add today's date (in mm/dd/yy or US format). Entries may be added or deleted through the **All info** tab. Entries are automatically saved in a site folder called _notes – the file bears the name of the page followed by a .mno suffix e.g. *index.html.mno* is the name of the file containing notes for *index.html*.

Page title

Before we add any content to the page, we must ensure that we give it a title. This is potentially confusing for beginners because the assumption here is that a title is a heading. It isn't! Look again at the menu bar above Code view.

Title contains by default the text 'Untitled Document' – under no circumstances should you ever release a page to the Web which contains this default setting. It makes you look thoroughly unprofessional and it does not help search engines when they try to index your site.

So what should the title be? Anything that reflects the content of the page (within reason – a short, punchy title is better than a long, rambling description). As this is the site home page, we could use the title Home Page; once you have a domain name for your site you might use yoursite.co.uk – Home Page. The possibilities are endless but make sure you do add something suitable.

Adding content

Let's add some basic text so we have something to see when we preview the page in a browser. You can add content either in Code or Design view. Adding to Code view requires that you know HTML so it is better at this stage, and quicker, to add content in Design view.

Position the cursor in Design view and click – this is to ensure that when you start typing, your words appear in the Design view window, not Code view. Now type 'This is my first web page'. You will see that Code view also contains the same text. This is what I was referring to earlier when I said that Split view helps you to see the changes Dreamweaver makes to the HTML as you make changes in Design view.

Now that you have made changes, the filename in the tab above Code view is followed by an asterisk. This reminds you that you have made changes but have yet to save them; if your computer crashed now, you would lose them. Save your files regularly.

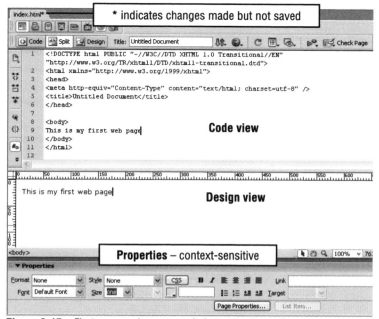

Figure 2.15   First page – changes made but not yet saved

Importing text into Dreamweaver

We will look first at importing text from a Word document. Position the cursor in Design view where the text is to be inserted and click **File > Import > Word Document...** and then navigate to the relevant document and click **Open**. The text will now be copied – be aware that Dreamweaver selects the formatting so you may need to amend the copied text.

If you just want to copy part of a Word document, then select and copy the text as you would normally do in Word, move to Design view, position the cursor then right-click and select **Paste**.

If you wish to add text just to pad out the page, which is often the case when developing new pages, then a good source is the Lipsum site at **http://www.lipsum.com**. You can create as much dummy text as you need and then, after selecting and copying it, move to Design view, position the cursor, then right-click and select **Paste**.

Displaying pages in a browser

Now you need to see how your page looks when viewed in a ~~...~~ sign view is ~~...~~ re advanced ~~...~~ nly reliable ~~...~~ r preferably

```
index.html*          * indicates changes made but not saved                    _ & x
 Code  Split  Design  Title: Untitled Document          C   Check Page
    1  <!DOCTYPE html PUBLIC "-//W3C//DTD XHTML 1.0 Transitional//EN"
    2  "http://www.w3.org/TR/xhtml1/DTD/xhtml1-transitional.dtd">
    3  <html xmlns="http://www.w3.org/1999/xhtml">
    4  <head>
    5  <meta http-equiv="Content-Type" content="text/html; charset=utf-8" />
    6  <title>Untitled Document</title>
    7  </head>
    8
    9  <body>
   10  This is my first web page.|          CODE view
   11  </body>
   12  </html>
```

~~...~~ ite browser.
~~...~~ eferences...)
~~...~~ el, you will
~~...~~ s – your list

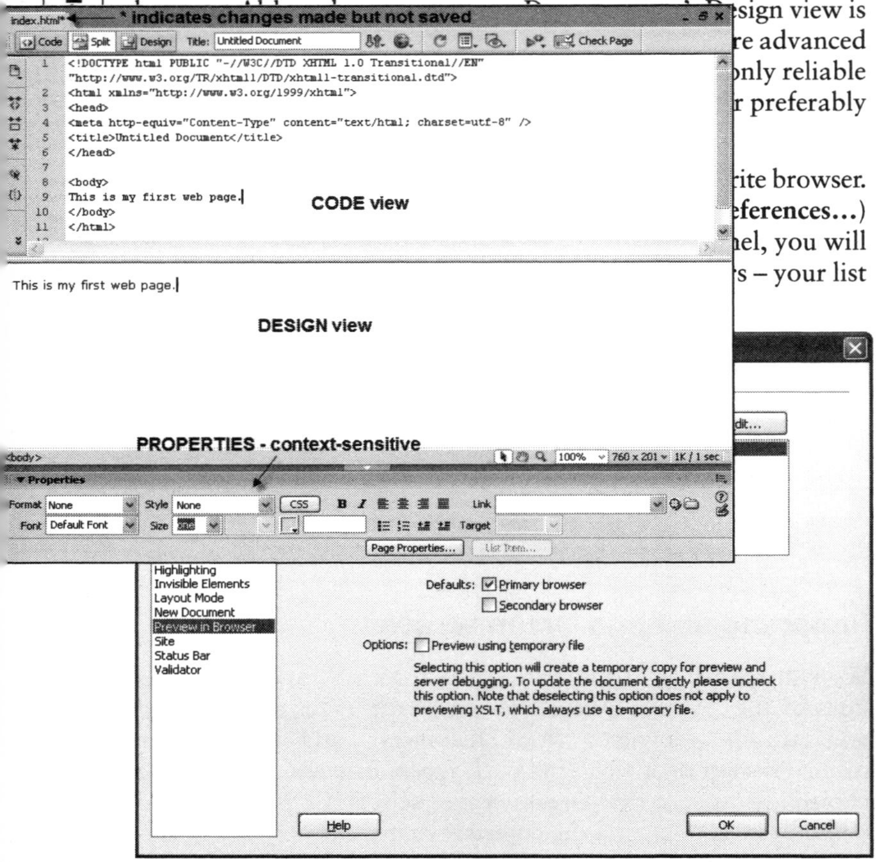

This is my first web page.|

DESIGN view

PROPERTIES - context-sensitive

```
<body>                                                     100% ∨ 760 x 201 ∨ 1K / 1 sec
▼ Properties
Format None  ∨   Style None  ∨  CSS  B I 三 三 三 三  Link                    ∨ ⊕ ☐
 Font  Default Font ∨  Size  None ∨        ☐  三 三 三 三  Target         ∨
                                     Page Properties...  List Item...
```

Highlighting	Defaults: ☑ Primary browser
Invisible Elements	☐ Secondary browser
Layout Mode	
New Document	Options: ☐ Preview using temporary file
Preview in Browser	
Site	Selecting this option will create a temporary copy for preview and
Status Bar	server debugging. To update the document directly please uncheck
Validator	this option. Note that deselecting this option does not apply to
	previewing XSLT, which always use a temporary file.

Help   OK   Cancel

Figure 2.16   Browser set up within Preferences

You need to tell Dreamweaver which browser you will be using to view web pages you have created. Click **Edit...** and you will see the **Edit Browser** dialog box.

Create a browser name (this is an internal Dreamweaver name only) and point to the browser executable file using the **Browse...** button. If you are not certain where this might be, it is highly likely it will be in the Program Files folder. In there the browser will

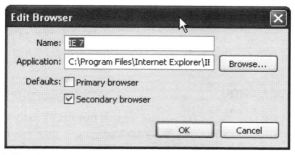

Figure 2.17 Edit Browser dialog box

be in a folder bearing its name, e.g. Internet Explorer. Open the folder and look for the executable file, which should end in .exe. if there is any doubt whether this is the correct file, double-click on it and the associated browser will open, if it is the right file.

Set it to be your primary browser (so that to open a page in it from Dreamweaver you just use [**F12**]). Click **OK** to see your default browser appear in the list with [**F12**] alongside the name and the checkbox labelled **Primary browser** checked (see Figure 2.16).

Click **OK** in Preferences and you will be returned to the workspace. With *index.html* open, press [**F12**] and the page will open in your chosen default browser.

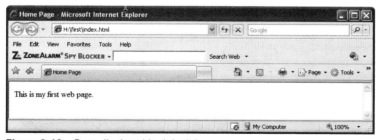

Figure 2.18 Page displayed in default browser

If the **Preview using temporary file** option is set, then you can press [**F12**] at any point when working with a page and see the results in the browser. The page does not have to have been saved first. A temporary filename is created and displayed, e.g. *H:\first\ TMPcimo2uc0tl.htm*. The temporary files are created in your site folder and you will need to remove them regularly.

If **Preview using temporary file** is not set, then every time you try to preview a page in a browser, if there are unsaved changes you will be prompted to save them first. In addition, the page name displayed will be a real filename, e.g. *H:\first\index.html*.

Browser usage

The browser you use to access the Web is not necessarily the one used by visitors to your site. Why should you be interested in the browsers your visitors use? Because browsers can, and do, behave differently. With simple HTML, such as the home page you have just created, you will be able to open a page in any browser and not see any differences in the display (subject to the default font set up in the browser – see box below).

Fonts and the web

You can set the font of the text in a web page, but if you do not, the browser will use its default. To see the IE7 default font, for example, click **Tools** then the **Fonts** button. This can be changed to any font. If you do not specify fonts, your careful design could be ruined if the page is displayed using a default of Tennessee Light SF! We will look at this in Chapter 3.

However, as the amount of content in your pages increases and/ or the generated code becomes more complex, this may no longer be the case. It is recommended therefore that you use a range of browsers to test your web pages so that, if any anomalies arise, you can fix them before you go live. You should install Internet Explorer 6 and 7, Firefox and Opera as a minimum. Try to install as many browser types as possible and make sure you use all of them when testing your pages.

If you do not use different browsers to test, the worst case is that your pages may not display properly (or at all) in some browsers.

Just as visitors to your site will use a range of browsers with different default font settings, so they may well be using computers with different screen resolutions. You need to keep this in mind so that you do not design pages using an ultra-modern screen size while ignoring those using older monitors.

Summary

We have covered quite a bit of ground in this chapter. You should now, with a bit of practice, be able to do all of the following:

+ Create a site folder
+ Create a site
+ Create an (X)HTML web page
+ Add a suitable title to your page
+ Test your page in a browser
+ Configure Dreamweaver to use a range of browsers
+ Access relevant Help.

Exercises

1 Add pages:

1.1 Create and save three additional pages for your site first. Make sure they are XHTML compliant.

1.2 Add some text to each page and save.

1.3 Make sure each page has a relevant title.

1.4 Preview the pages in at least one browser and ensure they appear as you would expect.

1.5 Find other ways to create pages than using the File menu.

2 Find the keyboard shortcut to access Preferences.

3 If you have not already done so, download and install at least two additional browsers. Configure them for use in Dreamweaver with one as the secondary browser (you should already have defined your normal browser as the primary). If you already use several browsers, then just configure them for use.

4 Where does the title appear when a page is displayed in a browser?

5 Find the keyboard shortcut to save files.

03 HTML

In this chapter you will learn:

- the syntax of HTML
- the purpose of attributes
- about HTML and XHTML
- how to configure Dreamweaver to use CSS for formatting
- about tag and attribute helpers
- about the HTML documentation in the reference section

Introduction

It may seem odd to include a chapter about HTML, but when you consider that generating HTML is a fundamental part of what Dreamweaver does for you, there is an argument for suggesting that an understanding of HTML would be advantageous. But why, you might say? If Dreamweaver does this for me, why do I need to know what it has done? Surely Dreamweaver is more knowledgeable about HTML than am I? Plus I don't want to learn HTML.

These are valid questions but there is of course an alternative response. Dreamweaver is a very complex program which contains a fantastic amount of useful functionality. Like any other complex program it does occasionally do things which you might not expect or understand. And so there are circumstances in which you might be glad that you do understand a little more about HTML.

This chapter does not attempt to teach you how to write HTML, but it will give you an overview of the structure of the HTML language as well as guiding you towards some of the resources available in Dreamweaver to help you address any HTML issues that may arise.

If you want to learn more about HTML, a good starting point is always W3 Schools at **http://www.w3schools.com/html**.

HTML – the language

HTML consists of tags and attributes.

A tag is a word, such as html, contained within less than and greater than symbols, e.g. <html>. The tag has a specific meaning to the browser, which will interpret it when the page is loaded (or opened). If the browser does not recognize the tag it will usually be ignored.

With several notable exceptions, which will become apparent as you learn HTML, nearly all tags also have a closing tag. This indicates to the browser that the tag it has been interpreting has now reached an end, e.g. </html> indicates the end of an HTML page. The closing tag is the same as the opening tag but the word (html in this example) is preceded by a /.

Failing to add a closing tag may cause unexpected and unwanted results. Naturally, Dreamweaver will automatically add closing tags when using its functionality.

An attribute is a value that is used with the tag; for example the attribute src, in conjunction with the <img> tag, will describe to the browser where an image may be found.

An HTML document is separated into two distinct parts – the head, as defined by the <head> tags, and the body, as defined by the <body> tags. The head contains all the tags that are not relevant to the display within the browser page (e.g. meta tags, title) while the body contains everything that you wish to display to the user (e.g. text, images, forms, tables). Both the head and the body are part of the overall HTML document, as defined by the <html> tags.

What follows is a simplistic explanation of the main tags and structure of a standard HTML page.

<html> and </html>

Every web page that you write will start and stop with the html tag, the tag basically tells your browser where your web page containing tags begins and ends.

```
<html>
All of your HTML code goes here
</html>
```

Figure 3.1   Example of a blank HTML document

<head> and </head>

The head tag contains information that is invisible in the main body of your page. It is a very important tag because it will contain amongst other things the title of your page that will appear in the browser's title bar.

<title> and </title>

Creates a title in the browser's title bar and will be the name of the page stored in Favorites or Bookmarks.

<body> and </body>

All tags that deal with page content (images, text, forms, links, etc.) go between these tags. The example below shows the structure of a page. Note that indenting is not necessary – this has been done for ease of reading. The same applies to having tags on separate lines. Remember that any code you create is easier to understand at a later date if you structure it in a readable way.

```
<html>
  <head>
    <title>Title of the page goes here</title>
  </head>
  <body>
    Page content goes here
  </body>
</html>
```

Figure 3.2 Structure of an HTML page showing the main tags

Tags are interpreted by browsers. All tags have a default behavior, e.g. <p>, which creates a paragraph in an HTML document, is by default aligned left; that is, the text will start on the left-hand side of the browser. If you want to change the default behavior of a tag, then an attribute has to be assigned to it. For example you can change the default background colour of the <body> tag by using the bgcolor attribute, as shown below.

```
<body bgcolor = "red">
```

or

```
<body bgcolor = "#FFFFFF">
```

Figure 3.3 Changing default tag behavior with attributes

The format of an attribute is as follows:

```
attribute_name = "value"
```

The attribute name is followed by an equal sign (spaces before and after it are optional) and the value is always in double quotes.

Dreamweaver does this for us, so we'll look in a minute at what happens when we create a new document and how attributes are attached to tags. But first we need to discuss XHTML because by default all of our Dreamweaver-generated HTML pages will be in XHTML format.

What is XHTML?

The X stands for extensible as XHTML is an extension of HTML. XHTML is based on XML so anyone familiar with the latter will recognize many of the specific language requirements of XHTML, the main ones being shown in the table below. Essentially it represents a stricter version of HTML, removing many of the anomalies which can make HTML code very untidy and incomplete.

While not yet a standard across the board, XHTML usage is becoming more commonplace. Whether it will ever become an enforceable standard (i.e. browsers will not render documents using anything other than XHTML) seems unlikely, or at least a long way off. However, XHTML does produce better quality code as a result of enforcing some sensible requirements.

Below are some of the key differences between HTML and XHTML. The XHTML requirements are derived directly from XML.

HTML	XHTML
No specific heading type required	Requires specific heading type, e.g.
	<!DOCTYPE html PUBLIC "-//W3C//DTD XHTML 1.0 Transitional//EN" "http://www.w4.org/TR/xhtml1/DTD/xhtml1-transitional.dtd">
	<html xmlns="http://www.w4.org/1999/xhtml">
Any case may be used for elements e.g. <TITLE>	Case must be lower for all elements, e.g. <title>
Elements may be closed or not e.g. 	All elements must be closed, even empty elements such as which should be rendered as
<html> alone defines the start of the page	<html> has been replaced by lines which define the XML version, encoding, the XHTML standard and other information for XML parsers
Tag attributes do not need to be in quotes e.g. bgcolor=red	All tag attributes need to be in quotes, e.g. bgcolor="red"

Use of deprecated tags still allowed e.g. <font>	Recommended to stop using deprecated tags such as <font> and to start using CSS
<title> may appear anywhere within the <head> tag	<title> should be the first tag to appear within <head>
<html>, <head> and <body> are not mandatory tags	Mandatory
Tags may be nested in any order e.g. hello	Tags must be nested correctly, e.g. hello

If you want to learn more about XHTML, try W3 Schools at **http://www.w3schools.com/xhtml.**

Dreamweaver and (X)HTML

Let's look at the creation of an HTML page in Dreamweaver.

When you create a new page (**File > New...**), the format will be automatically set to XHTML.

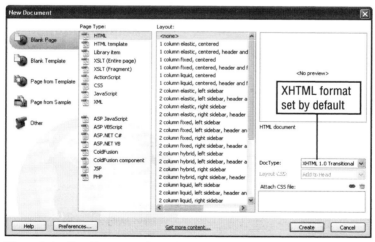

Figure 3.4 New Document dialog box showing DocType setting of XHTML

There are a number of alternative options available in the DocType drop-down menu but I would strongly recommend that you do not select anything other than the default until you have a clearer understanding of the implications of making such a change.

Click **Create** and the new page opens in Dreamweaver. To see the code generated for this blank page, select Code or Split view; at this stage, Design view will be empty as you have not yet added any content. The code will look like this:

```
1    <!DOCTYPE html PUBLIC "-//W3C//DTD XHTML 1.0 Transitional//EN"
     "http://www.w3.org/TR/xhtml1/DTD/xhtml1-transitional.dtd">
2    <html xmlns="http://www.w3.org/1999/xhtml">
3    <head>
4    <meta http-equiv="Content-Type" content="text/html; charset=utf-8" />
5    <title>Untitled Document</title>
6    </head>
7
8    <body>
9    </body>
10   </html>
11
```

Figure 3.5 Code generated when Dreamweaver creates a new HTML page

Notice that the cursor is positioned immediately after the <body> tag because Dreamweaver now expects you to start adding page content in Design view.

Line 1 is exclusive to XHTML. It contains pointers to information that could be used to validate the XHTML in this document.

Line 2 sees the xmlns (XML namespace) attribute added to the standard <html> tag. In conventional HTML, attributes are not used with the <html> tag.

Line 4 is a <meta> tag, which describes the character set used to build the page.

Line 5 contains the text Untitled Document – you must always change this to something meaningful which describes the page e.g. Products and Services.

Tags and attributes

The next stage is to add content in Design view. We will see, using some simple examples, how this affects the original HTML and also what happens when attributes are added.

Start by adding some text in Design view. Select the text, use the **Format** menu in the **Properties** panel and select **Paragraph** to place the text within a paragraph (a <p> tag).

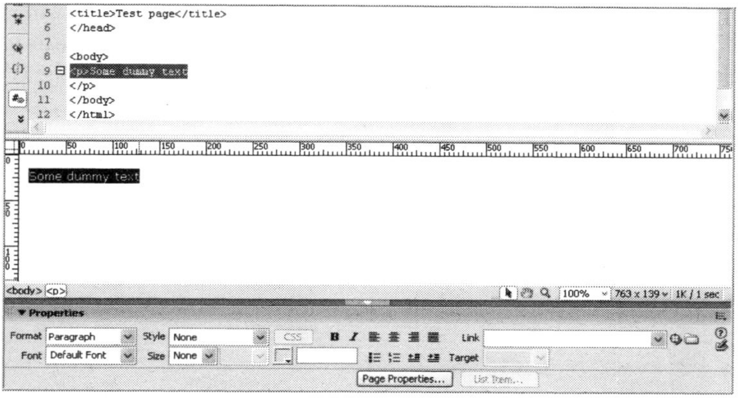

```
 5    <title>Test page</title>
 6    </head>
 7
 8    <body>
 9 ⊟  <p>Some dummy text
10    </p>
11    </body>
12    </html>
```

Some dummy text

<body> <p>

Format: Paragraph Style: None CSS **B** *I* Link
Font: Default Font Size: None   Target

Page Properties... List Item...

Figure 3.6 Text formatted as a paragraph

In Code view, note that Dreamweaver has placed the text within <p> tags. No attributes have been added yet, so the text is displayed in Design view left-aligned. We will change the alignment by clicking the **Align Right** icon ≣ in the **Properties** panel.

```
 8    <body>
 9 ⊟  <p align="right">Some dummy text</p>
10    </body>
11    </html>
12
```

Some dummy text

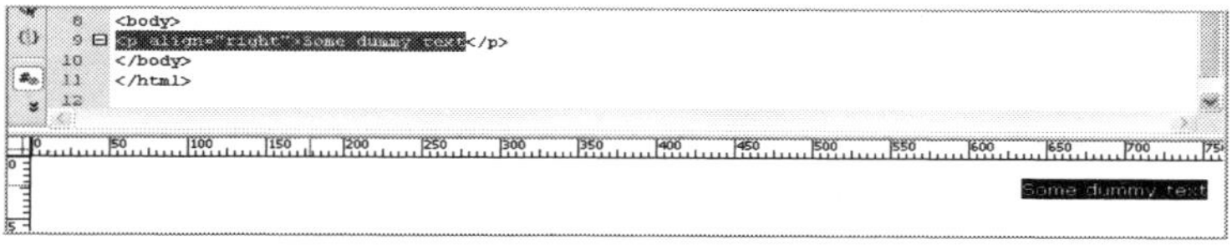

Figure 3.7 Alignment attribute added

In Code view, the attribute align="right" has been added to the <p> tag and the text has been right-aligned in Design view.

Generally speaking, most of the changes you make in the Properties panel will result in HTML tag attributes being created e.g. colour, width, height. You will recognize the attributes because they always follow the same format of attribute_name="value".

Fonts

There is one specific instance when Dreamweaver creates an attribute named class with an associated value which is, by default, called style*n* (where *n* is a number, starting at 1 and incrementing by 1 every time you add new formatting). That is when you apply any font type characteristics (size, font face or colour). If you select any of these (Size, Font or Text Color (the colour palette) in Properties), Dreamweaver will create an attribute of class="style*n*" and will add a <style> tag along with CSS selectors in the <head> area.

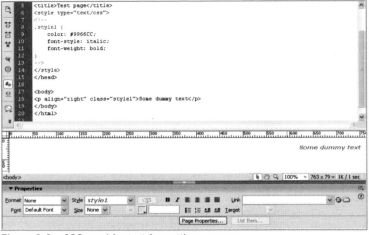

```
5   <title>Test page</title>
6   <style type="text/css">
7   <!--
8   .style1 {
9       color: #9966CC;
10      font-style: italic;
11      font-weight: bold;
12  }
13  -->
14  </style>
15  </head>
16
17  <body>
18  <p align="right" class="style1">Some dummy text</p>
19  </body>
20  </html>
```

Some dummy text

Figure 3.8 CSS used for text formatting

CSS is covered in more detail in Chapter 7 but it is worth stating here why CSS is being added rather than HTML.

When comparing HTML and XHTML, there was a reference to deprecated tags. Some HTML tags have been declared to be at the end of their life and, rather than continuing to use them, the alternative CSS selector should be used. One such tag is <font>. Whenever you apply changes which would require a <font> tag and an associated attribute (i.e. anything from Font, Size or the colour palette), Dreamweaver will use the CSS alternative.

This may seem a little confusing at first but you can just ignore this altogether if you wish. The action that Dreamweaver takes does have some implications relating to CSS, which we look at in Chapter 7. You can override this feature by going to Preferences (**Edit > Preferences**) and unchecking the box highlighted below. This would result in the <font> tag being used again where relevant. This is not a course I would recommend as the resulting code would not be valid XHTML.

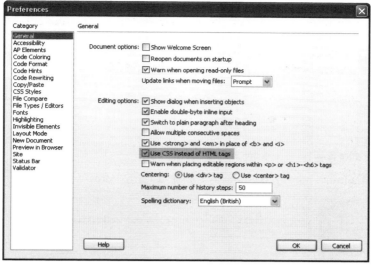

Figure 3.9 Preferences setting for text formatting

As you develop more complex pages, the underlying HTML will also be much more complex as well. Tinkering with code in Code view is not recommended unless you know what you are doing. However, it is always possible that Dreamweaver may do something which to you seems incomprehensible and amending code might represent the best, or only, way forward. If you do become stuck, there are additional Help facilities in Dreamweaver. Depending on your existing knowledge of HTML, some of these features will be of more use than others.

For example, the tag helper guides you if you decide to write HTML directly in Code view. I would suggest that you would only be writing code if you had a good grounding in HTML to start with. In the screenshot below you will see that I have typed this character '<' which indicates to Dreamweaver that I am about to write the name of an HTML tag. The pop-up helps you by showing available tags as you type. The more letters you type, the more filtered the list of available options in the pop-up, e.g. , if you were to type in the letters 'abb', then the only tag to appear would be **abbr** (see Figure 3.10).

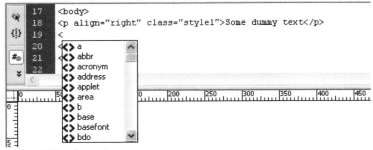

Figure 3.10 Tag help pop-up menu

A similar pop-up menu is available for attributes.

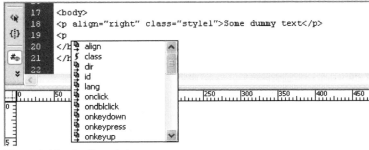

Figure 3.11 Attribute help pop-up menu

In the above example, I have typed '<p' followed by a space so Dreamweaver knows that, because I have not typed '>' to close the tag, I am about to add an attribute. The pop-up menu shows attributes valid for this tag and, as before, the more I type the more refined the list becomes.

Having typed the attribute name (align=), as soon as I type the opening quote " to indicate that I am about to add the attribute value, another pop-up shows the valid values.

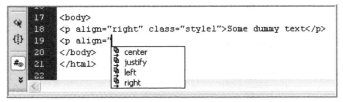

Figure 3.12 Valid attribute values pop-up menu

A context-sensitive reference is also available. With the cursor still positioned as in Figure 3.12 above, I selected **Window > Reference** and the information below was displayed.

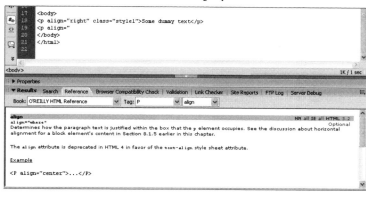

```
17    <body>
18    <p align="right" class="style1">Some dummy text</p>
19    <p align="
20    </body>
21    </html>
22
```

<body>   1K / 1 sec

▶ Properties

▼ Results   Search   Reference   Browser Compatibility Check   Validation   Link Checker   Site Reports   FTP Log   Server Debug

Book: O'REILLY HTML Reference   Tag: P   align

align   NN all IE all HTML 3.2
align="where"   Optional
Determines how the paragraph text is justified within the box that the p element occupies. See the discussion about horizontal alignment for a block element's content in Section 8.1.5 earlier in this chapter.

The align attribute is deprecated in HTML 4 in favor of the text-align style sheet attribute.

Example

<P align="center">...</P>

Figure 3.13   Reference example

The HTML reference document within Dreamweaver is not up to date but it will help you to understand the purpose of tags and attributes as well as showing examples of their usage.

Click the **Book** drop-down menu to see the other available reference documents.

Summary

If you have followed all of the activities in this chapter, you should now be able to:

◆ Read a simple HTML document and recognize tags and attributes

◆ Create Dreamweaver HTML using XHTML

◆ Describe the purpose of XHTML

◆ Describe how and why Dreamweaver uses CSS rather than HTML for formatting

◆ Write simple HTML using Dreamweaver's Help facilities

◆ Find help on HTML within Dreamweaver.

Exercises

1 Which HTML tags do you need for each and every document?

2 What is the purpose of an attribute?

3 Is this XHTML valid? If not, what is wrong with it?

```
<P align=center>This is a paragraph

<P>So is this</P>
```

4 What is special about the HTML <font> tag?

5 What do the tags <strong> and <em> do?

6 What is the purpose of writing <p align= "left">?

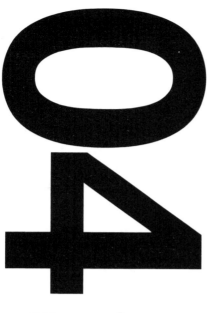

04

text and images

In this chapter you will learn:

- about the properties panel
- how to choose font styles
- about special characters
- how to apply colour
- how to source images
- how to place and edit images
- about other media types

An overview of the Properties panel

Before we start, let's remind ourselves about the Properties panel which is of major importance in this chapter. You will recall that the Properties panel appears below the Code and Design views, as in the sample screenshot below.

Figure 4.1 Properties panel

The Properties panel is context-sensitive which means that it will display the attributes of whichever page element you are working with. In the example above, the image in Design view has been selected so the display in the Properties panel relates to that image; you will see two settings of W and H (width and height) which show that the image is 800 pixels wide and 80 pixels high.

What happens if we want the text to be justified (align both left and right margins rather than just the left)? Then we need to modify the default behavior of the <p> tag to tell the browser to justify our text. This is done in the Properties panel. Let's look at an example.

First let's add some text to a new page and format it as a paragraph (Figure 4.2). What has happened is that the paragraph has been created, using an HTML <p> tag, and with the default behavior applied, i.e. left-aligned.

To amend the alignment of a paragraph, the cursor must be positioned anywhere in it in Design view; you could select it by dragging over all the text but this is not really necessary. You must select an element to change it within the Properties panel.

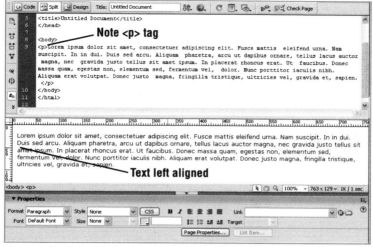

Figure 4.2   Default behavior of a <p> tag – left-aligned text

Next, click on the **Justify** icon. This has changed the text alignment
in Design view as well as modifying the <p> tag in Code view.

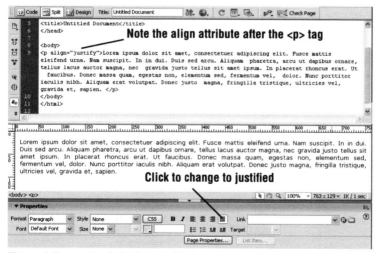

Figure 4.3   <p> tag behavior modified using the Properties panel

What you can amend in the Properties panel depends on whether
you are working with text, images, tables and so on – for example,
you would not expect to be able to adjust the font of an image!

Page Properties

The Properties panel allows you to change attributes of elements of a page – with Page Properties you can make changes that affect the whole page. Page Properties is accessed from the **Page Properties...** in the Properties panel.

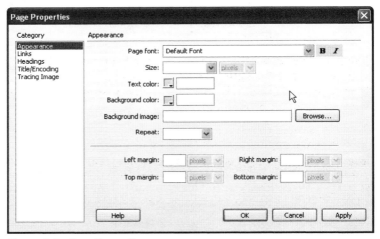

Figure 4.4 Page Properties

On the left, under **Category,** you can select the page settings you want to change. If we look initially at the screenshot above which concentrates on **Appearance,** we can change attributes of the text (Page font, Size and Text color), the page's Background color, a Background image and how, if at all, to Repeat the Background image and, finally the Left, Right, Top and Bottom margins around your content.

Let's see an example. We will start with a very simple page which contains text only.

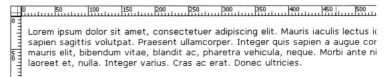

Figure 4.5 Text before changing Page Properties

Note the following:

- There is no background colour.

- There are margins between the text and the left-hand ruler and between the text and the top ruler.

- The text uses the default Dreamweaver font (which is defined in **Preferences > Edit>Preferences…>Fonts**).

- The text is coloured black and is not bold.

Using the Page Properties panel, as shown below, all of the above will be changed by setting **Page font,** clicking the **B** (for bold) button, **Size, Text color, Background color, Left margin** and **Top margin**. All other properties will be ignored.

There is no need to select anything in Design view as the change we will make applies to the whole page.

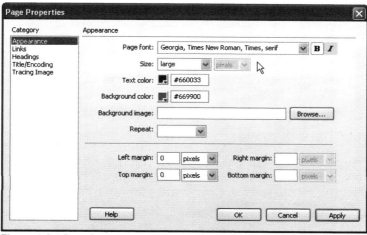

Figure 4.6 Page Properties (amended)

The text in Dreamweaver now looks like this:

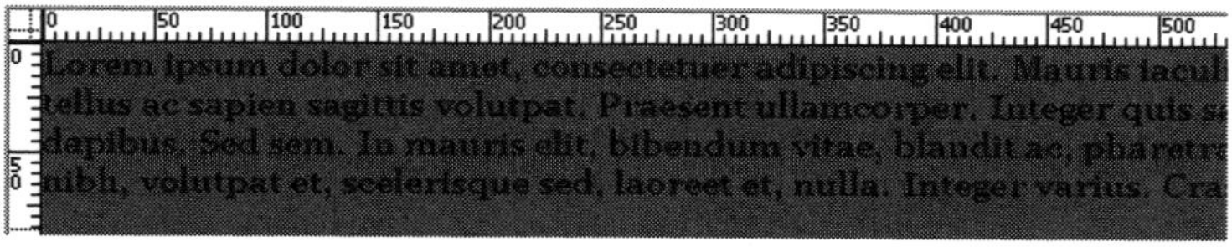

Figure 4.7 Text after changing Page Properties

Note:

◆ There is now a background colour.

◆ The margins between the text and the left-hand ruler and between the text and the top ruler have been removed (by setting the margin value to 0 pixels).

◆ The Georgia font is used for the text.

◆ The text is coloured and bold.

So, what has Dreamweaver done? First of all, these changes have been made to the whole page so that any text you now add will have the same characteristics as that shown. Dreamweaver will create CSS (Cascading Style Sheet) code from your entries in the Page Properties panel and add this to your page, amending its appearance. For the sake of completeness, let's see that CSS code. (We will address CCS in Chapter 7.)

```
1   <!DOCTYPE html PUBLIC "-//W3C//DTD XHTML 1.0 Transitional//EN"
    "http://www.w3.org/TR/xhtml1/DTD/xhtml1-transitional.dtd">
2   <html xmlns="http://www.w3.org/1999/xhtml">
3   <head>
4   <meta http-equiv="Content-Type" content="text/html; charset=utf-8"
5   <title>Text editing</title>
6   <style type="text/css">
7
8   body,td,th {
9       font-family: Georgia, Times New Roman, Times, serif;
10      font-size: large;
11      color: #660033;
12      font-weight: bold;                    ┌─────────┐
13  }                                         │   CSS   │
14  body {                                    └─────────┘
15      background-color: #669900;
16      margin-left: 0px;
17      margin-top: 0px;
18  }
19
20  </style></head>
21
22  <body>
23  <p>Lorem ipsum dolor sit amet, consectetuer adipiscing elit. Mauri
    Aenean sed tellus ac sapien sagittis volutpat.  Praesent ullamcorp
    condimentum dapibus.  Sed sem. In mauris elit, bibendum vitae, bla
    neque. Morbi ante nibh, volutpat et, scelerisque sed, laoreet et,
    erat. Donec ultricies.</p>
24  </body>
25  </html>
```

Figure 4.8 CSS shown in Code view

I will not launch into an in-depth explanation here. Suffice it to say that the CSS rules Dreamweaver has created reflect the options selected in the above Page Properties dialog box.

Choosing a font

The choice of fonts, even in the limited 'font sets' available in Dreamweaver, can be a little overwhelming. It can be a useful exercise first to look at how different fonts appear on the printed page. Here are some examples of standard fonts (all shown at 10 pt and bold) together with my brief assessments of the fonts: (which you are welcome to ignore or argue with!)

Arial (sans-serif)

The quick brown fox jumps over the lazy dog

Verdict: Designed for print rather than the Web but useful for headings.

Verdana (sans-serif)

The quick brown fox jumps over the lazy dog

Verdict: Looks good and should be widely available; specifically designed for the Web.

Times New Roman (serif)

The quick brown fox jumps over the lazy dog

Verdict: Perhaps a little old-fashioned for use on the Web.

Georgia (serif)

The quick brown fox jumps over the lazy dog

Verdict: Works well in combination with Verdana for a contemporary feel.

Serif fonts contain little hooks on the end of the main strokes of letters which can make reading them in a browser more difficult. These hooks are absent from sans serif fonts. So, as a general rule, use sans serif for the Web and serif for print media. The current trend on the Web is to mix the two – serif for page headings and sans serif for content text.

There are also fonts which fall into the category of fixed width which means that each letter occupies the same amount of space, e.g. the letter 'i' takes the same space as 'w'. Here is an example using Courier New – both sets of words contain the same number of characters and would, if using a standard font, occupy different amounts of space; with a fixed width font, the space required is the same.

```
four seven twelve
five eight eleven
```

Fixed width fonts are useful if you have a particular need to ensure that text is aligned column-by-column, e.g. displaying program code. In Dreamweaver, to ensure column alignment you may either select a specific fixed-width font or select the text and then apply the HTML preformat tag <pre> which automatically converts the font to fixed width – this may be done by selecting **Insert > HTML > Text Objects > Preformatted Text**.

Fonts

If you are familiar with word processing software such as Microsoft Word, then you know that changing your document's font can be achieved in a number of ways – by creating a new style, by changing an existing style or by selecting parts of your document and applying a different font; in each case, you may select from the range of fonts installed on your computer. To a large degree, you can do something similar with Dreamweaver but there is an important difference – if you use a specific font in a web page then the visitor to your page needs to have the same font installed on their computer to see the text as you intended it.

How can you ensure that visitors have the right font? Of course, you cannot guarantee anything as far as a visitor's computer is concerned, but by using one of the standard font sets as defined within Dreamweaver you can avoid many of the difficulties associated with font selection. You can use any font installed on your own computer but Dreamweaver has created a recommended set of grouped fonts which, because they are widely available on a range of computers, should ensure compatibility with your visitor's font set.

So what would happen if I decided to use a font outside the Dreamweaver groupings, e.g. Albertus Extra Bold? If your visitors do not have this font installed on their computers, they will see your page with the text displayed in their own browser's default font, which might be something like Times New Roman. This could of course make a considerable difference to the appearance of your page and may significantly detract from your carefully created design.

If we look at the Properties panel and click on the Font drop-down arrow, the available font groupings are displayed.

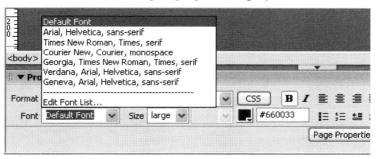

Figure 4.9 Font groupings

The reason that the fonts are grouped is to cater for different computers and for the fact that one or more of the fonts may not be installed. Thus, if we take 'Arial, Helvetica, sans-serif' this means that Arial is the primary font we wish to use for our page display. If the visitor does not have Arial installed, then a search will be made for Helvetica; if this is not present, the default sans-serif font will be used (the actual font applied may well vary from computer to computer).

All of the grouped fonts are in common usage on Windows and Mac computers, so selecting any group should guarantee that the visitor's default font is not substituted for your carefully selected font.

If you absolutely must use a specific font, then consider adding the text to an image (created in Fireworks or Photoshop) – in this instance, the visitor's browser will simply display the image and not worry about the font used. In the normal course of events, though, this is not what you would sensibly do.

Changing the font properties

We have seen that, using Page Properties, we may amend the font and this change will be included in our page as CSS code.

There is also the option of changing the font for specific parts of the page – for example, the heading, a specific paragraph or part of a paragraph/sentence. In each of these instances, the Properties panel should be used. In the following example, we will create a page with a heading and two paragraphs of text.

This also gives the opportunity to introduce the Format drop-down menu in the Properties panel.

Here is the text:

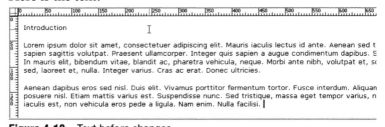

Figure 4.10　Text before changes

First of all, the text 'Introduction' will be converted to a heading. Position the cursor in Design view anywhere on the line which contains 'Introduction' then, from the Format drop-down menu select **Heading 1** – the result will now look like this:

Figure 4.11　Heading 1 created

Lines and paragraphs

You normally enter text by typing it in the Design view window. To create a new paragraph, press [Enter]. Dreamweaver will interpret this as a paragraph request and position the cursor, after a blank line, ready for input to the new paragraph. An HTML paragraph tag, <p>, will be added in Code view.

If you want to move to the next line without a line gap, then hit [Shift] and [Enter]. Dreamweaver will interpret this as a break request and will move the cursor to the first position on the next line – and add an HTML break tag, <br>, in Code view.

There are a range of heading options which have default sizes – from Heading 1 which is the largest to the smallest, Heading 6. Try them to see the different sizes applied.

Now let's amend the first paragraph by applying a different font, size and colour. To change the whole paragraph, all of the text needs to be selected; there are at least three ways to do this:

1 Drag the cursor over the whole paragraph in Design view.

2 Click on the <p> tag before the paragraph in Code view.

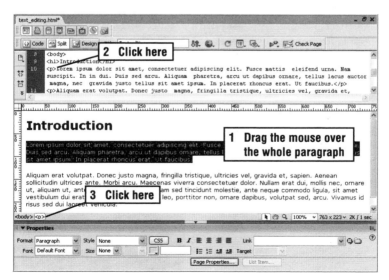

Figure 4.12 Selecting text

3 Click the <p> tag in the Status bar immediately below Design view – you first need to position the cursor in Design view anywhere within the paragraph you want to change.

Whichever option you take, the paragraph will be highlighted.

Font sizing

In a word processor, you will be used to being able to change the point size of text, where 10 or 12 points is fairly standard. With web fonts you have a much wider range of choices, encompassing fixed (or absolute) and relative sizes.

The issue of font sizing on the Web is complicated and this is not the right place to address it in detail. Dreamweaver gives you the choice of a numeric size (in pixels, points, inches, centimetres, millimetres, picas, ems, exs or %) or a word (e.g. small). For now, let's go with the word settings.

From the Properties panel, select 'Georgia, Times New Roman, Times, serif' from the Font menu, then 'large' from the Size menu, a shade of red from the colour palette, and finally click on the **B** and **I** icons to embolden and italicize the text.

To the right of the **B** and **I** icons are icons for aligning text. They signify left, centre, right and justify respectively. As a general rule, there is no need to use left alignment as this is the default value.

To select a colour, click anywhere in the palette icon. The palette will be displayed with Dreamweaver's defined colours. Click a colour to select it. When the mouse is over the palette it takes the form of an eye dropper. You will notice as you move the mouse

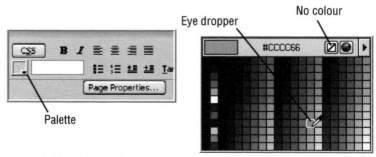

Figure 4.13 Palette selector and palette

that the colour will appear at top left in a rectangular box and alongside it will appear a code for the colour – in the example below, this is #CCCC66.

Note that the mouse will still pick up colours when moved away from the palette which can be a useful way of selecting colours – move the dropper tool away from the palette and the colour code shown in the top line (e.g. #CCCC66) will change to show the code of the colour underneath the dropper. (These colours may well not be web-safe colours – see page 73.) If you happen to hover over a colour you like, just click the mouse and the colour code will be recorded. If you wish to revert to the default colour, i.e. no colour at all, click on the **No colour** icon.

The final result will look something like this – you have applied a colour to the selected text and made the text bold and italic:

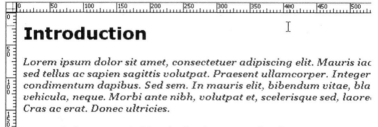

Figure 4.14 Text changes applied

In common with the changes we made earlier to the page properties, Dreamweaver has saved these changes in the form of CSS code which you can see if you look in Code view.

The same process may be followed if we want to make changes to the second paragraph. What if you want to change two paragraphs out of four on your page to have the same appearance? The easiest method is to select both paragraphs by dragging the mouse over them and following the same procedures as we used above.

You might be wondering why there is no icon for underlining text, which you would find in a word processing program. The answer is simple – if you underline text, a visitor will assume that it represents a hyperlink and they will try and use it as such. If this is not so, the visitor will become confused. Confusing your visitors is not to be encouraged. Therefore, underlining is not available as an option.

Lists

A list might represent a series of steps to be taken when installing software, which should be numbered, or perhaps a list of required ingredients for a recipe, which should not. Dreamweaver allows the easy creation of both ordered (numbered) and unordered (bulleted) lists.

Let's start with an unordered list.

Type some recipe ingredients into Design view and make sure that each item is on a separate line.

It does not matter if you use **[Enter]** or **[Shift]+[Enter]** to move to a new line – when the list is created, Dreamweaver will ignore these settings.

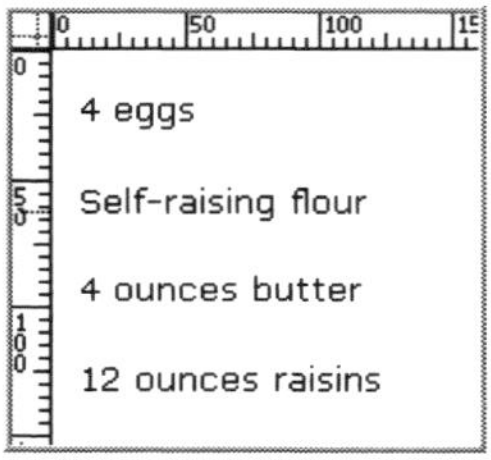

4 eggs
Self-raising flour
4 ounces butter
12 ounces raisins

Figure 4.15 List in Design view (unformatted)

To create the list, select the items then click on the unordered list icon in the Properties panel. Try also the ordered list icon.

CSS
Link
Target
Page Properties...
Unordered
Ordered

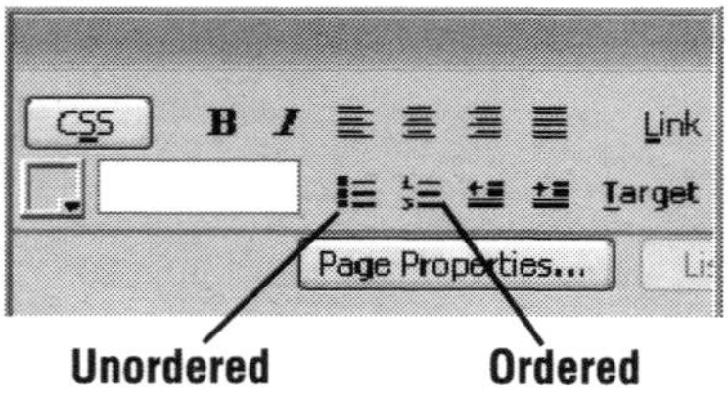

Figure 4.16 Unordered and ordered list icons

The end results will look like this in Design view:

• 4 eggs
• Self-raising flour
• 4 ounces butter
• 12 ounces raisins

1. 4 eggs
2. Self-raising flour
3. 4 ounces butter
4. 12 ounces raisins

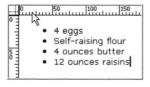

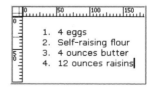

Figure 4.17 List items in Design view, formatted as an unordered list (left) and an ordered list (right).

Note that, in both instances, the list items have been indented from the left side of the page. This is the default behavior. The indentation can be changed using CSS. There are icons in the Properties panel, alongside the list icons, which allow you to increase or decrease the indent, but if you try to increase it you will find that it will revert to plain text; decreasing the indent is fine though.

Using special characters

So far the text we have added has been 'normal' in the sense that it consists of the letters A–Z. We may wish to add other characters, such as a copyright mark ©, a registered symbol ®, trademark ™, etc. Adding this type of character is straightforward and does not involve searching your keyboard!

The **Insert** toolbar contains a tabbed panel labelled **Text** – click on this and, at the right-hand side you will see a drop-down arrow (circled in the screenshot below)

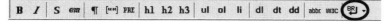

Figure 4.18   Text toolbar with special character icon circled

Your icon may not look like mine, as Dreamweaver will display here the last selection you made. Click the arrow and you will see a list of commonly-used special characters – if you don't click on the arrow but on the character itself, Dreamweaver will insert that character into your current page.

Click on a character to add it to your page. The option **Other Characters** will take you to another display with more choices.

Note that the **Line Break** is a special case as this is not a visible character at all, but an HTML tag, <br>. I am unsure why this has been included in the list of special characters.

Figure 4.19   Special characters menu

Remember that, when you select an item, Dreamweaver will insert it at the current position of the cursor. If you have positioned the cursor in Code view, the change will not automatically be displayed in Design view; Properties panel will display a Refresh button which needs to be clicked to see the change take effect. This does not happen if the cursor had originally been positioned in Design view, in which case any changes made are displayed immediately.

HTML and special characters

You might notice, if you look in Code view after inserting a special character, that the code has a strange format, starting with an ampersand (&) and ending with a semi-colon (;). This is the format in which all HTML special characters are coded.

Each character has a numeric id as well as a meaningful alphabetic id. For example, the Euro currency symbol is represented by both € and €. In some cases Dreamweaver uses the numeric code and in others the alphabetic code. Don't worry about this; all you need to know is that it will insert the correct code for the character.

A useful list can be found at **http://www.chami.com/tips/ internet/ 050798l.html**

Colour and Dreamweaver

I do not propose to give you a lecture about colour usage in the sense of which colours to use and which not to use – to some extent, there is an element of common sense involved (for example, don't use very bright colours, particularly not in combination, e.g. red text with a blue background); there is also an element of fashion involved as well as issues of accessibility (for visitors with colour blindness or other visual impairments).

Some accessibility guidelines have been established by the World Wide Web Consortium (Web Content Accessibility Guidelines at **http://www.w4.org/TR/WCAG10/**). Following these guidelines, useful tools have been created by Juicy Studio to enable you to analyse your chosen foreground and background colours for brightness and level of difference (see **http://juicystudio.com/ services/colourcontrast.php**).

We have already seen how colour may be added to web pages using the Dreamweaver colour palette, either at a page level (affecting background and text colour, using Page Properties) or at a lower level (affecting text colour, using Properties).

Let's take a look at the palette of colours which Dreamweaver provides. When we saw this for the first time in an earlier section, you may have been surprised at the limited number of colours presented.

Most modern computer monitors can display millions of different colour combinations but, in the not so distant past, this was not the case. There was also a problem with how different manufacturers' monitors displayed colour; for example, 'red' could look significantly different when displayed on different makes of monitor. A way round this was devised, in what seems to be a rare instance of manufacturer cooperation, whereby a palette of colours was set out which would be guaranteed to have the same intensity on every monitor and thus look the same.

Because colour support was fairly restricted at the time, there were only 256 colours to play with. This number was restricted even further by browser support issues so the final palette, which was labelled 'web-safe' because of its consistent appearance, was limited to 212 colours. These make up the Dreamweaver palette even now. Web-safe colours can be recognised from their codes which always consist of these pairs characters – 00, 33, 66, 99, CC, or FF. For example, 006699 is web safe while 226699 is not.

As the codes are hexadecimal (base 16, as opposed to the conventional decimal system which is base 10), the digits are not limited to 0–9 but extend to F (where there are additional values: A=10, B=11, C=12, D=13, E=14 and F=15).

The following simple example may help to clarify. The decimal number 42 is represented by 2A in hexadecimal.

$$2A \text{ (hex)} = 2 \times 16 + 10 = 42$$

Here is an example using a larger number; decimal number 128 which is equivalent to 80 in hexadecimal:

Decimal: $128 = 1 \times 100 + 2 \times 10 + 8$

Hexadecimal: $80 \text{ (hex)} = 8 \times 16 + 0 = 128$

Each hexadecimal code represents the intensity of the colours Red, Green and Blue. So 006699 is an intensity of 00 for Red (0%), 66 for Green (40%) and 99 for Blue (60%). Combined, they create a single colour. In all cases, you will note that Dreamweaver precedes each 6-character code with a hash symbol, #. The table below shows all of the web safe intensity values together with their hexadecimal equivalent.

Intensity%	Hex equivalent
100%	FF
80%	CC
60%	99
40%	66
20%	33
0%	00

The inevitable question is what will happen if I use a non-web-safe colour? The advances in monitor support for colour means that a 212-colour palette is now archaic. However, you may wish to stick with this palette if designing for mobile devices.

For the full range of colours, click the **System Color Picker** icon in the palette and use the slider controls to select a colour.

As we move forward, you will see that other page elements as well as text, such as tables, may also have colours allocated to them.

Images

Images add interest to your pages and are essential in many cases, such as when you are selling an item – as the old saying goes, a picture is worth a thousand words and you will find it is far quicker to add an image with Dreamweaver than it is to type 1000 words!

There are three types of image formats which are heavily used on the Web – the format is identified by the file suffix, .gif, .jpg, .jpeg or .png.

Graphic Interchange Format (**gif**) files are suitable for general purpose images, such as illustrations and line art, but not for photographs as their colour support is limited.

Joint Photographic Experts Group (**jpeg** or more often **jpg**) was designed with photographs in mind and is highly suitable for that medium.

Portable Network Graphics (**png**) takes the best features of GIF and JPEG and was designed specifically for the Web.

This is not the place to talk about the creation of graphics but the Adobe products which address this requirement are Photoshop and Fireworks.

Whatever the format of your image, it is important that the file size – its size in bytes not its dimensions – is not too large. As more and more consumers make the transition to broadband, there may well be a case for wondering why file size is important. Remember that not everyone is using broadband and if you ignore a percentage of your user base, then inevitably they will go elsewhere. The question as to the ideal file size is a difficult one to answer but if you aim for a maximum size of 30–40K you will not alienate too many people when they try to open your pages.

Adding images to the page

In the first chapter we saw the importance of a separate images folder for your site. If you do not already have an images folder, creating one is straightforward using the Files panel. Click on the line **Site – site name** (in the screenshot below, this reads **Site – hodder**) and then right-click to see the menu which contains **New Folder**. Select this option and assign a name, in this case images, to the folder.

As an aside, always be careful to select the correct folder before trying to insert a new subfolder. It is quite easy to insert folders in the wrong place if you are not taking care!

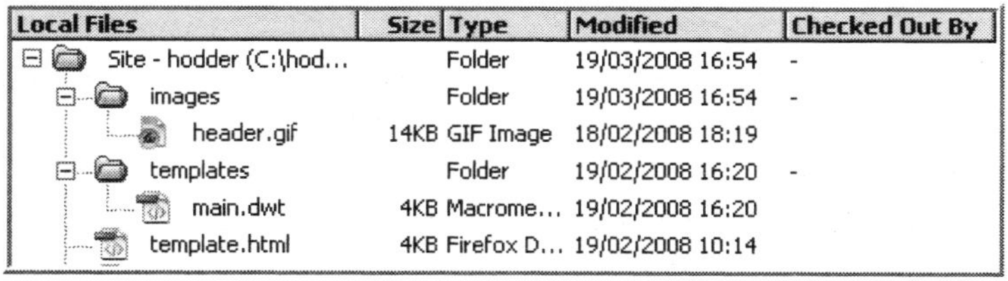

Local Files	Size	Type	Modified	Checked Out By
⊟ 📂 Site - hodder (C:\hod...		Folder	19/03/2008 16:54	-
⊟ 📂 images		Folder	19/03/2008 16:54	-
📄 header.gif	14KB	GIF Image	18/02/2008 18:19	
⊟ 📂 templates		Folder	19/02/2008 16:20	-
📄 main.dwt	4KB	Macrome...	19/02/2008 16:20	
📄 template.html	4KB	Firefox D...	19/02/2008 10:14	

Figure 4.20 Files panel showing site folders

If we take a look at the files panel, we can see the images folder and contents (in this case, a single image called *header.gif*).

Once we have an image or images in place we need to update our page by inserting one or more. There are a number of ways of doing this.

First make sure you have positioned the cursor in Design view where you want the image to go. Now, assuming you have identified your image and know where it's going, let's proceed.

Make sure in the **Insert** toolbar, that the tabbed panel labelled **Common** is selected, as here:

Common

Figure 4.21   Common toolbar

Hover over any of the icons and you will see a label indicating its purpose. The image icon will display the last option used. For the sake of this explanation, we will assume that **Images : Image** will be displayed when you hover over it as the last image-related action was to insert an image. Note that there is a down arrow alongside the symbol. Click anywhere on the icon to see the full range of options.

Figure 4.22   Image options

Click on the first option, **Image** and this dialog box will open:

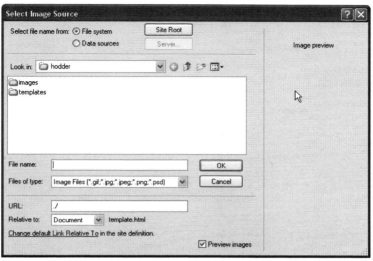

Figure 4.23   Image dialog box

Dreamweaver initially shows you the site root folder together with any subfolders, in this case *images* and *templates*. There are no images in the root folder so we must look for them in the *images* folder. Images are recognized, as you see in the box labelled **Files of type,** as having a suffix of .gif, .jpg/jpeg, .png or .psd (originating from Photoshop). There are of course other image types (e.g. .bmp) but these are not recognized as web image types by Dreamweaver.

Double-click on the *images* folder, which will display all relevant images within that folder. Select your image and click **OK.**

Note from the screenshot in Figure 4.24 that when you select an image, Dreamweaver will show you a thumbnail image on the right (under the heading **Image preview**) and also show the image dimensions (800 x 80), the type (GIF) the size (14K) and an estimated download time (1 sec).

After clicking **OK,** Dreamweaver displays an accessibility dialog box for the image. Accessibility, or ensuring that ALL users of your site are able to access the contents, is a very important issue and while it is a topic too large to address in full in this book, it will be discussed in context.

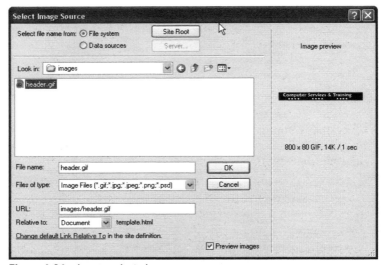

Figure 4.24 Image selected

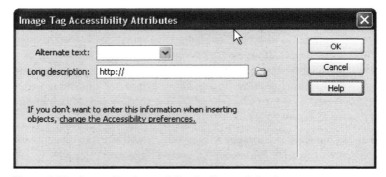

Figure 4.25 Image Tag Accessibility Attributes dialog box

Of course an image is fine for those of us with no visual impairment. What happens if you are not able to see the image, either partly or completely? Visually impaired users may be using a screen reader such as JAWS which translates your text into sound or Braille. However an image has no text, you may say. This is where the accessibility options come in.

Text may be added which is appended to the image so, if the image cannot be seen, there is text which describes it. Your text, for example 'Picture of an English rose garden in summer', should be descriptive of the image and is typed into the box labelled **Alternate text**. Should there be a need for a longer description of say 50 characters or more, then the text should be added to a separate page and the address (or URL) of that page added to the **Long description** box.

Unless you change the accessibility preferences by clicking the hyperlink **Change the Accessibility preferences** in the dialog box (which takes you to the default Accessibility settings in Preferences), you will be similarly prompted when adding tables, frames and other media types.

With an image inserted in the page, we will click on it to select it so that we may explore the options available in the Properties panel.

Figure 4.26   Image properties

You can see the image has been selected because of the resize handle at the bottom centre of it – selecting the image is the only way in which the relevant properties will be displayed in the Properties panel.

Let's look at some of the more frequently used properties in detail.

The first text box on the left which has no label and no content initially (it is directly below the text **Image, 14K** in Figure 4.26) is intended to hold your name for the image. Why do you need to name the image? As the need for more complex pages arises, it is easier if we have meaningful names for each element we have added to the page. As this is the logo for a company site, the name 'logo' would be appropriate or perhaps 'header_logo' (try not to leave spaces in names as this can cause problems; use an underscore '_' to join words).

W (width) and **H** (height) we have met already – Dreamweaver calculates this for you based on the actual size of the image. As there are resize handles, can we amend the image size? It is not really advisable to do so because Dreamweaver is not an image editor as is Fireworks or Photoshop. Though you can change the size, the results will usually be unsatisfactory. You might achieve satisfactory results if reducing an image but increasing its size will invariably introduce distortion.

There are however some changes that may be made to images in Dreamweaver – cropping, resampling, adjusting brightness/ contrast and sharpening (see page 84).

Src indicates the source of the image (where it is stored). This should always be in the *images* folder of the site. As file locations are shown relative to the root folder, this should always be along the lines of *images/image_name.suffix*.

Link would contain a hyperlink if you wanted the image to act as a link to another page. We will look at hyperlinks in Chapter 5.

Alt stands for 'alternate' and is important for accessibility reasons as we saw earlier. You should always complete the Alt attribute.

We will look at **Map** and its associated symbols in the next chapter.

V Space and **H Space** allow you to create vertical and horizontal space respectively round your image; the measurement is in pixels.

Low Src is intended for large images (in terms of file size) which may take a while to download completely. A low-source image is a very compressed version of the full one which will be displayed first; the full image will replace it when fully downloaded. If using this setting, you would need to create a second, smaller version of your image. This, of course, would need to be done using an image editor.

Border is to create a visible border round the image and is measured in pixels.

Align is concerned with how other elements are displayed with the image. We will look at this attribute in the next section.

What if I see this message when adding an image?

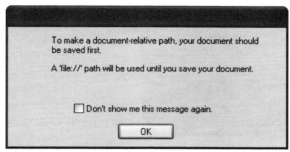

To make a document-relative path, your document should be saved first.

A 'file://' path will be used until you save your document.

☐ Don't show me this message again.

OK

Figure 4.27 Image import warning

This is quite common and indicates that you are adding an image to a Web page in Dreamweaver without first having saved the HTML file. As the file has not been saved, Dreamweaver is unable to determine the path to the image so it adds its own path. When you save the file, the image path should change in the Properties panel to something like *images/image_name.suffix*.

Positioning and configuring images

Let's look at the image shown in Figure 4.26. You will recall that we can alter the margins to the left of and above the image. Set these to 0 pixels and the logo will always appear flush with the left and top margins of the browser window. Let's not worry for now about centring the image – we will look at this when we get to Chapter 7 on CSS.

The image in Figure 4.26 was designed for a particular purpose – to form the heading of a page which will be 800 pixels wide, i.e. everything after it will also be a maximum of 800 pixels wide.

If we use a different image, which we will do below, we will be able to see how some of the properties previously described affect the overall appearance.

How can we control where the image is placed on the page? The answer is we have little control at this stage. It will be placed at the next position after the existing content. As it is unlikely that your page will consist of images alone, we will add some text. After inserting an image, the page looks like this initially:

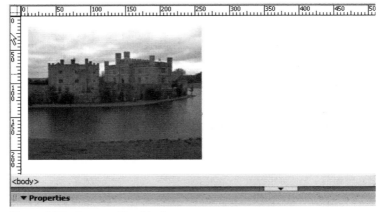

Figure 4.28   Image without text

When you add text, by default it is aligned at the bottom right of the image.

Figure 4.29   Image with text (default)

To alter the position of the text, the attributes of the image – not of the text – must be changed (which may seem rather odd). Select the image and in the Properties panel select **Left** from the **Align** list; the text is now aligned as shown below. If you add more text, it will eventually wrap around the base of the image – try it!

Figure 4.30 Image with text (left-aligned)

The left alignment refers to the image; try **Right** and the image and text will be swapped over. Try other variations of **Align**.

You might also, with the image selected, try setting **V Space** (to set the space above and below the image) and/or **H Space** (to set the space to its left and right) to create blank space around it.

As you experiment, you will appreciate that precise positioning of the text and image is not possible using the attributes we have just been looking at. So how would we position exactly? The answer is either to use a table or CSS (covered in Chapters 6 and 7).

Image editing

Image editing is possible in Dreamweaver, but only to a limited extent. It is better really to call it modification. Note that the functions work with image files with a .gif or .jpeg suffix only. In all cases, the image must first be selected to use the functions.

The functions are available through **Modify > Image**. Be aware that the end result of each of the operations below is likely to be a larger file in terms of bytes. Also bear in mind that the changes you make are automatically saved to the image file.

These options are also available via icons in the Properties panel – available when the image has been selected.

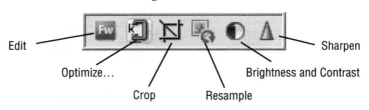

Edit

Optimize...

Crop

Resample

Brightness and Contrast

Sharpen

The **Edit** icon will differ depending on the image file suffix, i.e. for .psd image files, the icon will contain **Ps** (for Photoshop); for all other types, **Fw** (for Fireworks). To use this option, you must have Photoshop or Fireworks installed. As I cannot assume you have installed either, we will not look further at this option.

Optimize... – select this option and the Image preview dialog box will open (Figure 4.31). Note that changes you make will be saved to the image file so if you are experimenting make sure you have a copy of the original file.

A series of options is available from the Options tabbed panel (the default view) for changing the image, depending on which format is selected from the Format drop-down menu.

- Looking at the example in Figure 4.31, **Quality** is set to 79 (percent); if the slider is used to increase this percentage, then the file size (shown initially as 11.61K) will also increase. Changing to 100% changes this particular image size to 20.96K, or almost double. In fact, as a general rule, any changes you make to improve the image quality will also affect the file size so be careful not to make unnecessary changes which might have a consequent affect on the image download time.

- **Progressive Browser Display** will display the image at low resolution at first and increase the resolution progressively. This is useful if the image size is large.

- **Sharpen Color Edges** may improve the quality of the image.

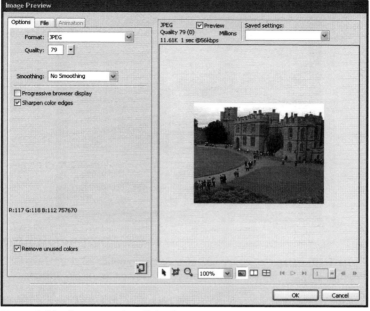

Figure 4.31   Image preview dialog box

+ **Remove unused colors** will, where possible, restrict the colour palette needed to display this image. This may result in a smaller image size and therefore quicker downloading.

+ Select the **File** tabbed panel to see the file sizes and also, if you wish, to change the display size of the image by clicking the Export area checkbox which then allows mouse movements to resize the image. Click **OK** and the new image will be exported to your page.

Crop – you may select a portion of the image to be displayed. A resizable box will overlay the image (Figure 4.32); move the borders of the box with the resize handles until the contents of the box include the portion of the image you wish to display.

When you have selected the area of the image you want, double-click anywhere in the box and the rest of the image will be removed. The image added to your page is a cropped version of the original. If you are unhappy with the display, use **Undo** to restore the original image and start again.

Figure 4.32 Image in Design view after Cropping option selected. Note the presence of resize handles which allow you to change the displayed size.

Resample – once selected, you may resize an image using the resize handles or by changing the width/height attributes in the Properties panel. Usually attempts to increase the image size will lead to a distorted result. Resampling attempts to recreate the look of the original image by adding or subtracting pixels after resizing. This only works with files with a suffix of .gif or .jpeg (.jpg is not supported) which have been resized, i.e. the Resampling option will not be accessible if the image retains its original size.

Brightness/contrast – this option will attempt to correct images which are too dark or too bright. The brightness and contrast is controlled via a dialog box which allows changes to be made using movable sliders. Assuming the image is showing in Design view, the changes you make will be applied to the image immediately if the Preview option is selected.

Sharpen – adjusts the contrast of elements within the image again via a dialog box. A movable slider controls the sharpness. Again, there is a Preview option to enable changes to be seen as they are made.

Integration with Photoshop

Photoshop image files are saved with a .psd suffix which is not an image type/format which browsers recognize. You cannot therefore include a .psd file directly in a Web page. So how can you use the image you have created in Photoshop? Quite simply, Dreamweaver will take care of the optimization into a format suitable for the Web.

To illustrate the process I have taken a copy of *Fish.psd* from the Photoshop Samples folder and copied it into my site images folder. If I now try and copy this image into my page in Design view, the Image Preview dialog box which we saw in Figure 4.31 will be displayed automatically.

We now have the option to create a version of this image in JPG, GIF or PNG format by selecting an appropriate value from the Format drop-down menu. As we saw earlier, the Quality setting has a great impact on the file size shown above the image. (In the

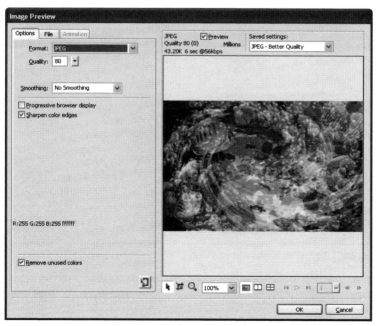

Figure 4.33   Photoshop .psd image file opened in Image Preview

above example, the file size is 43K; change the Quality to 100 and it rises to 183K or change it to 50 and it falls to 20K.)

Once you are happy with the settings, click **OK** and Dreamweaver will prompt you to save the file, which in this case will be called *Fish.jpg* by default – make sure you save it in the *images* folder. This new image is the one that will be included in your page. The Photoshop image remains in your images folder so you might choose to remove it as it has no practical use.

Create a Web photo album

This is a new feature in Dreamweaver CS3, allowing you to create a photo album quickly and easily, though you do need Fireworks as well. Before you start, you need to have your images ready in the normal place – the images folder. You also need to create a standard HTML page.

Click **Commands > Create Web Photo Album...** and the dialog box will appear (Figure 4.34).

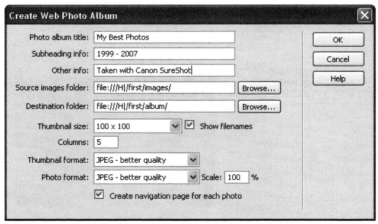

Figure 4.34   Web photo album dialog box

The first three fields allow you to enter title information. (See Figure 4.35 for an example of how these appear in the resulting web page.)

The **Source images folder** represents the location of the images to be used for the photo album – all images in the folder will be used. If you have any images in your folder which you do not want to be added to the photo album, now is the time to move them elsewhere.

At the end of the process, the **Destination folder** will contain:

1 An images folder, with the original, full-size images.

2 A thumbnails folder, with the images sized according to the criteria set out in **Thumbnail size** and **Thumbnail format**.

3 A pages folder (to hold the individual HTML pages which display an image each).

4 The final file will be *index.html*, an example being shown in Figure 4.35.

If it does not already exist, Dreamweaver will create the Destination folder for you.

Uncheck **Show filenames** and the name of the image will not be displayed on the page.

Columns dictates the number of columns used to display the images in *index.html*.

Thumbnail format and **Photo format** can be either JPEG or GIF formats for the thumbnails and large size images. You may scale the large images by entering a percentage value in **Scale**.

Figure 4.35   Index page for photo album as displayed in a browser

Finally, to create a page for each individual image together with navigation links, select **Create navigation page for each photo**.

Click on an image and you will see a page like this.

Figure 4.36   Individual image shown in an HTML page

Use the navigation to move through the images – click Home to return to *index.html*.

Image placeholders

When designing a site, it is possible that the final images may not be ready or available at the point when you are creating your pages. To make sure that the image is not forgotten about, you can add a placeholder – this is a space allocated for use by the image.

In this example, I will create a placeholder for the logo. Position the cursor as you would normally before inserting an image, and select **Image Placeholder** from the drop-down menu.

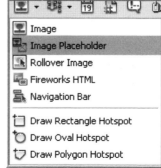

Figure 4.37   Image Placeholder menu selection

After selecting this option, you will be prompted to give the placeholder a **Name, Width, Height, Color** and **Alternate text.**

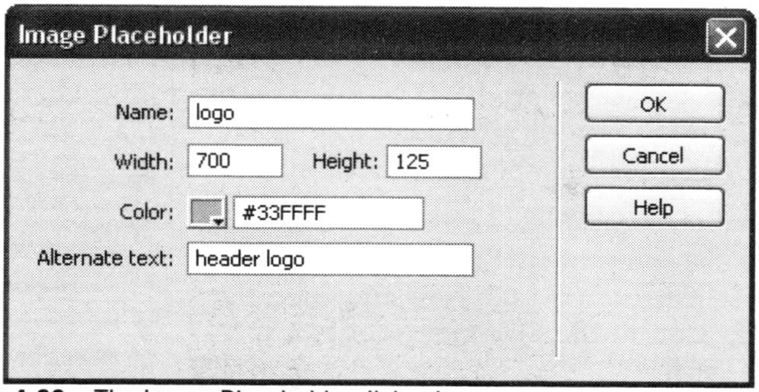

Image Placeholder

Name:	logo	OK
Width:	700	Height: 125	Cancel
Color:	#33FFFF	Help
Alternate text:	header logo	

Figure 4.38   The Image Placeholder dialog box

Note that the placeholder is not displayed when the page is opened in a browser – there will simply be a blank space. It is only therefore of real use within Design view.

logo (700 x 125)

Figure 4.39   Design view showing image placeholder

When you receive the final image, simply replace the placeholder – your final image should be in your images folder, so select the placeholder by clicking it as you would an image and, using the **Src** attribute in the Properties panel, navigate to and select the newly available image.

Adding other media

As well as images, there are other media types that you may wish to add to your pages. These include Flash and Shockwave files, Flash video, sound files and applets. Note that these are files which you create in applications other than Dreamweaver. Dreamweaver gives you the functionality to import or insert these media types into your pages, but making changes to them requires that you go back to the creating program e.g. Flash, Director.

Flash

Flash is, in Adobe's words, 'the industry-standard tool for creating interactive content'. You have undoubtedly come across the Flash player as a means of viewing web content produced by Flash CS3. Shockwave files are produced by Adobe's Director which, though a web authoring tool, is designed for the multimedia environment of, for example, games and e-learning.

To include a Flash file (which is recognized by its file suffix of .swf) in your page, position the cursor in Design view and select the **Media** icon in the **Common** tool bar, then click **Flash**.

Figure 4.40   Inserting a Flash file

When prompted in the **Select File** dialog box, select the Flash file and click **OK**.

A placeholder is added to Design view and the attributes are visible within the Properties panel.

As with an image, you may alter the size (**W** and **H**), and space around the inserted file (**V space** and **H space**). You may also preview it in Design view by clicking the **Play** button.

As with other site content, it is a good idea to create a separate folder for Flash files.

Shockwave files are imported in a similar fashion – just select **Shockwave** from the media menu.

To import Flash video files, position the cursor in Design view and select **Flash Video** from the media menu.

Applets are small self-contained applications written using the Java programming language. Select **Applet** from the media menu.

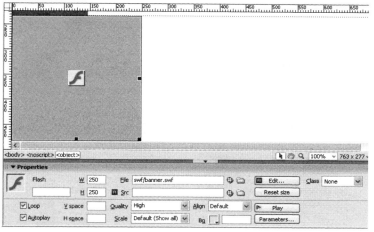

Figure 4.41 Flash file added to page

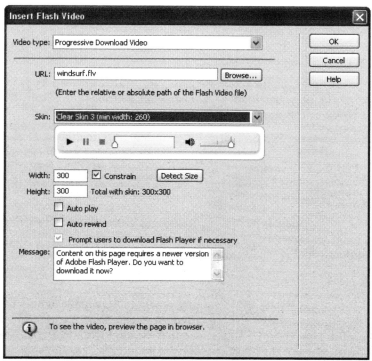

Figure 4.42 Insert Flash Video dialog box

ActiveX controls are also applications but they are Microsoft-specific i.e. they will run within the Internet Explorer browser on Windows platforms. This severely restricts their usage given the rising prevalence of alternative browsers such as Firefox.

Plugin refers to other media types (such as Apple's QuickTime) which may require a plug-in to allow the browser to display or run the embedded object.

You will now have the strong impression that inserting media files into your web page is simple with Dreamweaver!

Let's look at adding a Flash video file to a page (Figure 4.42).

* Setting the **Video Type** to **Progressive Download Video** allows it to start playing before the complete file has been downloaded to the visitor's system. This is advantageous if the file is large.

* **Skin** allows you to choose the appearance of the buttons used to control the video.

* You can either assign a size or let Dreamweaver calculate it by checking **Detect Size**.

* **Auto play,** as the name suggests, will start the video as soon as the page has loaded. **Auto rewind** will move the controls back to the start position at the end of the video.

* A **Message** is automatically included by Dreamweaver for display if the visitor's computer does not have a sufficiently up-to-date version of the Flash Player to run the video. A prompt will be displayed for the visitor to download the latest version.

The other **Video Type** option, **Streaming Video,** requires broadly similar parameters to be set, the major difference being that content is delivered exclusively over the Internet.

Sound

It is just as easy to include sound media in your page as it is to include visual media. One method of incorporating a sound file is via a conventional hyperlink; that is, the visitor will choose whether or not they wish to play the sound file. The alternative of course, is to embed the file in your page.

The sound file is inserted using the **Plugin** option – navigate to the file you wish to insert (.wav being an example of a sound file suffix). Make sure when you insert it into your page that the necessary controls are visible when you select **Play** (no controls show when you insert the file initially) – you may well have to resize the sound file in Design view so that it looks like the screenshot below as the default size is only 32 × 32 pixels.

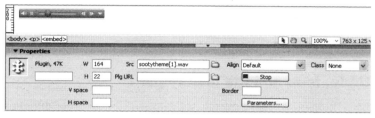

Figure 4.43 Sound file (.wav) playing in Design view

Though when inserted, the **W** and **H** were set by Dreamweaver to 32 and 32 respectively, I have changed them to 164 and 22 in order to show the full controls. The purpose is to ensure that your visitor is able to control the operation of the sound file.

You may have encountered web pages which automatically play sound when the page opens and there are no visible controls. How is this achieved? Going against the advice above about making the controls visible, we will now do the opposite. Set both **W** and **H** to 0, so that though the file is visible in Design view, it will not be visible when the page is displayed in a browser.

Because there is nothing visible in the browser, the visitor cannot play the sound file, so it must be set to autoplay. To do this, click the **Parameters...** button in the Properties panel and enter a **Parameter** of *autostart* and a **Value** of *true*, as in Figure 4.44.

You could also add a **Parameter** of *loop* and a **Value** of *true*. Why might this not be a good idea? Because the visitor has no means of stopping the sound file playing over and over again. This could be extremely annoying and is liable to irritate your visitors no end.

To give full control to the visitor, create a subsidiary page as in Figure 4.43 above and provide a link to it from one of your main site pages. This way the visitor will choose whether or not they even want to open a page containing a sound file.

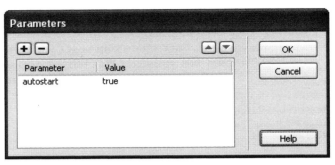

Figure 4.44 Parameter settings for sound file

Undo, redo and the history panel

Being human, we make mistakes. Dreamweaver provides different ways of recovering from errors. One is the standard Undo which is available with most applications (**Edit > Undo** or **[Ctrl]+[Z]**); if you subsequently change your mind, restore the action with Redo (**Edit > Undo** or **[Ctrl]+[Y]**). I have not tried to determine how many actions Dreamweaver will allow you to Undo or Redo, but practice suggests it is quite a few.

The History panel is rather more sophisticated. Up to 50 steps are retained by default. You may alter this in the **Preferences** panel –
under the **Category** of **General**, look for the **Maximum number of history steps** box.

To access the History panel, select **Window > History** (or **[Shift]+[F10]**). If you have been working on your document, there will be entries in the panel showing the changes you have made during the current editing session. The entries are in order with the last change having an arrow alongside. Drag the arrow upwards to undo changes.

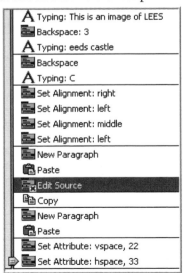

Figure 4.45 History panel

You can replay instructions, copy them to the clipboard or save them as commands using the icons below the History panel.

Replay

Using the History panel, you can select one or a series of actions which you can then **Replay**. Multiple steps may be selected using [**Ctrl**]-click.

Commands

There may well be repetitive actions which you wish to carry out on a number of pages. For example, the insertion of an email hyperlink or the insertion of a table with specific width, height and spacing attributes. To save having to repeat these tasks for every page, Dreamweaver offers the Commands function whereby you may save the code behind an action as a named command which may be run (not unlike a macro in a word processing program). Note that commands are not site-specific; they may be run on any page in any site.

The starting point for creating a command is the History panel, as this simplifies the creation process. Let's assume that I have created a table in a page – don't worry that we have not yet covered the subject of tables, the important point here is how Dreamweaver records the action and allows us to save it for future use. The History panel will look like this:

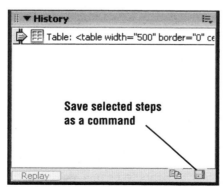

Figure 4.46 Table insertion shown in the History panel

To save the table insertion as a command which may be reused, first click on the entry in the History panel. This will enable the **Save** button (which in Figure 4.46 is greyed out because an entry has not yet been selected). Click the button and you will be prompted to enter a name for the command. Enter a name which has some relevance to its purpose, e.g. *aaa* would be accepted but is not meaningful. Click **OK** and the command will be saved.

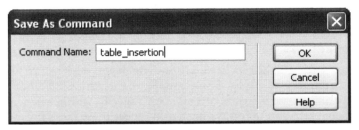

Figure 4.47   Save As Command dialog box

To execute a command in this or any other page, open the **Commands** menu and your commands will be shown at the bottom of the menu; click on one and it will be executed. In the case of my command **table_insertion**, a table will be inserted at the position of the cursor.

Dreamweaver will also record, in a temporary file, your actions as you enter them – click **Commands > Start Recording** and when you have finished click **Commands > Stop Recording**. There is no naming option because the commands are held in memory. To replay the stored commands, click **Commands > Play Recorded Command**. This is only recommended if there is something you wish to repeat during this Dreamweaver session only. The command will not be saved when you exit Dreamweaver.

Summary

If you have followed all of the activities in this chapter, you should now be able to:

+ Insert images as well as text into your pages

+ Use the Properties panel to change default settings of images and text

- Add special characters such as copyright
- Make sure your images are accessible to all users
- Change the appearance of a page using Page Properties
- Select a font to use for a page or a page element
- Align images and text
- Add image outlines (or placeholders) to your page in advance of images being ready
- Add sound and video media
- Create an easy-to-navigate photo album
- Undo and redo changes you have made
- Save commands and re-use them in other pages.

Exercises

1 When designing a page, how would you determine the estimated download time of that page for a visitor to your site?

2 Where and how would you edit the size (width/height) of an image?

3 Which image property would you set in order to wrap text around the right-hand side of an image?

4 In order to ensure accessibility of your images (to visually impaired users, for example), which image attribute should you always set?

5 Define two ways to insert an image.

6 Which of the following image-related issues should be considered when considering page download speeds?

   a. Remove unnecessary images from the page

   b. Make the images smaller in appearance i.e. alter the width and height attributes in Properties

   c. Maximise compression using an image-editing program such as Fireworks

   d. a and c

05

links

In this chapter you will learn:

- about site navigation using hyperlinks
- about links to external sites
- about intra-page, or anchor, links
- how to link to email
- how to attach links to images, Flash buttons and text

What is a hyperlink?

Let's first be clear about the purpose of a hyperlink or link. Quite simply it is a means for the visitor to move from the current page to another page of the same site, a page of an external site, a different section of the same page or to send an email (normally to the site webmaster or administrator).

Because the visitor needs to take some action, normally clicking a mouse, the link needs to be visible and obviously a link. Traditionally the link has been recognized by being blue, underlined text. However, links do not have to have these characteristics and many sites do not follow this tradition; therefore, your links need somehow to be obvious either through their position on the page or their behavior when a mouse moves over them.

We will start with the 'traditional' link, i.e. blue underlined text.

Standard link

In this context, 'standard' means a link which, when clicked will take the visitor to another page of your site or an external web page. As we will need several pages in order to implement and test our links, let's start by creating some additional pages.

You should already have a page called *index.html* which was created in Chapter 2. To create additional pages, go to the Files panel. Click on the site name, e.g.

then right-click and select the option **New File**. A file will be created called *untitled.html*; as the filename will still be selected, overwrite the word 'untitled' with something more meaningful e.g. *about, contacts, links*. Make sure you do not overwrite the .html portion of the filename or the page will not be viewable in a browser or editable in Dreamweaver.

Add three additional pages so that there are now a total of four HTML pages in your site. Content is unimportant at this stage – add a heading to each so that you can distinguish one from another.

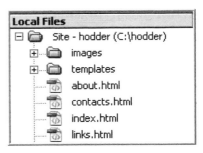

Figure 5.1 Site panel showing HTML files

Let's start by adding a link from the home page (*index.html*) to the About Us page (*about.html*). Open *index.html* and position the cursor in Design view at the point you wish the link to appear. In the Common toolbar, click the hyperlink icon . This dialog box will appear:

Figure 5.2 Hyperlink dialog box

Enter the **Text** that will appear on the page to indicate the link, in this case 'About Us'.

In **Link,** enter the name of the page to which you are linking, *about.html*.

Title refers to text that will appear when hovering over the link so, though optional, it is helpful to your visitors.

The **Access key** allows non-mouse users to activate the link with a letter.

The **Tab index** allows navigation of links using the keyboard.

Click **OK** and Design view will now look like this:

Figure 5.3 Hyperlink added. The default settings for the link are blue underlined text.

Test the link to make sure it works. Save your file (*index.html*) and open it in a browser (press [**F12**]). Click on the link and the page you have linked to should open.

A navigation bar is an extension of this process. As we have four pages, we need to add to each the same navigation bar (with some subtle differences) to allow easy movement from page to page.

Still in the *index.html* page, we will add some text which will form our navigation for each page. I have used '::' to separate the text; this is not mandatory, you can use anything you like. I have also positioned the navigation bar above the heading. You normally expect to see navigation bars above or to the left of the main page content.

Figure 5.4 Link text added

Each piece of text needs to be converted into a link, using a different method from the one we used to create the link shown in Figure 5.3 (we could use that technique but the one we will use here is just as good).

Start by selecting the text 'Home', then look in the Properties panel for the Link box – this will hold the address of the page, in this case *index.html*. There are several ways to create the link:

♦ Type in the filename.

♦ Drag the crosshair icon over the filename in the **Files** panel and release the mouse button.

- Open the files folder using the **Browse for file** icon and select the file.

- Drag the filename from the **Files** panel into the **Link** box.

My preference is to use the crosshair icon.

Your page should now look something like this in Design view.

Figure 5.5   First link created

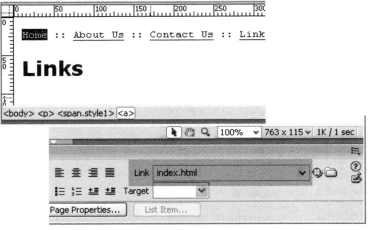

Figure 5.6   Home link selected showing corresponding address in Link box

Figure 5.7   All links created

Click on each link in turn in Design view and make sure that the filename that appears in the Link box is the correct one.

Save *index.html*, open it in a browser and test each of the links in turn. Make sure each link opens the correct file, e.g. clicking 'About Us' opens *about.html*.

So we have updated *index.html*, but we also need to include the navigation in each of the other three pages. Why? So visitors can go from any page in our site to any other in it without having to return to the home page. To achieve this, we can simply copy the code we have created already and paste it into our other pages.

To copy the code from *index.html*, in Design view, select all of the links, right-click and select **Copy**. Go to each of the other pages (*about.html*, *contacts.html* and *links.html*) and position the cursor in Design view where you wish to paste the links; right-click and select **Paste**. That's it – done. You now have a navigation bar in each of your pages. Remember to save all of the files.

There is one more thing to do before we test our navigation. You may already have worked out that on every page each link is active (or clickable), but is it sensible to have a clickable link labelled 'Home' if we are already on that page? The visitor may become confused seeing such links, so on each page we will deactivate the link specific to that page. This is quite straightforward.

If we take *index.html* as an example, in Design view click anywhere on the link **Home** and you will see *index.html* in the Link box in the Properties panel. Select *index.html* in the Link box and delete it using your keyboard delete button; hit [**Enter**] to confirm and the text 'Home' which previously appeared as a link will now just appear as conventional text.

Figure 5.8 Page-specific navigation – Home is no longer a link for this page, index.html

Dreamweaver's navigation bar

What we created in the last section is a navigation bar which will work perfectly well. You are probably aware that links may appear differently depending on their state. There are four states – *link* (when the link has not yet been used), *visited* (the link has been used), *hover* (the mouse is positioned over it) and *active* (the last link used on this page). Each link state may have its own defined attributes (e.g. text and background colours; underlined or not underlined) other than the defaults which are used for the examples in the previous section.

Browsers have defined colours which will normally be used when the web page itself does not specify any particular colour settings for link states. Here are two examples:

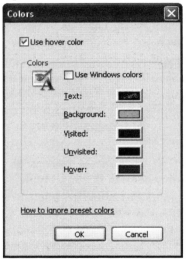

Figure 5.9 Firefox (below) and IE (right) link state colour settings. Though typically these settings are used only when the web page has no specific settings, it is possible to override these with custom settings for consistency.

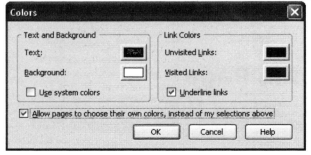

There are numerous ways to create a customized navigation bar which enables you to set the attributes for each link state – Dreamweaver's navigation bar and CSS.

The navigation bar relies on the use of images for each state so ideally you need four different images to represent each of the states; however, one is the minimum. As creation of images is outside our scope, I will just point you in the direction of this functionality. When you have prepared your images, use **Insert > Image Objects > Navigation Bar.** You then decide on how the navigation bar will look by assigning each image to a link state.

The alternative method, probably more widely used, is to use CSS which can achieve the same effects without the need to create image files. We will look at this option in Chapter 7.

External site links

The navigation bar we designed earlier was intended for our site only but there may be cases where we want the visitor to access pages outside our site, e.g. we have recommended a tutorial on a particular site. In this case we do not use a navigation bar but a standard link – if there are a number of such links, we might well incorporate them into a separate page which we could call *links.html.*

The difference between internal and external links is that the former are relative and the latter are absolute.

A relative link is used when we refer to pages in our site (internal links) and so we do not need to specify the full address, e.g. if our site domain name is **dummy.com,** and we want to provide a link from the home page to a links page, we can use **links.html** when defining that link rather than **http://www.dummy.com/links.html**. A relative link takes the current page as a starting point – it's like saying 'Fred's house is two doors down the street on the left-hand side' because the starting point is your house. Relative links are used for links to pages in your site only.

An absolute link provides the full address because the page we are linking to is not part of your site. In the example of Fred's house, no information was given about the city or country just the fact that it is two doors down on the left. If the person you were talking to was not in your house, you would have to provide more information such as 'Fred's house is in London, England and the address and post code are…'. An example of an absolute address is **http://www.anothersite.com/products.html**.

Creation of an external link follows the same steps as for the standard internal link. The difference is the address itself. Here is an example:

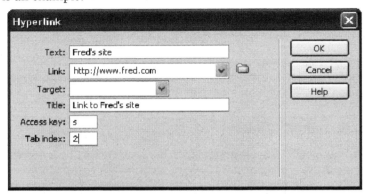

Figure 5.10   External link – http:// must be included with the link address

Anchor links

Anchor links provide the means by which visitors may move around within the current page – an example would be one which contains a large amount of information necessitating vertical scrolling. With anchors, we can create points in the page to jump to and also links to allow the visitor to return to the top of the page.

I will create a dummy page to show how this works. The page will consist of blocks of text which I will split up into three, with each block representing a topic. At the top of the page will be a set of links (acting as a menu) which will allow the visitor to jump to the topic which interests them, and below each topic will be a link to return the visitor to the top of the page (and to the menu).

My text consists of a heading (Topic 1 in heading 2 format) and four paragraphs of text. This is repeated twice so I now have three topics numbered 1, 2 and 3.

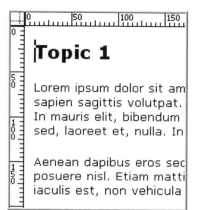

Figure 5.11 Text before adding anchor links

With the cursor positioned alongside the heading, as shown, click the anchor icon 🔱 in the **Insert** toolbar. You will be prompted to add an anchor name – for the first topic enter 'topic1'.

You can call the anchor pretty much what you like but, as always, I would advise against including spaces in the name.

Click **OK** and an anchor symbol will appear alongside the heading.

Figure 5.12 Anchor added. The anchor icon indicates that this heading can now be reached by using a link quoting the anchor name. Add anchors for the other two topics – make sure they are called 'topic2' and 'topic3'.

Note that the gold anchor symbol will not appear when the page is displayed in the browser.

The anchor alone is not sufficient – they provide points in the page to jump to but we also need standard links at the top of the page which will allow the user to jump to their selected topic. As there are three topics, three links are needed. These are standard links with one significant difference as we will see.

1   Add the text for the links and then select the link text for the first topic (Topic 1 in the example in Figure 5.14).

2   Click the hyperlink icon in the Insert toolbar and complete the dialog box as below – note that the Link box contains #topic1. The # must be present for an anchor link.

3   Click **OK** and the first link has been created – repeat for the
    other two links (making sure you add the correct Link name
    for each one – #topic2 and #topic3 respectively).

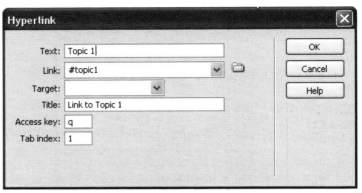

Figure 5.13   Anchor link

The page in Design view will now look something like this:

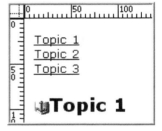

Figure 5.14   Links added to top of page.
Save the page and open in a browser. When
you click any link at the top of the page, the
browser should jump to the relevant topic.

Although the visitor can now go directly to the topic of interest,
they will still have to scroll to return to the menu of topics at the
top of the page. We can make this process easier by adding links at
the foot of each topic; first we need a point at the top of the page
to return to so we add an anchor link with the name of 'top'.

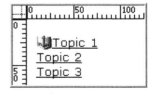

Figure 5.15   Menu anchor. Anchor added
alongside first link. Call the anchor top.

At the end of each topic add the text 'back to top' and create a link
from this text – select the text and add #top to the Link box.

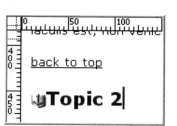

Figure 5.16 Back to top link. The text back to top should now be a link which, when clicked, returns the visitor to the menu at the top of the page.

Finally, save your file and test the links in a browser.

Email links

If you want visitors to your site to be able to contact you, the options open to you are an email link or a form (see Chapter 8). The email link contains your email address and will, when clicked, open the visitor's email program with your address already in the To: box.

Creating an email link is straightforward. Position the cursor in Design view where you wish the link to go and click the **Email** icon in the **Insert** toolbar. This dialog box will be displayed:

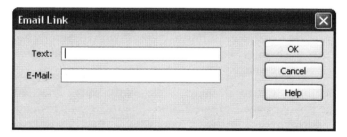

Figure 5.17 Email dialog box. Enter the Text to appear on the page, e.g. 'Email me' and the E-Mail address, e.g. info@abc.com

Click **OK** and the **Text** you entered appears in Design view. Save the file and test in a browser. Click the link and your email program should open with the specified **E-Mail** address already in the **To:** box.

You can also assign a value to enter into the Subject line of the email program by adding text after the E-Mail address. At the end of the address, type a question mark, '?', followed by 'subject=' and then the subject of the email, 'Your site', in Figure 5.18.

Figure 5.18 Add subject to E-Mail address. The format of the message after the E-Mail address is important.

You can also add copy and blind copy addresses after an ampersand, e.g. '&cc=fred@fred.com&bcc=manager@info.com'. The complete content of the E-Mail box might thus read:

info@abc.com?subject=Your site&cc=fred@fred.com &bcc=manager@info.com

Attaching links to images

It is common practice to attach links to images – news sites such as the BBC provide links via both text and image. How do you know that an image has a link associated with it? Simply because the cursor changes shape from a pointer to a hand when you hover over the image.

Attaching a link to an image is straightforward. First, add an image to your page and select it. In the Properties panel, add the link address in the Link box either by typing it, using the crosshair icon or the browse icon.

If the link is external, you will have to type the whole address (remember the http://); if the link is internal, you can use the crosshair or browse icons. You may also, after selecting the image in Design view, right-click and select the **Make Link** option – either select from the available file list or type in an address.

Save your file and test in a browser – click on the image and you should then be taken to the specified page.

Flash buttons

Dreamweaver provides a means of adding Flash buttons, which you might want to use instead of text links. The buttons are designed to act as links, as we will see when we add one below. Although Flash is the underlying technology, you do not need to have Flash installed on your computer in order to add these buttons. Nor do you need to know anything about Flash to use this functionality.

We will design a navigation menu similar to that in Figure 5.8 using Flash buttons. Note that the document you will be updating must first be saved if it is a new file or Dreamweaver will display a message asking you to do so when trying to insert a button.

Start by positioning the cursor in Design view where the first button is to be inserted; next select **Insert > Media > Flash Button** to see this dialog box:

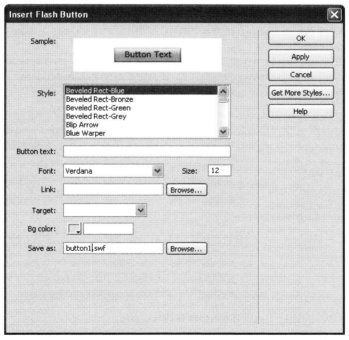

Figure 5.19   Flash button dialog box

Sample will display a button based on the selected **Style** – in this case the Style is *Beveled Rect-Blue*.

Button text represents the text displayed in the button i.e. what the visitor will see.

Font and **Size** allow you to set the button text's appearance.

Link is to specify the page or URL (internal or external links respectively) which this button will open when clicked by the visitor.

Target determines where the link will be opened:

_blank	a new window
_parent	the parent frameset
_self	the same window as the current page – this is the default setting
_top	the top frameset window

Save as will automatically contain *buttonx.swf* (where *x*, starting from 1, is the next number in sequence). Use the **Browse** button if you want to overwrite an existing button. Like other site assets, it would be worth considering placing any Flash buttons in a separate folder for ease of finding and maintenance.

Use the **Apply** button to see the button added to your page while the dialog box remains open – allowing you to make and test adjustments without the need to keep reopening the dialog box.

Get More Styles... does not actually lead you to an Aladdin's cave of additional button templates but to Adobe's online Exchange – the place where add-ons or extensions to all Adobe products may be found.

Click **OK** to insert the button. You will be prompted for Flash Accessibility Attributes:

* Title (which will enable visitors who are unable to see the button to determine its purpose via their specialized software)

* Access key (alphabetic shortcut)

* Tab index (number of tabs required to reach this button).

The page in Design view and the Properties panel will now look like this:

Figure 5.20   Flash button inserted

With the button selected, the Properties panel will display the attributes. As the button fully occupies the defined width and height, setting the Bg colour would result in a slightly coloured border only, as there is no visible background. You may adjust its width and height (either by changing the W and H values in Properties or by dragging the resize handle at the bottom right of the button) and there should be no loss of image clarity. If resizing the button would distort the image, the button itself is not resized though the overall image size does change. This in turn means that the background to the button is now made visible. In the example below the W and H values have been changed to 673 and 66 respectively and consequently there is now a visible background. The button could not be resized to fill this space without distortion.

Figure 5.21   Flash button resized

In common with all other page elements, you should consider allocating a name to the button – see the empty box to the left of the H attribute. As usual when naming an element, make sure you allocate it something meaningful, e.g. *submit_form*.

- To make any changes to the button's configuration, click **Edit...** and you will be returned to the dialog box as displayed in Figure 5.19 (page 113).

- **Reset size** returns the button to its original size if you have made W and/or H changes and wish to discard them.

- As with an image, you may define V space and H space to put vertical and horizontal space around the Flash button – note that this is not counted as the background, it is simply 'whitespace'.

- **Quality** should be left as the default High setting to ensure the image looks at its best when displayed.

- **Align** is the same setting as is used for an image and controls the alignment of surrounding elements such as text.

- **Play** will display the button in Design view as it will appear in a browser; after clicking this button, the text 'Play' will turn to 'Stop'. Click **Stop** when you have viewed the button.

- We saw above that changing the button's size might result in Dreamweaver displaying the background if the button will not scale without distortion. If you have a particular need for the button to occupy the defined space completely, without displaying any background, then use the **Scale** property – set it to *Exact fit* and the button will fully occupy any space; the results may not look too good however.

- Using the **Bg** colour palette allows the background colour, where visible, to be set.

- **Parameters** allows you to define additional parameters for the Flash button.

Flash text

Flash text can be used for any text, not just link text. However, as we are focusing on links in this section, we will look at how to produce a link using this functionality. Bear in mind though that Flash text has a wider usage.

The advantage of inserting Flash text is that you may use any font without having to worry about your visitor having the same font installed on their computer. As with the Flash button, Flash text is added to a .swf file which by default is called *textx.swf* (where *x*, starting from 1, is the next number in sequence).

Let's add some text using the font Napa Heavy SF (don't worry if you do not have this; the purpose of this exercise is to demonstrate insertion of Flash text so any non-standard font will do).

Position the cursor in Design view and select **Insert > Media > Flash Text**. In the dialog box (Figure 5.22), choose a **Font** and enter a **Size** (in pixels), justify the text if you wish, choose a **Color** and a **Rollover color** (the text will take this colour when the visitor's mouse is moved over the text). Add the text 'View latest bargains' (this is just dummy text for the purposes of this exercise), in **Link** enter an existing page address and choose a **Bg** color – leave the **Save as** filename set to the default.

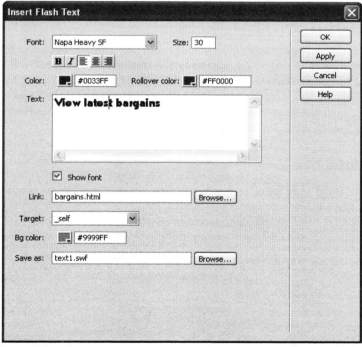

Figure 5.22 Flash text dialog box

- Click **Apply** to see the text in Design view before closing the dialog box.

- Click **OK** when you have finished experimenting with font and colour settings.

Figure 5.23 Flash text inserted

You may resize the text by using the resize handle; in this case, the text will always expand to fit the available space, unlike the behavior of the Flash button. As we have set a Rollover color property, click the **Play** button and hover over the text in Design view to see how the text will display when a visitor moves the mouse over it.

Hotspots

We have seen how a single link can be attached to an image. Hotspots allow the image to be split into areas, each with its own link. So for example, a map might be split into sections with each section linked to a tourism site for the country or area selected.

Hotspots may be rectangular, circular or polygonal. When an image is selected in Design view, the hotspot tools may be seen in the Properties panel.

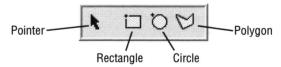

Figure 5.24 Hotspot icons

We will use a photograph of Leeds Castle to illustrate usage of the icons. A rectangular hotspot will be added which will link to the Leeds Castle website.

1 Add an image to the page and make sure it is selected.

2 Click the rectangle hotspot icon in the Properties panel.

3 Move the cursor over the image and, using the mouse, draw a rectangle over the castle; the end result will look something like this:

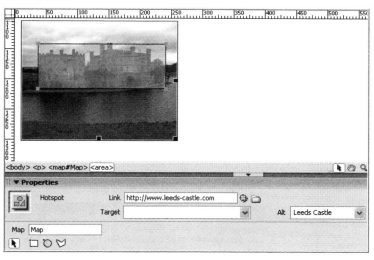

Figure 5.25 Rectangular hotspot added

Note, in the Properties panel, the full address in **Link** (as this is an external site) and the use of a description in **Alt** (for accessibility). Save and test in a browser – when you hover over the area defined by the rectangle (which will not be visible in the browser), the cursor will change to a hand shape. Now try the circle and polygon shapes as well.

Note that you can add multiple hotspots to an image.

Site map

Dreamweaver's Site Map functionality allows you to view the layout of your site together with the links that have been created. This can be accessed via the **Files** panel.

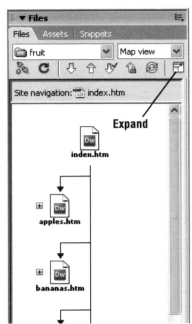

Expand

Figure 5.26 Map view selected in the Files panel. To build the map, Dreamweaver will look first for a file called index.htm or index.html – the default home page name. If this file is not present, no map will be built. To see an easier-to-read layout, click the **Expand** icon.

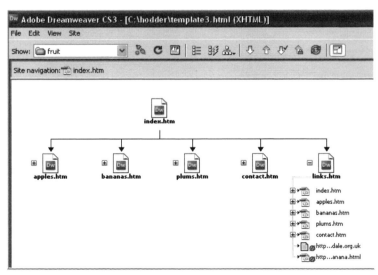

Figure 5.27 Site Map in expanded view

Click the **+** button next to a filename to see the links (internal and external) for a specific page. In the example above, I have opened the links page – you can see the internal and external links from that page where internal links are represented by just a page name while external links start with 'http'.

Summary

If you have followed all of the activities in this chapter, you should now be able to:

* Create a navigation bar for your site
* Create links to external sites and email addresses
* Create anchor links to aid navigation within a page
* Add a link to an image
* Add hotspots and associated links to an image
* Create Flash buttons with links
* Create Flash text with links
* View the site map.

Exercises

1   Into which field in the Properties panel do you type the destination address of your hyperlink?

2   What would you type into the field you identified in question 1 to link to an anchor called 'toc' on the same page?

3   How would you remove a hyperlink without removing the text from the page, i.e. disable the link?

4   How would you centre (or 'center') an image on the page?

5   What does the Reset Size option (circled in the screenshot below) in the Properties panel do? It will only appear when you change an image's width and height values from their original settings.

Figure 5.28   Properties panel – reset image size

W 222

H 200

06

tables

In this chapter you will learn:

- about static and liquid tables
- about formatted table contents
- how to use a table for page layout
- how to use spacer images to control column sizes
- about nested tables

Should I be using tables?

In word processing, tables are used to present information such as sales figures. In the web environment, tables are capable of more than just presenting data; they may also be used to lay out web pages. They are easy to use and Dreamweaver has a number of functions which allow you to progress from simple data tables, which are usually symmetrical (so many rows by so many columns), into the more advanced layout tables, which are typically asymmetrical.

Before we go any further it is safe to say that the use of tables is no longer universally favoured, with CSS (which we look at in the next chapter) being the preferred page layout method. CSS provides improved accessibility (page contents can be organized in order of relevance/importance which means that visitors using specialized software are able to read the relevant page content without needing to wade through navigation bars, footers, etc.) and leaner code (no need for the endless HTML <tr> and <td> tags associated with tables). The leaner code is a direct result of one of the primary purposes of CSS – to separate format from content.

That being said, my view, based on experience and observation, is that CSS contains a number of pitfalls both for those new to the language and for the more experienced practitioner. The way browsers interpret CSS does vary, not just between browsers, but sometimes between versions of the same browser. Tables are universally supported by current browsers and you should not see significant differences when viewing the same page in different browsers. This is certainly not the case with standard CSS, i.e. where no browser-specific workarounds have been applied. The situation though is improving with new browser releases, so watch this space!

The reality is that, while tables continue to work and be supported by browsers, many, many sites continue to use them. Will tables be deprecated at some point like the HTML <font> tag? That is entirely possible, but until that, as yet unknown, date comes about tables will still be around.

Terminology

Tables have their own terminology – rows, columns and cells. The diagram below identifies each element.

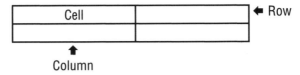

Figure 6.1 Components of a table

From the Dreamweaver perspective, each of the components of a table can be individually referenced. Each component also has its own HTML tag: <table> for the overall table, <th> for a table heading, <tr> for a row and <td> for an individual cell. Have a look in Code view when you create a table.

Table usage

In Chapter 4 on images it was apparent that we did not have complete control over the positioning of an image on the page, nor could we completely control where text was positioned alongside it. These issues are better addressed using a table, as control can be exercised over each row, column or individual cell.

As well as being created as individual stand-alone elements, tables may also be 'nested', i.e. inserted within a cell of an existing table (see page 135).

Table sizing

As tables give us more control over the layout of a page and the positioning of its contents, we need to be able to control the size of the table. There are two methods of sizing – static and liquid. The one you use depends on the effect you want for your website.

Static means that you define a fixed width for the table, in pixels, e.g. 600. If your visitor resizes their browser window so that it is only 500 pixels wide, this will have no effect on the table display, but horizontal scrolling would be needed to view the remaining 100 pixels of the table.

Liquid means that the table size is defined as a percentage of the available browser window space. Thus if we set the table size to 80%, whatever the size of the visitor's browser window the table will always (or at least until the window becomes too small to accommodate the table) occupy 80% of the available space.

Adding a table

Before adding a table you need to know what you will be inserting into it, so that you know how many rows and columns you need and the space (width and height) required to take your content. You can add anything in a table that you can also add to a standard page, e.g. images, text, links. The difference is the content is placed within individual cells, which makes your page layout easier to control.

As well as considering the overall table size, you need also to consider the individual column widths. When you insert a new table, the dialog box will ask for a table width. When inserting the table there is no means of pre-defining the width of cells – this information is added later. By default, Dreamweaver will initially display each of the cells with exactly the same width. If we do not set a width for each cell, Dreamweaver will decide, when content is added, how wide each should be and the browser will follow suit – this is not ideal.

Dreamweaver's method of determining cell widths can be somewhat disconcerting when you first encounter it – let's look at an example. I will create a two-row, two-column table with a width of 600 pixels and a two-pixel border for ease of visibility.

1 Position the cursor in Design view and click the **Table** icon in the **Insert** toolbar. This will bring up the **Insert table** dialog box (Figure 6.2).

2 Set the **Rows** and **Columns** (you may add more later).

3 **Table width** may be either static (pixels) or liquid (percentage). In this case, static is preferred.

4 **Border thickness** sets the width of the border; enter 0 (zero) for no visible border.

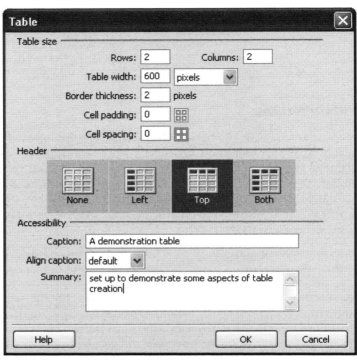

Figure 6.2 Insert table dialog box

5 **Cell padding** and **Cell spacing** we will look at in a moment – set to 0 (zero) for now.

6 Choose a **Header** setting and the highlighted table cells will become table headers – this means that the content you add to these cells will automatically be centrally positioned within the cell. The HTML tag applied is <th>. You would only use this option if you wanted column headings for your table; and not purely for page layout.

7 Don't ignore the **Accessibility** section as you need to cater for all visitors. **Caption** will create a header immediately above the table. Again, this is only used for a 'conventional' table, i.e. not for page layout. The position may be changed using **Align caption**. **Summary** provides a text explanation of the purpose and/or content if the visitor is unable to see the table; the summary text is not visible in the browser.

8 Click **OK** and the table will be created.

The screenshot below shows the code in Code view, the table in Design view and the overall table attributes in the Properties panel. The table is selected, as is evident from the resize handles. As yet, there is no content and the columns have not been assigned a width.

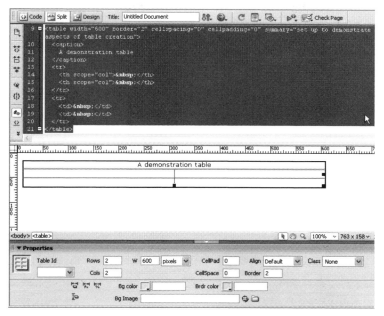

Figure 6.3 Table inserted, showing attributes in Properties panel

First, to demonstrate the function of table headers, I will add some content to the first row.

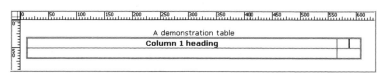

Figure 6.4 Column heading added in Column 1

After entering the heading text, I pressed [**Tab**] to move to the next column to add the second heading. Note how Dreamweaver has changed the table display. It now looks as though the columns have completely different widths, as it has decided that the first column should have more space because of its text contents, while the second column is narrower because it has (as yet) no content. When content is added, the display will look rather different.

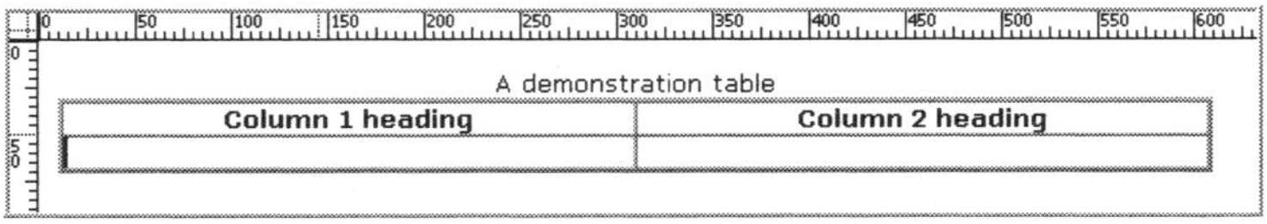

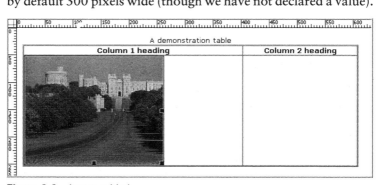

Figure 6.5 Column heading added in Column 2

After adding Column 2's heading, I clicked the cursor in the first column of the next row – at that point, Dreamweaver re-displays the table and we have reverted to equal-width columns.

To illustrate what happens when content is added, I will add an image to the first column of the second row. The table is 600 pixels wide and I am about to add an image 250 pixels wide. What do you think will be the result? In theory each column is by default 300 pixels wide (though we have not declared a value).

Figure 6.6 Image added

Therefore, there should be no impact if a smaller-width object is inserted. However, this is not the case. You can see that the same thing has happened as for the column headings. Dreamweaver has decided that the first column requires more space than the second because of its content. This situation will continue until we do something about it.

We need to allocate width values to each column. Note that this only needs to be done once, i.e. for the cells in the first row. Once a value for a cell has been set, all cells below it in the same column will also take that value.

Position the cursor in the first cell (the one with the heading Column 1 heading), which will display that cell's attributes in the Properties panel.

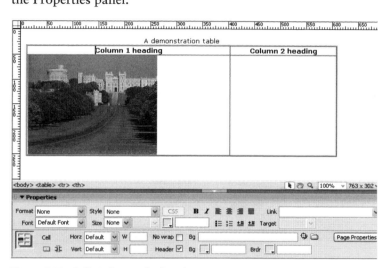

Figure 6.7   Cell attributes displayed

Look for the attribute **W** (width). Enter a static value in that cell, e.g. '300' for 300 pixels; there is no need to enter the word 'pixels'. If you wished this column to have a liquid width, then the numeric figure would be followed by a percent symbol, e.g. 45%.

Select the second heading cell and enter a value in **W** as well. This may seem obvious but the total width of the cells, when adding together the values in the W attributes, should equal the width allocated to the table. In addition, it is not a good idea to try to mix static and liquid values in the same table, e.g. if the table width is set to 75% and you set the cell widths to 250 and 450; the table can be resized to fit the visitor's browser but you want the cells to maintain their static width – the two are incompatible.

Having changed the **W** values for each cell to 300 (pixels) and added some dummy text to the second cell, the display in Dreamweaver now looks like Figure 6.8.

Figure 6.8   Columns sized and text added

Confusingly, despite applying column widths, Dreamweaver still displays the table incorrectly. This is corrected by the browser – the important thing is to set the column widths. This is probably the first instance we have encountered where Design view is not WYSIWYG. This highlights yet again the need to rely on browsers alone to determine how the page will look to a visitor.

A demonstration table	
Column 1 heading	Column 2 heading
	Lorem ipsum dolor sit amet, consectetuer adipiscing elit. Mauris iaculis lectus id ante. Aenean sed tellus ac sapien sagittis volutpat. Praesent ullamcorper. Integer quis sapien a augue condimentum dapibus. Sed sem. In mauris elit, bibendum vitae, blandit ac, pharetra vehicula, neque. Morbi ante nibh, volutpat et, scelerisque sed, laoreet et, nulla. Integer varius. Cras ac erat. Donec ultricies.

Figure 6.9   Display corrected by the browser – in this case, Firefox

Other table format options

Colour the border – in Design view, click anywhere in the table so that <table> appears in the Status bar at the base of Design view. Click it and you will see the table attributes displayed in the Properties panel. There is a palette labelled **Brdr color** – select a colour and the border colour will change.

Remove the border – again, select the <table> tag in the Status bar. In the Border box, change the value to 0 (zero) and press [Enter]. The border shown in Design view will change to a sort of dashed line – this is intended to help you, the designer, to see the outline of the table while you are creating pages; the outline is visible only in Dreamweaver.

Change the font – to change the font in a cell, click anywhere in that cell and its attributes will be displayed in the Properties panel. Select a font from the Font drop-down list. To change the font for a row, after clicking in a cell of that row, click <tr> in the Design view Status bar to select the row. Now change the font in Properties.

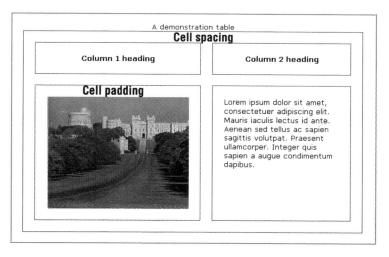

Figure 6.10 Table layout showing where the cell spacing and cell padding attributes are applied

Alter cell spacing – the **CellSpace** attribute, as shown in Figure 6.10, allows you to specify space between cells, and between cells and the border of the table. The value, specified in pixels, will be applied to each side of the cell (top, bottom, left and right). Follow the steps above to select the table attributes (select the <table> tag in the Status bar) and look for **CellSpace** in Properties – see Figure 6.3 (page 127). Change the value to something numeric and press [Enter]. You should now see space between the cells.

Alter cell padding – the **CellPad** attribute allows you to specify space between the border of the cell and the cell content. The value is applied to all sides of the cell. Look for **CellPad** in Properties. Change the value to something numeric and press [**Enter**]. You should now see space between the content and cell borders.

An interesting point to note about CellSpace and CellPad: when you look in the Properties panel, if either or both of these attributes is blank you might assume there would be no cell padding or cell spacing in your table. However, you would be wrong as the default setting is not 0. To be sure that you have no cell padding or cell spacing, make sure you enter a value of 0 (zero) in either or both boxes. You should also bear this in mind when inserting a new table, as we did earlier.

CellSpace and CellPad may only be set for the whole table, not for individual cells. If this is something you want to do, then CSS is the answer (using the margin and padding attributes).

As you will appreciate, the CellPad and CellSpace values affect the overall space available for text, images, etc. in your table. They also affect the column widths in the sense that if you start with this configuration:

Table width: 600 pixels

Column 1 width: 300 pixels

Column 2 width: 300 pixels

Cell padding: 0 pixels

Cell spacing: 0 pixels

then the cells will indeed be 300 pixels wide.

If you change the configuration to:

Table width: 600 pixels

Column 1 width: 300 pixels

Column 2 width: 300 pixels

Cell padding: 20 pixels

Cell spacing: 20 pixels

then cells cannot possibly still be 300 pixels wide because the cell spacing has to be included as part of the overall table width. As we want each column to be 300 pixels, we must adjust their widths to take account of the spacing. Effectively we have content which requires 660 pixels now, not 600. The table width will not expand to accommodate this; the contents will be adjusted to fit within the defined width of 600 pixels. What will happen in the above example is that the first cell will take 300 pixels, leaving the remainder, 240 pixels, to the second. This is not what we want.

The actual space available for content after applying cell spacing of 20 pixels will be: 600 – 20 (left hand) – 20 (between cells) – 20 (right hand) = 540 pixels. The two cells must share 540 pixels, or 270 each. So we should amend the **W** setting in Properties for each cell width from 300 to 270. The screenshot in Figure 6.11 shows a page layout with cell spacing and cell padding values.

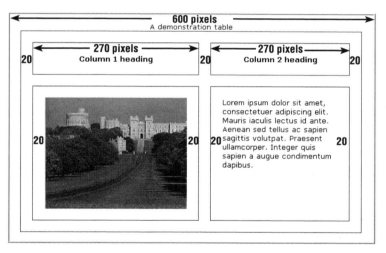

Figure 6.11   Cell padding and cell spacing values set

With the cells resized to 270 each, we still have a problem relating to the image, which is 250 pixels wide. As you can see above, the cell padding at each side adds up to 40 pixels; add the image width and we have 290 pixels. What will happen? Well, the image will simply take the space it needs – it will not be cropped or truncated. This will result in the second column having 250 pixels only.

What is the answer? We have three obvious options:

◆ Remove the cell padding given the usage of cell spacing

◆ Resize the image

◆ Resize the table.

As we have seen, there are many things to take into account when working with tables. However, some of the obvious traps have now been covered so we should not fall into these again.

Add background colours – the process to follow is similar to that for changing the font used in a cell or row. The difference is that the attribute to choose in Properties is the Bg colour palette. To avoid confusion, you will see two attributes labelled **Bg** in Properties – one is to set a background image, the other is the colour palette; it is easy to tell them apart but not so easy to explain why they have the same name.

Position content – when adding content to a cell, the content takes a default position in the cell. That position is left (from the horizontal perspective) and middle (from the vertical perspective). Look at the text in Figure 6.12.

Figure 6.12 Default alignment of cell contents

Let's look at how to change the text in the second cell so that it is aligned with its top and right borders and is justified.

Click anywhere in the cell and look for the attribute **Horz** (horizontal alignment) in Properties – change the setting to **Right** and the text will be aligned with the right-hand cell border rather than the left. Change the **Vert** (vertical alignment) attribute to **Top** and the text will align with the top of the cell rather than the middle. Finally, click the **Justify** icon to align correctly the left and right-hand text columns.

Nesting tables

It is possible to nest tables, i.e. place one inside another. We will look at an example in which we will create a navigation bar. Why use a nested table? Simply to have more control over the position and formatting of our navigation bar and individual links.

We will start with a simple two-column table which is to have a navigation bar in the left-hand column and the other column will hold text, images, etc. Therefore we need one row only, with the table width set to 600 pixels. Column 1 will be allocated 150 pixels and Column 2 set at 450 pixels.

To insert a nested table, click in the first cell and insert a table with five rows and one column (as five links will be added, arranged vertically). The size of the table may be set to 100% which means that it will completely fill the 150-pixel column.

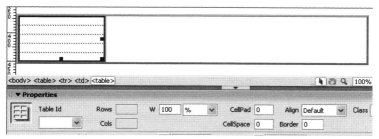

Figure 6.13   Table nested in cell of another table

Formatting is straightforward. Select <table> in the Status bar (be careful which, as there are two – you want the second one, as shown in Figure 6.13) and you may then change the background colour using the Bg colour palette. **CellPad** may also be set (to 5 pixels in this case).

You can see that this is very easy to do and can help to simplify the layout of your pages.

Figure 6.14 Nested table formatted

To make working with tables even easier, try opening the **Layout** tabbed panel in the **Insert** bar and clicking the **Expanded** button. Viewing and selecting individual table elements is now even more straightforward.

Deleting rows and columns

You cannot delete individual cells from a table as this would have a potentially detrimental impact on the display in a browser.

- **To delete a row** – click in any cell of the row you wish to delete and then use **Modify > Table > Delete Row**.

- **To delete a column** – click in any cell of the column you wish to delete and then use **Modify > Table > Delete Column**.

Practical application

In the examples above, we have looked at various aspects of table creation and management. We now turn to a practical example where the table is to be used for the overall structure of a page.

The first use we will put a table to is to create a header, navigation bar, content and a footer for a web page. This means we are going to remodel the home page, *index.html*, which we created in Chapter 5 (see Figure 5.8, page 105). This will enable us to look at a number of table attributes as we proceed.

The overall layout of the page will look like the one in Figure 6.15 (the table is defined by the borders).

We will need initially two rows and two columns. The table will be 800 pixels wide (static). We will use an image as the page header – this will not be included in the table for reasons explained later.

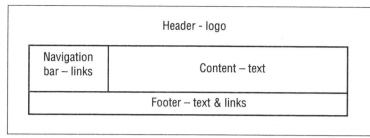

Figure 6.15 Nested table formatted

The table shows: Header - logo (top row spanning full width); Navigation bar – links and Content – text (middle row); Footer – text & links (bottom row).

Figure 6.15 Nested table formatted

The first addition to the page will be the image, which measures 800 pixels by 80. I have decided I do not want white space above and to the left of the image, i.e. I want it to start at the very top left hand corner of the browser window (this is equivalent to X,Y coordinates of 0,0). How do I fix this? The answer is by selecting the **Page Properties...** button in the Properties panel and setting the Top and Left margins. Note that the image in row 1 as shown in Figure 6.18 is positioned starting at coordinates 0,0.

Position the cursor in Design view below the image and click the **Table** icon in the **Insert** toolbar. This will bring up the dialog box (Figure 6.16).

Notes:

- 2 rows and 2 columns
- Width set to 800 pixels
- No border
- No Cell padding or Cell spacing
- No Caption as it would be displayed above the table – this is not appropriate when laying out a page
- Use of a Summary for screen readers

The values of Border thickness, Cell padding and Cell spacing should always be set to 0 (zero) when they are not required. Leaving the values blank means that Dreamweaver will supply a default value which is not 0. This is a particular issue in the Properties panel, which we will see later on.

137

tables

06

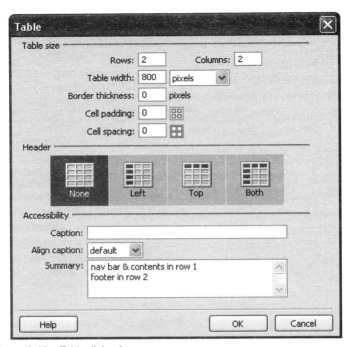

Figure 6.16 Table dialog box

Click **OK** and the table will be inserted. It will look like this in Design view:

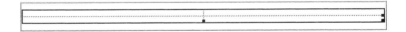

Figure 6.17 Blank 2-row, 2-column table in Design view

The table is automatically selected as it has just been added – note the thick black line around the table together with the resize handles. Within the table you should just be able to see the dotted lines which separate the cells.

To enter data into a cell you must first select the cell by clicking into it. You are then ready to enter images, text, etc.

We will now set widths for all cells for the sake of completeness. Position the cursor anywhere in the first cell of row 1 and, in the

Properties panel, look for the **W** (width) attribute, which will be blank. Enter '100' (no need to enter pixels or px) and hit **[Enter]**. Set the second cell width to 700. Of course, as we have already seen, this does not mean that the table is completely static because if I was to place an image in row 1 cell 1 with a width of 150 pixels, the cell would expand to that width. This emphasizes the need to plan your table content before creating the table.

Now we can add a vertical navigation bar in the first cell of the first row of the table that will look like this:

Links have been added for each of the four pages that exist in this site. Position the cursor in the first cell of the first row of the table and add the link text – remember, to eliminate line gaps between the links use **[Shift]+[Enter]** to move to the next line (this inserts an HTML break, <br />, rather than a paragraph, <p>).

Figure 6.18   Navigation links added

Add the relevant page address for each piece of text in the Link box in the Properties panel.

Don't worry about the vertical positioning of the links for now – we will address this in a minute.

Let's now focus attention on the contents area, the second cell in the first row. Into this we will add a heading and some dummy text (its meaning isn't important yet). You can get dummy text from **http://www.lipsum.com**. Our page now looks like this:

Figure 6.19   Content added

A background colour for the whole table which blends with the header logo would improve the look of the page. Moving the navigation links to the top of the first cell would look better as well. The first change can be made by selecting the table, the second, the row.

First click the <table> text below Design view in the Status bar. Look for **Bg** (be careful here as there are two Bg entries – make sure you choose the one with the colour palette). Select a shade of blue from the Bg palette.

Position the cursor anywhere in row 1 of the table in Design view. You will see the row attributes in the Properties panel – we are interested in **Vert** (vertical alignment). Select the **Top** attribute (to align all cell contents in this row to the cell top).

Figure 6.20   Navigation aligned and background colour added

You can see that the text in the navigation and contents cells lies immediately next to the cell borders. This can be changed by altering attributes of the whole table – the attribute we will use is cell padding which, as the name suggests, allows the space between the cell border and content to be configured; the setting we used initially was 0 – see Figure 6.15.

To select the table, the easiest method is to click on the text <table> in the Status bar at the foot of Design view. This will select the whole table and display the table attributes in the Properties panel. Look for the CellPad attribute and change it to 10 and click enter. 10 pixels of space will be added inside each cell (note that this also has the effect of changing the text layout in the contents area because we have reduced the cell width by 20 pixels – 10 on each side).

Finally, let's justify the text in the contents area. Select the whole cell (position the cursor in the cell and click <td> in the Status bar), then click the **Justify** icon in the Properties panel.

Figure 6.21   Cell padding of 10 pixels added to the table

Now we will add the footer which will occupy both cells in the second row; therefore, we need to merge the cells. First select the row. There are, as ever, several ways to do this – drag the mouse over the two cells or position the mouse in the first cell of the second row and click <tr> in the Status bar below Design view (there are other ways as well – see if you can find them).

With the row selected (indicated by a black border around the whole row), click the **Merge selected cells using spans** icon in the Properties panel. Row 2 now consists of a single cell. Enter your text – what follows is an example (text is centred in the row using the **Align Center** icon in Properties):

> Privacy policy | Terms of use | Site map © C S & T 2007 - 2008

Figure 6.22   Footer added with text centre-aligned

To separate the contents from the footer, we will insert a horizontal rule (a ruled line across the page; see Figure 6.23). Before adding the rule make sure that you add a paragraph or line break into the cell or, when you insert the rule, you will have difficulties inserting any other content (unless you amend the HTML in Code view). Position the cursor in the footer row and, from the menu bar, use **Insert > HTML > Horizontal Rule.**

By default, the horizontal rule will extend across the available space, e.g. the whole page, a table cell. Select the rule and you can change some of its attributes in the Properties panel.

▼ Properties						
	Horizontal rule	W		pixels	Align	Default
		H				☑ Shading

Figure 6.23   Horizontal rule attributes

Width and height can be set using the **W** and **H** attributes. The width may be set as a fixed size (pixels) or as a percentage of the available display space (%). If not occupying all of the available space, the alignment may be changed using **Align** – although only Left, Center and Right are available as options. **Shading** may be turned on or off.

Dreamweaver does not give you the option to change the default colour of the horizontal rule, so if you want to change the colour you have to add the attribute manually in Code view. Here is an example with the required additional text:

```
<hr align="right" width="440" size="5"
noshade="noshade" color="#FF0000" />
```

The final page will look like this when displayed in a browser:

Figure 6.24   Page displayed in browser – page background is white

Adding to the table

You may need to add to your table after it has been created and Dreamweaver provides you with several ways of doing this.

Using the **Insert** menu, with the cursor positioned in an appropriate place in the table, select **Table Objects** – you then have four options – **Insert Row Above**, **Insert Row Below**, **Insert Column to the Left** and **Insert Column to the Right**.

Using the **Modify** menu, again with the cursor positioned in the table, select **Table > Insert Rows or Columns...** to see this dialog box:

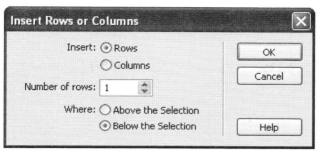

Figure 6.25   Insert rows or columns dialog box

Select the button for either **Rows** or **Columns** and set the number to be added.

Choose **Above the Selection** or **Below the Selection** (for rows); **Before current Column** or **After current Column** (for columns). The advantage of using this method is that you can add multiple rows or columns with a single command.

If you reach the last cell at the end of the last row and want to continue the table in a new row you could just press [**Tab**] and Dreamweaver will automatically add a new row for you.

Layout mode

There is an alternative method of adding tables, which does not require you to specify rows and columns in advance – this is layout mode, in which you draw the tables and cells yourself. You are not constrained to have contiguous cells (i.e. immediately next to each other), thus allowing a fairly free approach to page design. Using this method also means you can easily create much more complex tables.

To enter layout mode, use **View > Table Mode > Layout Mode**.

To use the layout mode functions open the Insert bar panel labelled **Layout**.

Draw Layout Cell

Draw Layout Table

Figure 6.26 Layout bar

The two icons we will use to create a table are at the right-hand side, **Draw Layout Table** and **Draw Layout Cell**. To use these, you must first position the cursor in Design view, otherwise they will remain greyed out. Click on the left-hand icon, **Draw Layout Table**, and you then draw the outline of a table. Once the table has been drawn, Design view will look something like this:

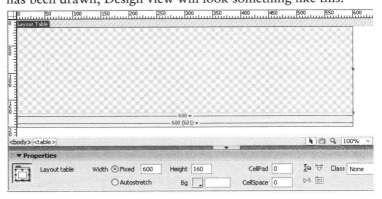

Figure 6.27 Table drawn using Draw Layout Table

Note that the Properties panel displays different attributes to those displayed when working with a table in what Dreamweaver calls standard mode. Access to all of the standard attributes can be gained by exiting from layout mode using the exit hyperlink which appears at the top of the document window.

To add cells, click the **Draw Layout Cell** icon and draw. The cells may not overlap each other, but there is no need to create cells for the whole of the available table space; if you want a few cells only, you are not stuck with a rigid formula of rows and columns.

In the following example, there are four cells for content (shown with white background). To achieve this effect working with tables in standard mode would be complicated.

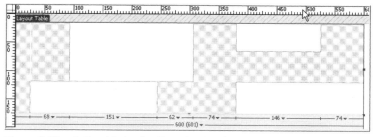

Figure 6.28 Cells added using Draw Layout Cell

Content is added as with a standard table.

There is one point to consider if you decide to use this method of table creation. The resulting HTML code will be 'bloated' – it will contain a considerable amount of code to achieve the desired end result. This code is potentially less friendly to visitors with accessibility issues making use of tools such as screen readers; in short, the content, which is after all the most important part of your page, is difficult to extract from the sea of code.

Working with layout mode makes it straightforward to create a table with one column which will resize as the browser window is resized, which is like having a dynamic table but in this case only part of the table is dynamic. Why would you want to do this? There may be elements of your page which you do not want the browser to resize such as some critical text or an image, while the remainder of the page can be resized to fit in with the visitor's selected page size.

This method introduces the concept of the spacer image, which requires a little explanation. The spacer image is to all intents and purposes an invisible image, typically only one pixel high, which is used to force a table cell to a minimum width that cannot be affected by the size of the browser window. Dreamweaver can create a spacer image for you – it will be inserted into the selected table cell.

Also introduced here is the concept of **autostretch** which, as the name might suggest, when applied to a column will allow the column to increase and decrease in size according to the dimensions of the browser window, i.e. it is dynamic.

Let's look at an example. Click the **Draw Layout Table** icon and create a table roughly 600 pixels wide. Then click the **Draw Layout Cell** icon and add two cells, each of around 300 pixels.

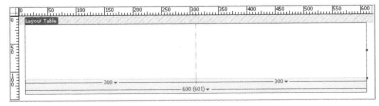

Figure 6.29 Two-column table

Add some text to each cell, save the page and view in a browser. The table is fixed size and will not be affected by resizing the browser window.

Click the down arrow at the base of the right-hand column and choose the option **Make Column Autostretch**.

Figure 6.30 Column options

To allow one column to autostretch, Dreamweaver will ensure that your other columns remain static. To do this, it will insert spacer images in each of the other columns so that they will retain their size. After selecting **Make Column Autostretch** you will see the **Choose Spacer Image** dialog box.

Figure 6.31 Choose Spacer Image dialog box

Click **OK** to select the default and Dreamweaver will create the spacer image file for you. Make sure, when prompted, that you save it in your images folder.

When you repeat these steps subsequently, Dreamweaver will automatically add your spacer image without asking. Now look at the table in Design view and its appearance has changed.

Figure 6.32 Foot of table after adding spacer image to left-hand column and applying autostretch to right-hand column

Note that the left-hand column remains at a fixed size of 300 pixels, but there is now a double bar on either side of the size; this indicates the presence of the spacer image and that this column now has a minimum width set to 300 pixels. Similarly, look at the right-hand column – the wavy line indicates an autostretch column. Finally, note that the table width has been reset to 100% to allow the right-hand column to expand and contract to fill the available browser space.

View the page in a browser and while the left column will retain its static width when the browser window size changes, the right column will change.

As a final point, you should be aware that autostretch may be applied to one column only.

Summary

If you have followed all of the activities in this chapter, you should now be able to:

• Add a table to your web page

• Size a table to be static or liquid

• Format the table contents by row, column or cell

• Use layout mode to create a page layout

• Configure a table to have static and liquid elements.

Exercises

1 It is possible to set the background colour of individual table cells but not of a whole row. True or false?

2 You have added text to a cell; how would you justify it?

3 All table elements may be selected using the mouse alone, e.g. you can select a row by clicking when pointing to it. This requires good mouse control. There is an easier way, which displays the table in an expanded (hint!) format. Try and find it.

4 When you create a table cell, Dreamweaver adds this " ". If you look in Code view, you will see this between <td> and </td>. But what does it do? Use a search engine to look for " ".

5 In terms of the Properties panel, what are the main differences between Layout and Standard view when dealing with a table?

6 What is the difference between the **Modify > Table** commands **Insert Rows or Columns...** and **Insert Row** or **Insert Column**?

Frames

Frames, or framesets, offer an alternative to tables for structuring pages, but they have long been a controversial topic in web design circles. The main difference between a frameset and a conventional page is that the frameset consists of a number HTML pages – one to specify the overall layout and one each for, say, a navigation bar, contents area and footer. The other significant difference is that when the visitor clicks a link, the browser opens the link page in a specified area of the frameset, usually the main contents area. The frameset itself is not reloaded; the only visible change is to the contents area.

The main reason for using frames is their ability to keep certain areas of the page static (e.g. navigation, header/footer) while the content changes. This is important from two perspectives – navigation and branding.

Against that are many reasons for not using frames:

* Accessibility may suffer if the visitor's software is unable to process all of the frame pages.

* Search engines may not be able to index all of the frame pages.

* Valuable screen space may be taken up with scrollbars, reducing the space available for content.

* Linking to external sites may be problematic – some sites do not wish their content to be viewed within the frame of another site for reasons of branding and potential plagiarism.

* Complexity – as you need a number of HTML pages to create a single visible page, there is a maintenance overhead.

Dreamweaver continues to offer the functionality to create frames, but as they are only used for very specific reasons, we will not be covering them in this book.

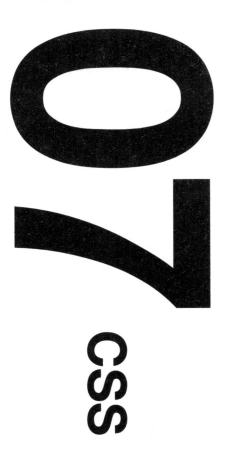

07

CSS

In this chapter you will learn:

- how to configure Dreamweaver to use CSS instead of HTML

- how to create and attach style sheets

- how to navigate around the styles panel

- about different selectors

Introduction

Using HTML tables is not the only way to lay out your pages or to format the content of pages. The alternative is to use Cascading Style Sheets (abbreviated to CSS) which provides a means of separating content (your text and images) from the format (font, sizes, etc.) in the code of a web page. As well as providing a greater range of formatting options than HTML, CSS's separation of format from content is advantageous from an accessibility as well as a maintenance viewpoint.

In addition, there are parts of the HTML language (such as the <font> tag) which are deprecated or scheduled for removal from the HTML language specification in the future. Any such tags should therefore no longer be used – the replacement for deprecated tags is CSS.

CSS – an overview

CSS is a separate language from HTML but Dreamweaver can create CSS as well as HTML without us needing to know the nuts and bolts of either language. However, as with HTML, having knowledge of CSS would be helpful when issues arise, as inevitably they will. A great starting point for familiarisation with CSS is the W3 Schools tutorial at **http://www.w3schools. com/css**. Dreamweaver itself also provides Help in a number of ways, which we will see in this chapter.

The issue that can trip up new, and indeed longstanding, users of CSS is browser support. We saw earlier that browsers interpret HTML; they also interpret CSS. Unfortunately, they tend to have their own individual interpretations of CSS and, suffice it to say, this is a topic of great and often heated debate in the web arena. Dreamweaver provides a means of checking for browser compatibility but, as ever, the best test is to open your page in a variety of browsers. Though this may sound a little off-putting, as new versions of browsers are released the levels of hope increase in the web community that the old (and significant) problems are being gradually eliminated.

Like HTML, CSS is not a programming language though it does have its own specific syntax as defined by the Worldwide Web

Consortium (or W3C, **http://www.w3.org**) – CSS has been the subject of two major releases, being referred to as CSS1 and CSS2. CSS2 has been around for a number of years now; CSS3 is in the pipeline – for more details on the CSS roadmap see the W3 website.

CSS2 is a style sheet language that allows authors and users to attach style (e.g. fonts and spacing) to structured documents (e.g. HTML documents). By separating the presentation style from the content, CSS2 simplifies web authoring and site maintenance.

CSS2 builds on CSS1 and, with very few exceptions, all valid CSS1 style sheets are valid CSS2 style sheets. CSS2 supports media-specific style sheets so that you may tailor the presentation of documents to, for example, printers – when you print a web page, with CSS you can configure the appearance of the page, e.g. removal of images. CSS2 also supports content positioning, which we will be looking at in more detail later in this chapter.

All levels of CSS – level 1, level 2, and any future levels – use the same core syntax, so once you have become familiar with the language you should not need to revise your existing knowledge when a new version of CSS is released.

You might already be asking yourself, do I really need to use CSS? The short answer is no, you don't have to, but as you develop sites you will find it restricting to ignore this significant technology. Best to embrace it from the start!

CSS has its own syntax (language rules) which means that if you have struggled to learn HTML you now need to get to grips with another set of attributes. On the plus side, knowledge of CSS will make your life much easier as you develop sites.

Why do you need to know CSS if Dreamweaver creates/writes it for you? Well the argument is somewhat similar to the one I used to justify learning HTML – to understand better what Dreamweaver has done and to make changes if necessary. You also need to understand at least a little about the workings of CSS to use the built-in functionality to advantage.

Another question you may be asking yourself is why do I need CSS as well as HTML? Because CSS can do many things which HTML cannot, such as positioning elements to an exact point on the page (without using a table), using a wide array of sizing for elements such as text, creation of navigation reflecting all possible link states without needing to use images, and so on. The list is huge.

One of its most significant advantages is the ability to use a single file (a style sheet file) to control the format of a site rather than having formatting applied to each page which is the case with HTML. This makes amendments very easy. Suppose you have a site of 50 pages and you decide to change the font from Georgia to Helvetica on each page. With HTML this would require amendments to each and every page; with CSS, to the contents of one file only. This reduces the risk associated with making changes and of course makes them quicker to implement.

The syntax of CSS

In HTML we talked about attributes which modify the default behavior of tags. In CSS, the terminology is different, as we now refer to rules. Let's look at the makeup of a rule.

```
RULE:     p { color: #FFFF00; }
SYNTAX:  selector { declaration; }
```

A CSS rule consists of two main parts: selector ('p') and declaration ('color: #FFFF00'). The declaration has two parts: property ('color') and value ('#FFFF00'). The brackets round the declaration and the semi-colon at its end are very important but Dreamweaver will add these for you.

The CSS rules are present in your page in three possible forms:

* Within <style> tags in the <head> area of an HTML document -- either as separate rules or as an imported style sheet file.

* In a separate style sheet file which is included in the HTML page using the <link> tag.

* As inline code embedded with the HTML code.

Whichever method is used, the underlying syntax is the same.

Let's look at a simple example which will contrast HTML formatting with CSS. Remember that one of the key benefits of CSS is its ability to separate formatting from the content, something which HTML is unable to do. Why is this important? Because it makes maintenance of the page much easier as the formatting of the code is completely separate from the content and therefore easier to find, update and edit.

```
<!DOCTYPE html PUBLIC "-//W3C//DTD XHTML 1.0
Transitional//EN" "http://www.w4.org/TR/xhtml1/
DTD/xhtml1-transitional.dtd">

<html xmlns="http://www.w4.org/1999/xhtml">

<head>

   <meta http-equiv="Content-Type"
   content="text/html; charset=utf-8" />

   <title>HTML formatting</title>

</head>

<body>

   <h1>HTML formatting</h1>

   <p><font color="#FF0000">Demonstrates HTML
   formatting</font></p>

</body>

</html>
```

In the above example, which represents a very simple HTML page with a heading and a paragraph of text, the <font> tag has been used to change the text colour in the paragraph to red (#FF0000). This illustrates perfectly the fact that HTML format and content are both to be found within the <body> tag. Imagine if there was much more content with associated formatting; how difficult would it be to find the individual attributes and change them? Also how easy would it be to miss one when the format is embedded with the content code?

Taking the same example and applying CSS, we can see clearly the separation of format and content.

```
<!DOCTYPE html PUBLIC "-//W3C//DTD XHTML 1.0
Transitional//EN" "http://www.w4.org/TR/xhtml1/
DTD/xhtml1-transitional.dtd">

<html xmlns="http://www.w4.org/1999/xhtml">

<head>
```

```
<meta http-equiv="Content-Type"
content="text/html; charset=utf-8" />
<title>CSS formatting</title>
<style type="text/css">
   p {color: #FF0000; }
</style>
</head>
<body>
   <h1>CSS formatting</h1>
   <p>Demonstrates CSS formatting</p>
</body>
</html>
```

The <font> tag has been removed and a new section, contained within the <style> tags, has been added into the <head> section. Now if we want to change the text colour we know where to find the code – it will always be in the <head> area, not mixed up with the HTML.

In Dreamweaver terms, the selector portion of the CSS rule may be a class, a tag or advanced. These terms are defined below:

- **Class** – a custom rule which may be applied to any code but requires you to specify where in the page it should be applied. May be used more than once in a page.

- **Tag** – redefines the default behavior of an HTML tag and as such will be automatically applied whenever that tag is used.

- **Advanced** – covers class-like rules which should only ever be used once in a page as well as selectors controlling hyperlink states.

Let's look at examples of each of these in turn, using the code we created above.

Class

```
<!DOCTYPE html PUBLIC "-//W3C//DTD XHTML 1.0
Transitional//EN" "http://www.w4.org/TR/xhtml1/
DTD/xhtml1-transitional.dtd">
<html xmlns="http://www.w4.org/1999/xhtml">
<head>
  <meta http-equiv="Content-Type"
  content="text/html; charset=utf-8" />
  <title>CSS formatting</title>
  <style type="text/css">
    .para {color: #FF0000; }
  </style>
</head>
<body>
  <h1>CSS formatting</h1>
  <p class="para">Class applied to this
    paragraph</p>
  <p>Class NOT applied to this paragraph</p>
  <p class="para">Class applied to this
    paragraph as well</p>
</body>
</html>
```

A class, also known as a 'custom class' because you create it and apply it, is always defined with a full stop as the prefix. You decide what name to give to the class, though it should be something meaningful and not contain special characters or embedded whitespace. I have chosen the name 'para' because I am going to apply the class to selected paragraphs only. In fact, in the sample code above you will see that there are three paragraphs; para is applied to two of them with the attribute **class="para"**. You do not need to put a full stop in front of the class name when it is quoted in an attribute. Note that this attribute is in exactly the same format as a standard HTML attribute, i.e. attribute_name="value". The second of the three paragraphs will not display the text as red because the class has not been applied.

Tag

```
<!DOCTYPE html PUBLIC "-//W3C//DTD XHTML 1.0
Transitional//EN" "http://www.w4.org/TR/xhtml1/
DTD/xhtml1-transitional.dtd">
<html xmlns="http://www.w4.org/1999/xhtml">
<head>
   <meta http-equiv="Content-Type"
   content="text/html; charset=utf-8" />
   <title>CSS formatting</title>
   <style type="text/css">
      p {color: #FF0000; }
   </style>
</head>
   <body>
   <h1>CSS formatting</h1>
   <p>Class applied to this paragraph</p>
   <p>Class also applied to this paragraph</p>
   <p>Class applied to this paragraph as well</p>
</body>
</html>
```

A tag, also referred to as redefined HTML, changes the default behavior of an HTML tag; in the case above, the tag being redefined is <p>. So in this example, the CSS selector uses the name of the HTML tag but note that you do not need to specify the <>. Because we are redefining an HTML tag, any instances of it which are found within the <body> will be affected. There are three <p> tags in the example code and each of them will feature red text when displayed in a browser. There is no need in this case to add an attribute to the <p> tag as the CSS is applied automatically when it is found.

Advanced

Advanced covers two CSS rule types – ID selector and pseudo classes. ID selectors work in the same way as a class, the main differences being the name is prefixed with a # when the selector is defined, the ID selector is intended for single usage in a page (a custom class may be used multiple times) and it is invoked with the **id** attribute, e.g. **<p id="para">**. There is nothing actually to stop you from using an ID selector multiple times in a page but this is not its purpose. An example is given below.

```
<!DOCTYPE html PUBLIC "-//W3C//DTD XHTML 1.0
Transitional//EN" "http://www.w4.org/TR/xhtml1/
DTD/xhtml1-transitional.dtd">
<html xmlns="http://www.w4.org/1999/xhtml">
<head>
   <meta http-equiv="Content-Type"
   content="text/html; charset=utf-8" />
   <title>CSS formatting</title>
   <style type="text/css">
      #para {color: #FF0000; }
   </style>
</head>
   <body>
   <h1>CSS formatting</h1>
   <p id="para">ID Selector applied to this
   paragraph</p>
   <p>ID Selector NOT applied to this
      paragraph</p>
</body>
</html>
```

'Pseudo classes' in this case refers to link states – link, visited, hover and active. The link itself is defined by the HTML <a> tag and the pseudo classes are named a:link, a:visited, a:hover and a:active. Wherever an <a> tag is encountered in the page, these pseudo classes will automatically be applied.

```
<!DOCTYPE html PUBLIC "-//W3C//DTD XHTML 1.0
Transitional//EN" "http://www.w4.org/TR/xhtml1/
DTD/xhtml1-transitional.dtd">
<html xmlns="http://www.w4.org/1999/xhtml">
<head>
   <meta http-equiv="Content-Type"
   content="text/html; charset=utf-8" />
```

```
<title>CSS formatting</title>
<style type="text/css">
   a:link {color: #009966; text-decoration:
   none;}
   a:visited {color: #FF6633; text-decoration:
   none;}
   a:hover {color: #CC00CC; text-decoration:
   underline;}
   a:active {color: #990000; text-decoration:
   none;}
</style>
</head>
<body>
   <h1>CSS formatting</h1>
   <a href="#">Dummy link</a>
</body>
</html>
```

In this example, there is a single link defined in the page with the text 'Dummy link'. Each of the four states is defined with a different text colour as well as an indication of whether the link text is to be underlined or not. The rule **text-decoration: none** indicates that underlining is to be turned off. When the visitor hovers over the link though there will be underlining because **text-decoration: underline** has been applied to the a:hover pseudo class.

All of the examples shown in this section implement page-level CSS. This means that the CSS rules apply only to the page in which they have been entered. This is not the only, or the best, way to implement CSS as we will see in the next section.

Methods of applying CSS

There are three ways in which CSS may be applied to your page: in-line, page level and style sheet.

Given that CSS separates format from content thus improving ease of maintenance and accessibility, adding in-line CSS is by far the least favoured method. In essence it means adding CSS in with the HTML or using CSS as if it was HTML formatting.

Here is an example of inline CSS:

```
<p style="color: #FF0000; font-face: Arial, Hel-
vetica, sans-serif">Inline CSS applied to this
paragraph only</p>
```

Using the HTML attribute style, the CSS selectors are defined as attribute values following the syntax rules we looked at earlier. I have only included this for the sake of completeness; we will not be looking at in-line CSS again, even though Dreamweaver does add in-line CSS for certain operations.

We explored page-level CSS with detailed examples in the last section. This is preferable to in-line CSS as it allows separation of format and content but it still presents a maintenance issue, i.e. we would still have to amend every page to change the font. At least with this application of CSS we know that the rules will be in the same place in each page.

The third option, and by far the best, is to add all of your CSS into a style sheet file which may then be attached to every page in your site. This means that when changes are required you only have to change the entries in the file – no changes are needed to the pages themselves.

The code required to add a style sheet is simple:

```
<head>
    <meta http-equiv="Content-Type"
    content="text/html; charset=utf-8" />
    <title>Style sheet attached</title>
    <link href="stylesheets/main.css"
    rel="stylesheet" type="text/css" />
</head>
```

No other code needs to be added to the page. The content of a style sheet looks like the example in Figure 7.1.

The file is a simple text file containing CSS selectors only – you do not need to use <style> tags.

Any text editor can be used to create, amend or update style sheets.

```
main.css

Code    Split    Design    Title:

  1    p {
  2        font-family: Georgia, "Times New Roman", Times, serif;
  3        font-size: large;
  4        font-style: italic;
  5        line-height: 1.4em;
  6        color: #330066;
  7    }
  8    .para {
  9        font-family: "Courier New", Courier, monospace;
 10        font-size: xx-large;
 11        font-style: italic;
 12        font-weight: bold;
 13        color: #990033;
 14    }
 15    #paragraph {
 16        font-family: Geneva, Arial, Helvetica, sans-serif;
 17        font-size: small;
 18        line-height: 1.8em;
 19        color: #CC0066;
 20        padding: 23px;
 21    }
```

Figure 7.1   Sample style sheet contents

We need to address now how Dreamweaver applies CSS, so we will concentrate on page level and style sheet methods only. By default, Dreamweaver will use CSS rather than HTML for page formatting – look in **Edit > Preferences > General** at the **Use CSS instead of HTML tags** setting which should be checked. Look also in **Edit > Preferences > CSS Styles** – although these will not necessarily mean much at this stage, it is worth remembering that you can control to some extent the format of the CSS created by Dreamweaver.

Applying CSS

So far in this book we have paid little or no attention to Code view, concentrating on Design view. However, it would now be advantageous to look at Code view as well. As a reminder, to view Design and Code views simultaneously open a page and click the **Split** icon at the top of the document window. You can resize the views by dragging the border at the top of Design view either up or down.

Let's start with something very simple: changing the appearance of some text.

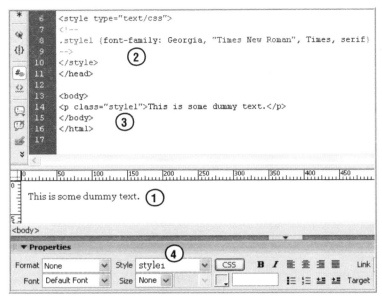

Figure 7.2 Adding CSS to text

Type some text into Design view, select it and change the font. Now look at Code and Design views. The notes that follow refer to the numbered sections in Figure 7.2.

1 Add text in Design view.

2 Select the text and, in the Properties panel, choose a Font. Dreamweaver automatically creates a class (custom class) with the default name of *.style1*. This is a class selector, defined by the dot before the selector name, which was mentioned earlier. The font to be applied by this selector appears within brackets.

3 The style created is linked to the selected text, i.e. by the addition of the attribute **class="style1"**.

4 The style name, style1, now appears in the Style drop-down list in Properties panel, so it may be reused. Dreamweaver will automatically assign a style name in the format *stylen*

(where *n* is the next number in sequence) to any CSS-related formatting operations you carry out. This can become a little irritating as Dreamweaver adds more and more style*n* classes – you can always prevent this by either (a) creating styles in advance and applying them as required or (b) unchecking the option **Use CSS instead of HTML tags** in Preferences. The first option is preferable.

As an aside, and we have seen this earlier, if you want to change the font for the whole page, you can do so via **Page Properties…** The resulting CSS would be applied to the <body> tag and thus to the whole page.

Let's suppose that we want each paragraph in our page to look the same without the need for selecting text each time. This is where it becomes helpful to have a little understanding of HTML because when we say 'paragraph' we are referring to HTML's <p> tag. We will see now how to change the font for every <p> tag, and by definition all paragraphs, in the page.

It is easier to start with a new page and add three paragraphs of text. There is no need to select any text as we will work with the CSS Styles panel on the right-hand side of the page. To make the panel visible, select **Window > CSS Styles**.

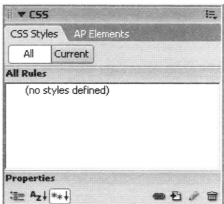

Figure 7.3 CSS Styles panel – at this stage, no styles have been added to the page, so the main panel is empty.

Click the **New CSS Rule** icon ⬚ at the foot of the panel. The **New CSS Rule** dialog box will be opened, as shown in Figure 7.4.

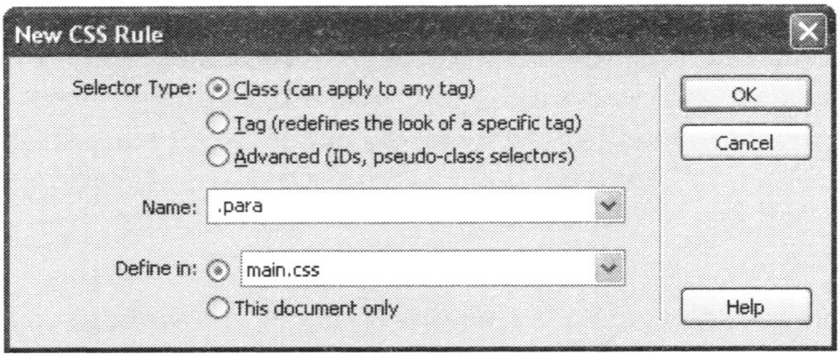

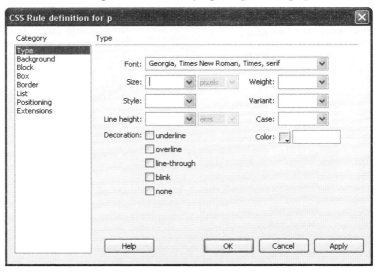

Figure 7.4 New CSS Rule dialog box

In this case, because we are going to change the <p> tag, we need to select **Tag**. From the Tag drop-down list, select **p**. Finally click the button labelled **This document only** as we will look later at site-wide style sheets.

A further dialog box will now be displayed, which will allow us to choose the settings we want every <p> tag in our page to have.

Figure 7.5 CSS Rule definition for <p> tag

On the left-hand side, under **Category**, you may choose from different CSS selectors which are grouped according to their general purpose. **Type** relates to text selectors. To change the font, use the **Font** drop-down list and select one of the options. Click **Apply**

and you will see the changes take effect in Design view while the
CSS Rule dialog box remains open; if you don't like the look of
the chosen font, change it to another. When you are happy, click
OK and Dreamweaver will add the necessary CSS to your page.

```
6   <style type="text/css">
7   <!--
8   p {
9       font-family: Georgia, "Times New Roman", Times, serif;
10  }
11  -->
12  </style>
13  </head>
14  <body>
15      <p> Lorem ipsum dolor sit amet, consectetuer adipiscing elit. Fusce
```

```
0      50    100   150   200   250   300   350   400   450   500
```

Lorem ipsum dolor sit amet, consectetuer adipiscing elit. Fusce mattis eleifend urna.

Figure 7.6   Code and Design views after applying <p> tag change

Note that, in contrast with the first example, there is no leading
full-stop before the 'p' in Code view; this indicates that it is, as
we already know, an HTML tag rather than a class. Similarly,
line 15 of Code view does not contain any reference to a class;
all instances of the <p> tag will take the defined style.

What if we want to change the defined style for the <p> tag? Look
in the CSS Styles panel and there is now an entry labelled **p**.

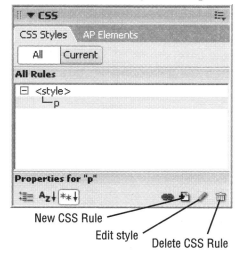

New CSS Rule

Edit style   Delete CSS Rule

Figure 7.7   Editing a style

Click on **p**, then on the **Edit Style...** icon and you can add to, or amend, the style via the dialog box as shown in Figure 7.5.

To delete the style, click on the **Delete CSS Rule** icon.

Style sheets – creating and attaching

Let's suppose that, after experimenting, we have defined a number of property values for the <p> tag and want to make these changes available to other pages in our site. Dreamweaver provides the means of exporting styles to a style sheet file.

1   Click on the **p** entry in the CSS Styles panel, then right-click and choose **Move CSS Rules...** A dialog box will ask you where to move the rules.

2   Click the button labelled **A new style sheet...** and click **OK**.

Figure 7.8   Move To External Style Sheet dialog box

You will be prompted to name the file and to save it in your site. It is suggested that you create a new folder called *stylesheets* and save the file there, to make site maintenance easier. It does not matter what you call the style sheet; I called mine *main*. It will have a suffix of *.css* which indicates that it is a style sheet file.

Look in the **CSS Styles** panel now and you should see something like this:

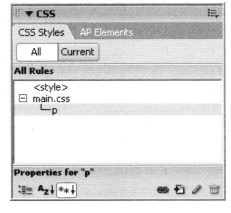

Figure 7.9   Style sheet called main.css created

Note that the **p** definition we created earlier has now been moved into the *main.css* file.

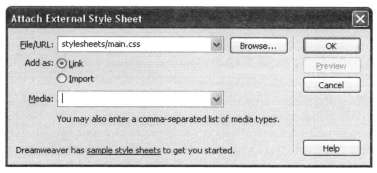

Figure 7.10   Style sheet file saved to new site folder

Having saved the style sheet file, we now want to add it to other pages in our site. Note that it has automatically been added to the page we are currently working with. Create a new page, add some paragraphs of text and then, from the CSS Styles panel, click the **Attach Style Sheet** icon to open the **Attach External Style Sheet** dialog box.

Figure 7.11   Attach External Style Sheet dialog box

Use the **Browse** button to find the style sheet file you have recently created – it should be in the *stylesheets* folder. The choice of **Link** and **Import** relates to the HTML used to attach the style sheet – leave set to the default Link. Click **OK** and the style sheet is attached to this page as well. Look in Code view and you will see this line in the HTML.

Figure 7.12   Style sheet attached using HTML <link> tag

Repeat this for all other pages.

You may subsequently wish to make additions to your style sheet file. This can easily be done by following the steps to create a new rule. When the dialog box opens (see Figure 7.13), your style sheet filename should appear in the definition drop-down box. Make sure you check the button labelled **Define in** and all subsequent changes you make will be added to this file.

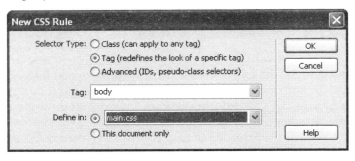

Figure 7.13 Updating an existing style sheet file

If we wish to change existing rules in the style sheet, simply select the rule you wish to change in the CSS Styles panel (all rules will appear below the style sheet name, as in Figure 7.9) and click the **Edit Style...** icon. You can then edit or add to the existing rule.

There is another way to produce a style sheet without creating styles in a web page. First create a blank style sheet – **File > New... > CSS** and click **OK**. Working in the CSS Styles panel you may then add styles just as we have already done; make sure that when creating the rule you check the button labelled **This document only** and any rules added will be written to your file. The file may then be attached to web pages as previously described.

Class and advanced rules

The example we have worked with so far has been an HTML tag. Let's look at how we define class and advanced rules as well.

Class, as we discussed earlier, refers to a custom style definition which you decide where to use in your page – unlike the Tag which is automatically applied based on usage of the associated HTML tag. Why do you need a class as well as or instead of a tag? Because, for example, you may not want every paragraph to have the same style – you may want only one paragraph to have a specific style.

To create a custom class you need to define a name for the class as in Figure 7.14.

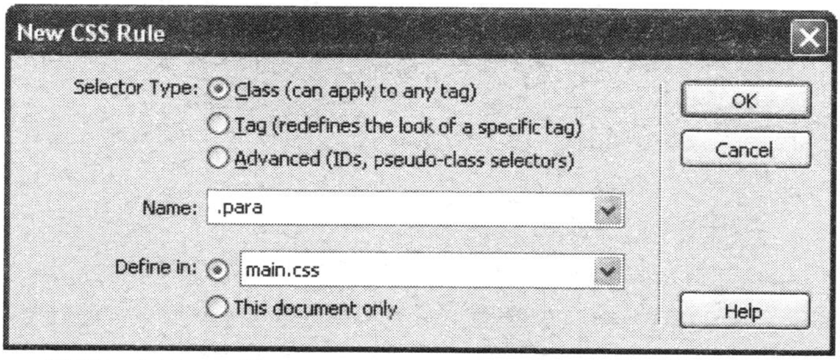

Figure 7.14 Add new Class

Click the **Selector Type** labelled *Class* and, in the **Name** box, add the class name. I have chosen to add the rule or rules which I will create to the existing style sheet file *main.css*.

Note the leading dot before the Name *.para*. The dot is mandatory. The name you use for the class may be almost anything but I would suggest using text which reflects the intended application of the class. In this case, *.para* suggests that this class will be used to define a paragraph style. The remainder of the rule definition process is exactly the same as we followed for Tag. After I have added the rules, *main.css* will now have this content:

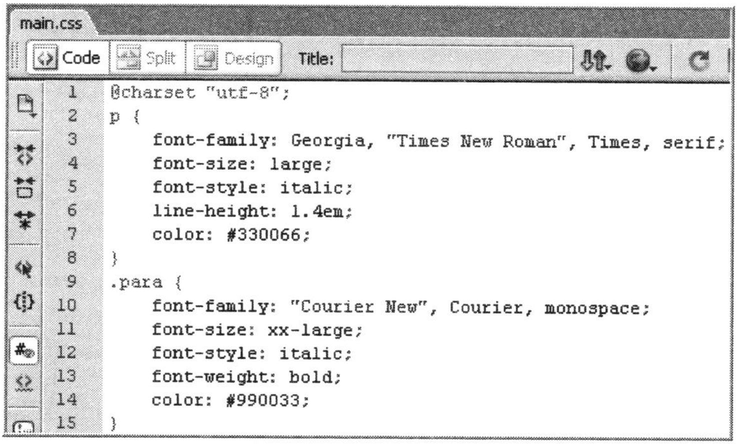

```
1  @charset "utf-8";
2  p {
3      font-family: Georgia, "Times New Roman", Times, serif;
4      font-size: large;
5      font-style: italic;
6      line-height: 1.4em;
7      color: #330066;
8  }
9  .para {
10     font-family: "Courier New", Courier, monospace;
11     font-size: xx-large;
12     font-style: italic;
13     font-weight: bold;
14     color: #990033;
15 }
```

Figure 7.15 main.css with custom style .para added

Once complete, there will be one significant difference, which we can see in the Properties panel on the Style drop-down list.

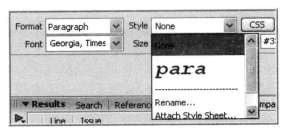

Figure 7.16 Properties panel showing addition of new custom class para

Dreamweaver shows the custom class name with the style applied, i.e. this is how any text would look after applying the style.

Now we will apply the style. If you have followed what we have been doing so far, then you will have a page containing three paragraphs of text which have been formatted by creating a CSS rule for the <p> tag. We will now change one of these paragraphs by attaching the new para style.

Click anywhere in the paragraph you wish to amend and then, in the Properties panel, select the para style from the Style drop-down list. The paragraph will now have the defined custom style rather than the <p> tag style.

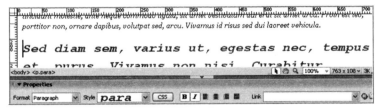

Figure 7.17 Custom class para applied

With the cursor positioned in the amended paragraph, click the CSS button to the right of the Style list in the Properties panel and the CSS Styles panel will display the settings for the class. If the CSS Styles panel is undocked (refer back to Chapter 1 for details) then we can see all of the content more easily by expanding the panel's width.

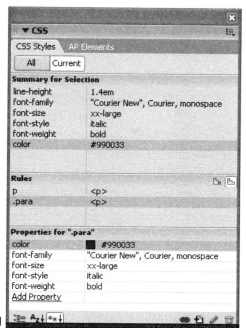

Figure 7.18 Expanded, undocked CSS Styles panel

The panel is context-sensitive, so this display results from clicking the CSS button when the cursor is in the amended paragraph.

- The **Summary for Selection** shows the CSS rules that have been applied to the selected paragraph.

- **Rules** lists the rules in the current style sheet file.

- **Properties for ".para"** shows the rules created for that style. If you click **Add property** link, definitions may be added.

There is one particular issue to note here – the line-height rule shown in **Summary for Selection**. This does not appear in the Properties for ".para" so where did it come from? The answer is from the <p> tag definition.

When the <p> tag setting was created, we knew that it would be automatically applied to all instances of that tag – in this case, our three paragraphs of text. However, we wanted to modify the second paragraph with the custom style .para. The .para style takes precedence over the p style but, any rules defined for the

<p> tag will be inherited by the custom style if the latter does not redefine the particular selector. This may make more sense if we look at the Properties for "p" which have been applied to this paragraph. Click on **p** in the **Rules** section – see Figure 7.18.

Properties for "p"	
~~color~~	■ #330066
~~font-family~~	Georgia, "Times New Roman", Times, serif
~~font-size~~	large
~~font-style~~	italic
line-height	1.4em
Add Property	

Figure 7.19 Properties of p applied to this paragraph

The rules which have been struck through do not apply because .para defined similar rules which take precedence. The only rule not struck through is line-height because this was not defined as part of the .para style.

The advanced category

We will now look at the advanced category of CSS rules. This may be split into two topics – ID selectors and pseudo classes. The former are not unlike custom classes except they are intended for once-only usage in a page (custom classes may be applied multiple times); the latter relate to link states.

To create an ID selector, first click the **New CSS Rule** icon at the foot of the CSS Styles panel to open this dialog box:

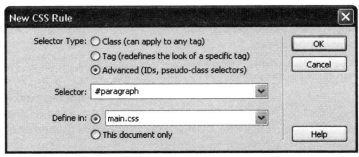

Figure 7.20 Creating an ID selector

Note that the **Advanced** button has been selected and the entry typed in the Selector box is prefixed with a # – this is a mandatory prefix for ID selectors. The remainder of the steps to create the rules are exactly the same as for a Class.

Having created **#paragraph**, we will now apply it to the third paragraph of our text. The rule will not appear in the Style list in Properties panel – it may only be applied using the CSS Styles panel. (This is not completely true – you can also do it by making changes in Code view, but this approach requires that you have knowledge of the correct syntax.)

Click anywhere in the paragraph you wish to change in Design view, then right-click the name of the style, #paragraph, in the CSS Styles panel and select **Apply**. Your paragraph should have changed to reflect application of the new style.

Pseudo classes

We will now turn to pseudo classes which relate to hyperlink states. By applying CSS rules we can change the visual appearance of links. For example, we might want to change the link state so that it does not appear as blue, underlined text. Many sites now use alternatives, though there is no reason why you should not use the tried and tested default which everyone can recognize easily. If you are going to use a different style then remember that your links need to be obvious to visitors – this may be because they appear in a navigation bar or because the text colour separates them from the rest of your text.

If your page does not specify CSS rules for the different link states, then they will behave as defined by your browser.

We can combine this topic with working on the pages created in previous chapters. The last time we worked on our site home page it looked like this:

Figure 7.21   Page before applying CSS

The point has already been made that CSS is an alternative to tables, so our first change will be to set the table's cell padding attribute back to 0. The reason for doing this? We are going to add CSS rules to configure the cell padding so we do not need the HTML attribute to be set. Our list of changes which will be applied using CSS rules is as follows:

* Change the default link states.

* Create space between the cell borders and the navigation bar contents.

* Create vertical space between the links in the navigation bar.

* Create space between the cell borders and the main contents.

To change the cell padding, click anywhere in the table in Design view and then click <table> in Design view's Status bar. This will bring up the table properties in the Properties panel. Change the CellPad attribute to 0 and hit [**Enter**].

Let's start adding the CSS. Dealing with the link states first, in the **New CSS Rule** dialog box, click **Advanced** and then click the drop-down selector list. Four classes are shown: 

```
a:link
a:visited
a:hover
a:active
```

Figure 7.22 Pseudo classes list

The order is important and worth remembering. Always create pseudo class rules in the order specified.

If you create say, a hover link rule before a visited rule, you may get unexpected results. Remember the order – LVHA (link, visited, hover, active). Also bear in mind that these rules will be applied to any links found in the page. Create a rule for each link state in turn – I recommend that you keep the same font and size for each state.

Underlining is controlled through the Decoration setting. This should be cleared to turn off underlining; **underline** explicitly sets underlining on. Repeat for a:visited, a:hover and a:active – alter just the colour and whether or not underlining is on. Then save and test. The change that will be most immediately obvious will be to hover state – when the mouse is positioned over the link you should see the link text change colour.

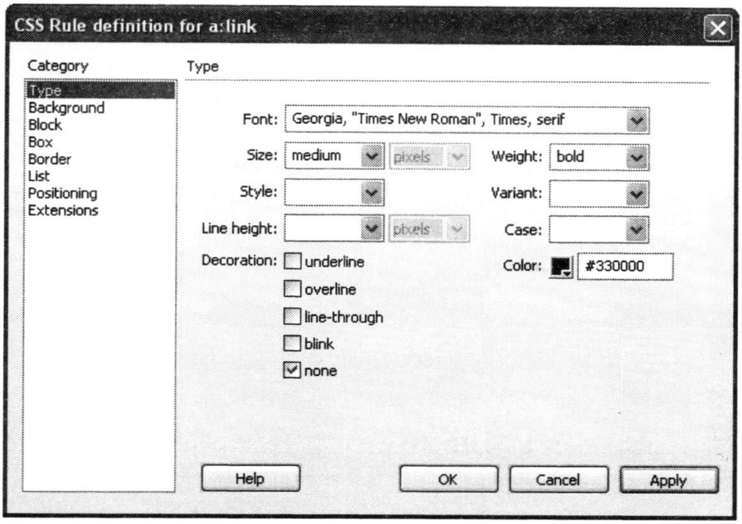

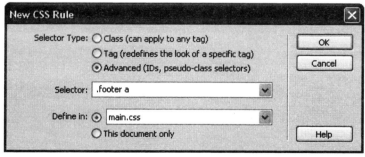

Figure 7.23 Sample configuration for a:link pseudo class

These changes will also have affected the links in the footer area. If you want to retain the appearance of the footer links, one method would be to create a custom class for links in the footer area setting the required font size, underlining, etc. This class would then be applied to the whole table cell in which the links sit and would override the link state rules created above.

Figure 7.24 Creation of link rules for custom class footer

Note that **Advanced** must be selected because of the format of the selector; there is a space between *.footer* and *a*. This syntax indicates that the style created will only apply to links within areas of the page associated with the footer class.

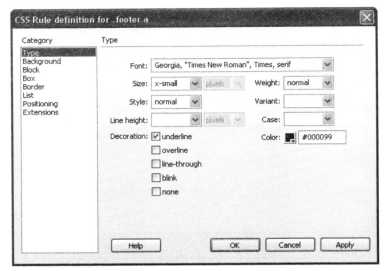

Figure 7.25 Rules for links within footer class

Open the page and see how the links behave. The navigation bar links should appear and behave differently from the footer links.

Let's now address the spacing issues around the links and text. We want to go from this:

to this:

What has changed? The appearance of the links, the space around them and the positioning/formatting of the main content text. The links and main text are still within a table, in individual cells. Because we may wish to make further selective changes, we will create a custom class for each – called .nav and .content.

There are two changes to be made in .nav – the space between the cell borders and the link text and the vertical space between link text. These screenshots show the relevant settings.

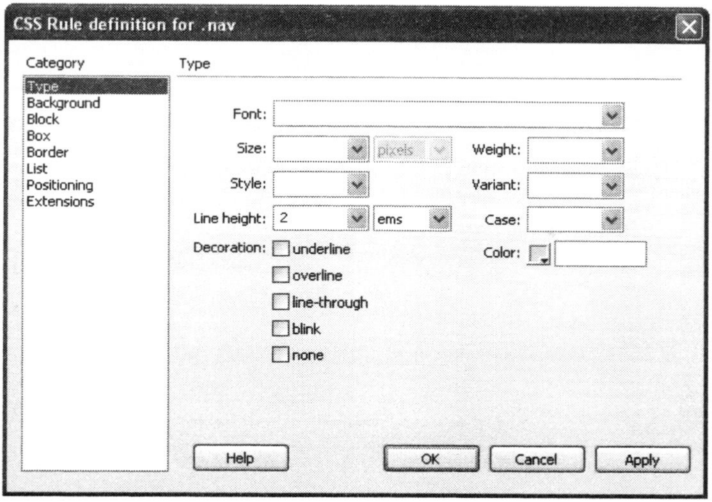

Figure 7.26 .nav vertical spacing

Line height, as the name suggests, affects the vertical space occupied by each line – 2 ems means in effect a double height line.

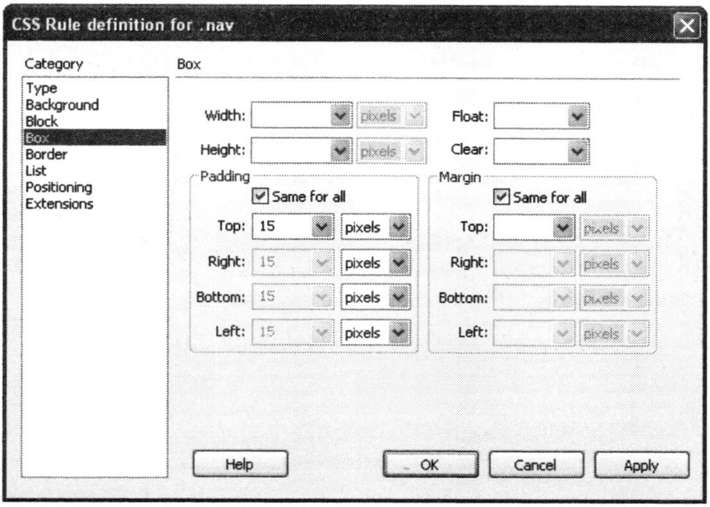

Figure 7.27 .nav spacing

The Box category affects, in this case, the whole navigation panel, treating it like a separate 'box'.

Padding is set to 15 pixels for each part of the navigation panel. This is equivalent to the HTML CellPad attribute.

The .nav style now needs to be applied to the cell which holds the links. Click anywhere in the navigation cell in Design view and select **nav** from the **Style** drop-down list in the Properties panel.

Next, the .content style. The settings are illustrated in the next three screenshots.

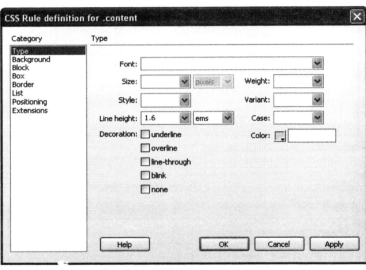

Figure 7.28   .content vertical spacing

Apply the style in the same way as you have just done for .nav. If you need to make any further changes to the look of the navigation bar or the contents, you can make changes to the style which is applied to each.

You have now completed the CSS styling of a page.

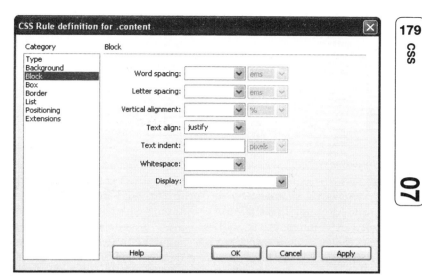

Figure 7.29 .content text justification – Justify aligns text on left and right.

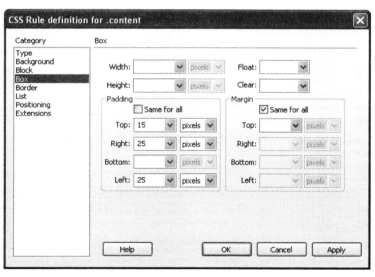

Figure 7.30 .content spacing – Different settings have been used for right/left and top. Bottom has no setting so there will be no space immediately before the footer. You could set Bottom to 0 pixels to be absolutely certain.

CSS properties in Dreamweaver

You will notice when creating CSS rules that there is a large range of available properties. This section examines each category and gives brief explanations of each property.

There is a huge amount of information here and a similar amount of space would be needed to display examples of each property – this would also have the effect of converting the main topic of the book from Dreamweaver to CSS.

This explanation of CSS properties does not include any comments about browser support. You may find, depending on the browsers and versions, that some of the properties may be treated differently. Although this situation is changing with the release of new browser versions, you should be aware of possible variations. Your best recourse then is to use a search engine to look for instances where other users have encountered a similar problem – this is almost always bound to be the case, so don't despair.

Dreamweaver groups related properties into Categories.

Type

Font – select the font for your chosen element using one of Dreamweaver's predefined font combinations. If you wish to use a different font, consider either embedding the text in an image or creating a piece of Flash text.

Size – you can choose from numeric values or named values; if you select the former you will then need to choose the unit of measurement, e.g. pixels or points. The named values do not allow you to select a unit of measurement.

Note that the named values (xx-small, x-small, small, medium, large, x-large and xx-large) are equivalent to the old HTML font size range of 1 to 7.

The values larger and smaller allow you to increase or decrease the font size for the chosen element relative to the base font. As an example of its usage, the body tag is often assigned a font size value which will apply to all of the page contents – the base font. This size may be modified for page contents through the use of values such as larger and smaller – these values are applied to the defined base font.

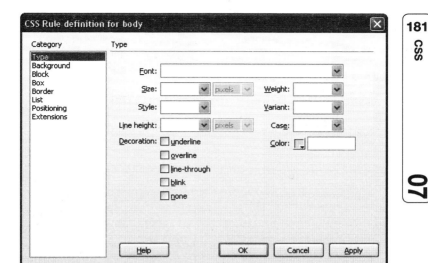

Figure 7.31 Type category

The numeric values allow the choice of units of measurement. There are three categories of measurement: absolute, relative and device-dependent. Absolute is the same on any device (in, mm, cm, points, picas); relative depend on the font in use (ems, exs and %); device-dependent change according to the monitor (pixels).

The different units of measurements are:

• **pixels** – a single dot (picture cell), and the unit of measurement used to determine the height and width of computer screens, e.g. 800 × 600. The actual size of a pixel will depend on the type of monitor and resolution.

• **points** and **picas** – you should know points (or pt) from word processing. These are standard measurements – there are 72 points to 1 inch, 12 points to 1 pica and 6 picas to 1 inch.

• **in, cm** and **mm** (inches, centimetres and millimetres) – 1 inch = 2.54 centimetres = 25.4 millimetres.

• **ems** and **exs** – equivalent to the size of the letters 'm' and 'x' in the chosen font.

• **%** – this unit is relative to the base font or a parent font.

Weight – refers to the thickness of the font, e.g. **bolder** would be thicker than **bold**. You may also set values from 100 to 900.

Style – essentially this is the way to set the text to italics; the two values oblique and italic will have the same result.

Variant – the only setting is small-caps which will change the text display to small capital letters.

Line height – used to set the vertical distance between lines. You choose a numeric value and then select from the drop-down list which contains the same units of measurement as Size.

Case – *capitalize* sets the first letter of each word to a capital letter; *uppercase* sets the whole word to capitals and *lowercase* will remove any capitals and convert them to lower case.

Decoration – the choices are fairly self explanatory. This property is used most often for hyperlinks. To remove the default underlining, choose none; to restore underlining, choose underline.

Color – use the colour palette to set the text colour.

Background

Background color – use the colour palette to set the background colour for this element.

Background image – set as the background for the element.

Repeat – setting that determines how the image defined in Background image is tiled (or repeated) on the page.

* *no-repeat* – the image will be displayed once only

* *repeat-x* – tiles the image across the page (horizontally)

* *repeat-y* – tiles the image down the page (vertically)

* *repeat* – tiles the image horizontally and vertically.

Attachment – determines the action of the Background image when the page containing this element is scrolled.

* *fixed* – the background remains in place while the other page elements move up and down with the action of scrolling

* *scroll* – the default setting, the background moves with the rest of the page elements when scrolling

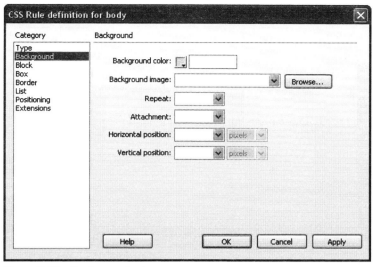

Figure 7.32 Background category

Horizontal position – allows the precise positioning of a Background image. The position is calculated using as a starting point the left-hand side of the browser window (known as the X axis). Enter a numeric value and choose from the drop-down list of units of measurement. You may also choose *center* or *right* to move the image from its default left position.

Vertical position – similar to Horizontal but calculates from the top of the browser window (the Y axis). You may use center or bottom to move the image from its default top position.

Block

Word spacing – controls the space between words, using the same units of measurement as Size (with the exception of %) in the Category Type.

Letter spacing – controls the space between letters, using the same units of measurement as for Size (with the exception of %).

Vertical alignment – used to control the alignment of text alongside another page element such as an image (similar to the settings available for image alignment in the Properties panel).

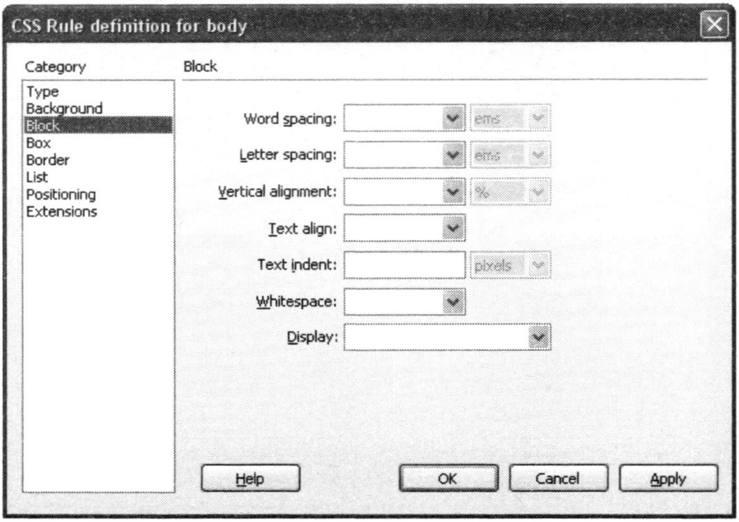

Figure 7.33 Block category

Text align – aligns the text in the same way as a word processor might do. The values are self-explanatory with the exception of inherit which means that this element will take the Text align value from its parent element.

Text indent – indents text from the left margin of the browser page. Only the first line of a paragraph, for example, will be indented. Again, uses the same units of measurement as Size.

Whitespace – determines how linefeeds are treated within your text. *Nowrap* ignores linefeed characters while *pre* works like the HTML <pre> tag, maintaining linefeeds and spaces (useful, for example, for displaying text which has to follow a particular display format).

Display – a large number of options are available which cannot all be described here. There are a number, prefixed *table-*, which equate to HTML table-type tags e.g. *table-cell* is equivalent to the <td> or <th> tag. *Block* and *inline* are perhaps the most used, the former treating the selected element as a block (an HTML example of a block element is a <p> tag which has space before and after) while the latter treats the selected element as a follow-on from the previous element i.e. on the same line.

Box

Width – used to set the width of an element on the page. Enter a numeric value and you may choose from the list shown in Size. Note that using the % setting typically means that the element will expand or contract as the containing element (which may well be the browser window itself) is resized. The setting auto will, if used for an image, default to the image's actual size.

Height – similar to Width in terms of the options available; this time though we are dealing with the height of an element.

Float – determines how an element is displayed relative to a parent element. A good example would be the alignment of text with an image. If an image is set with the float value of *right*, then any text following it would be positioned to its left and aligned with its top. A setting of *left* would do the opposite.

Clear – used to remove the effect of a Float or Floats. Using the first image example from Float, a Clear setting of *right* would see the following text positioned below the image rather than being aligned with its top.

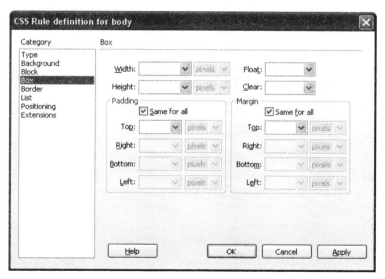

Figure 7.34 Box category

Before looking at Padding and Margin, a visual explanation would be helpful. This image has been taken from the W3C document 'Cascading Style Sheets, level 2 CSS2 Specification'.

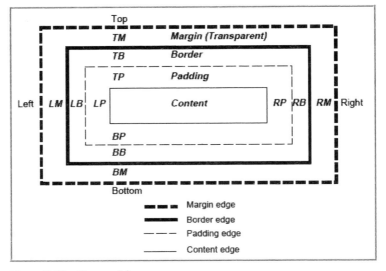

Figure 7.35 Box model

The diagram puts into context the application of borders, padding and margins with respect to the content.

* 'Margin' defines the space between the previous element (or the browser window) and this element.

* 'Padding' defines the space within the element, i.e. between the border of the element and the actual content.

The theory is the same as for the HTML table attributes, **cellpadding** and **cellspacing**, where the former sets the space from the cell border to the content and the latter sets the space from the table border to the cell border.

Padding – with *Same for all* selected, enter a numeric value, select a unit of measurement and the same value will be set for Top, Right, Bottom and Left. Deselect *Same for all* and you can set individual values.

Margin – exactly the same functionality as for Padding.

Border

Style – sets the appearance of the border for this element; the values are self-explanatory. Either set the same value for each border (**Top, Right, Bottom** and **Left**) or set individual values by deselecting **Same for all**.

Width – sets the width of the border using predefined values (*thin, medium, thick*) or the Size options.

Color – sets the colour of the border.

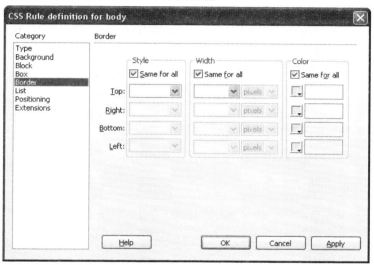

Figure 7.36 Border category

List

Type – defines the type of bullets used for a list, e.g. *square* would specify an unordered list where list items are preceded by a ■. Choosing *decimal* would specify an ordered list with list items preceded by 1, 2, 3, etc.

Bullet image – instead of using the predefined bullet types, you may instead specify an image.

Position – defines whether the bullet is incorporated within the following text or is offset to the left as would normally be the case (inside for the former; outside is the default setting).

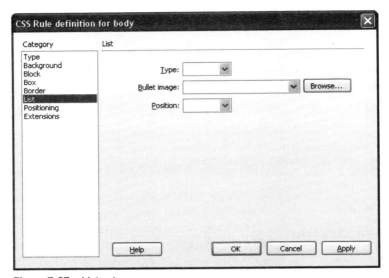

Figure 7.37 List category

Positioning

Type – sets the type of positioning that will be used for this element. The most used are *absolute* which places it at a specific point, calculated from the top left-hand corner of the browser window, irrespective of the positioning of other elements; and *relative*, which positions it in relation to the last element added to the page.

Width and **Height** – set the overall size of the element.

Visibility – control the element's appearance. *Visible* and *hidden* are self-explanatory.

Z-index – a numerical value typically used to control the stacking, or overlapping, of elements. Think of a deck of cards which have been spread out overlapping on a table. The higher the Z-index number, the higher in the stack this element will be.

Overflow – if the content you have defined for this element is too large to fit into the space allotted, this informs the browser what to do with the additional content. *Visible* and *hidden* are again self-explanatory, though *visible* means in effect that the defined sizing is overridden as all of the content is displayed irrespective of element settings; *scroll* and *auto* will force the addition of scroll bars and will add them as necessary, respectively.

Placement – defines the coordinates for the element's position. Depending on the intended position, it would be usual to set *Top* and *Left*, or *Bottom* and *Right* but not all four.

Clip – defines the part of the element to be hidden from view.

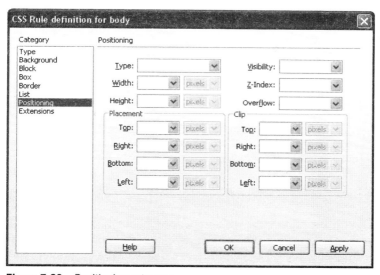

Figure 7.38 Positioning category

Extensions

Before – if set, the browser will insert a page break before this element.

After – if set, the browser will insert a page break after this element.

Cursor – defines the cursor appearance when hovering over this element.

Filter – a range of options for changing the appearance of the element.

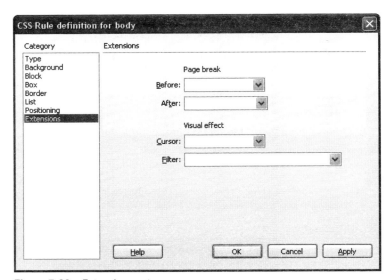

Figure 7.39 Extensions category

Style sheets for different media

One of the additional advantages of CSS is the ability to attach style sheets which are applicable to certain media only. For example, when a visitor prints one of your pages you may wish to make the page printer-friendly, i.e. just the text and no images, navigation bars, etc.

Figure 7.40 Page in Design view

We will take a simple example where images will not be displayed when the page is previewed and/or printed. The starting point is a page with a heading, two images and some text with a background colour set. This is fine for the browser display, the CSS rules having been saved in a style sheet file as normal. However, if the visitor wants to print this page we will assume they want the text only. (This may well not be the case for some sites, of course.)

Therefore, an additional style sheet file is needed which will apply when printing only.

The new style sheet file will contain one rule only, to remove images when the page is either printed or previewed. We will create the style sheet file now and call it *print.css*.

1 Select **File > New... > Page Type** of CSS and click **Create**.

2 Save the file as *print.css* and then click the **New CSS Rule** button at the base of the CSS Styles panel.

3 The rule will apply to the whole page so the **Selector Type** should be **Tag** and the Tag selected should be *img*. Make sure that **This document only** is checked so that any changes are added to *print.css*.

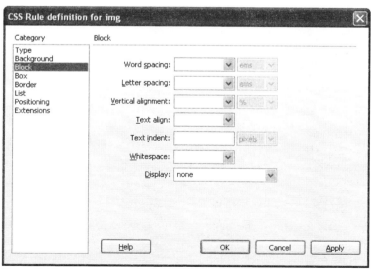

Figure 7.41 img rule

4   Setting **Display** to *none* will mean images will be ignored when this style sheet is applied.

5   Click **OK** and make sure the style sheet is saved.

6   The style sheet file must now be attached to the page. Go back to the page containing the images and attach the style sheet *print.css* using the **Attach Style Sheet** icon at the base of the CSS Styles panel.

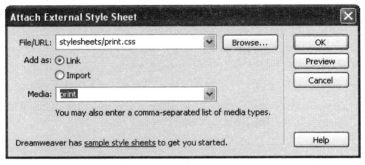

Figure 7.42   Attach a style sheet which applies to print media only

7   Using the **Browse...** button, make sure your new file name appears in the File/URL box.

8   Leave the **Add as** option set to **Link**.

9   Select **print** from the **Media** drop-down menu. You will see that there are a number of other possible choices available, depending on the media type you are aiming to use.

10 Click **OK** and the file will be added to your page.

If you look in Code view, there are now two style sheets linked to your page.

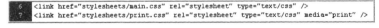

```
6  <link href="stylesheets/main.css" rel="stylesheet" type="text/css" />
7  <link href="stylesheets/print.css" rel="stylesheet" type="text/css" media="print" />
```

Figure 7.43   Print style sheet print.css added; note media= "print" attribute

You can test how the page will look when the visitor prints or previews it by opening the Style Rendering toolbar (**View > Toolbars > Style Rendering**). Click the **Render Print Media Type** button and the display in Design view will mimic the page's appearance when previewed or printed.

Render Print Media Type

Figure 7.44   Style Rendering toolbar

The page should now look like this in Design view:

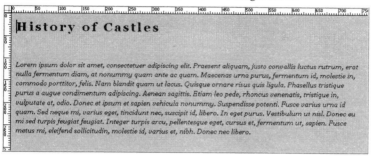

Figure 7.45   Simulated printing layout in Design view

You may of course wish to make other changes to the print layout. For example, you might want to change the text formatting or font used. This would require more changes to the *print.css* file.

Predefined CSS

Dreamweaver provides a number of predefined pages which make use of CSS styling. To access these pages, select **File > New...** and choose a layout from the column headed **Layout** (you would normally leave this set as <none> when creating a new, blank HTML page). You will see a representation of the page layout on the right-hand side, as in the example in Figure 7.46.

Of course, with this approach you need to feel reasonably happy with CSS as you would probably want to make changes to such basic settings as the colour and font. On the plus side, you have a ready-made page which, after a few custom changes, is available faster than if you coded the page from the start. The other significant plus is that built into the code is the ability to recognize and cater for different versions of Internet Explorer – it is probably enough to say that different versions of IE have introduced a variety of CSS-related challenges to developers over the years.

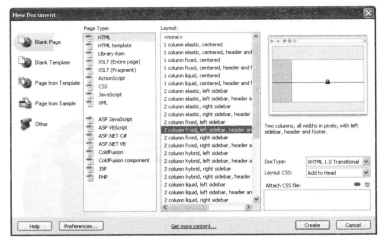

Figure 7.46 Predefined CSS layouts

We will create a new page based on the Layout highlighted in Figure 7.46 – *2-column fixed, left sidebar, header and footer*. The box **Layout CSS** towards the bottom-right allows you to define where the necessary CSS will be placed – in the document's <head> area (**Add to Head,** which means it will, at least initially, be usable in this page only), **Create New File** (referring to the creation of a new style sheet file) or **Link to Existing File** (an existing style sheet file).

You may also choose to attach an existing CSS style sheet file (**Attach CSS file**) to this new page, i.e. the CSS generated by the creation of this page will not be added to this existing file – it will co-exist in the page. Note that it is possible to have multiple style sheets attached to a single page, as we saw in the example relating to printing above.

I will choose the option **Create New File** from **Layout CSS**. Click **Create** and you will be prompted to save the new CSS file which, in reality, is Dreamweaver's own CSS file used to create the page format. The file is called *twoColFixLtHdr.css* and the initial page in Design view looks like this:

Figure 7.47 2-column fixed, left sidebar, header and footer – before changes

The page is laid out using HTML <div> tags. A <div> tag defines a block of page content and is used to create stand-alone sections within a page. Each division may be formatted and positioned separately, though the conventional usage, as is the case here, is to create logical page divisions which, when added together, create a complete and seamless page.

To illustrate how this works requires us to look at the HTML code for Figure 7.48. First though, here is the page marked up with the names of the <div> sections. Container, as indicated by the arrows, actually holds all of the other <div> sections.

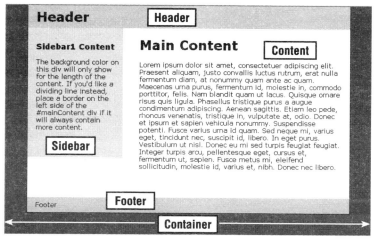

Figure 7.48 2-column fixed, left sidebar, header and footer – as displayed in a browser, annotated with <div> names

I have, for ease of reading, removed much of the text from the <p> tags – you should be able to see how the code matches up with the sections of the page above:

```
<body class="twoColFixLtHdr">
<div id="container">
  <div id="header">
     <h1>Header</h1>
  </div>

  <div id="sidebar1">
     <h3>Sidebar1 Content</h3>
     <p>The background color ….</p>
  </div>
  <div id="mainContent">
     <h1> Main Content </h1>
     <p>Lorem ipsum dolor sit amet,  …</p>
  </div>

  <div id="footer">
     <p>Footer</p>
  </div>
</div>
</body>
```

You can see from this example that immediately after the <body> tag, there is a <div> with an id of *container* – as the name suggests, this <div> contains the contents of the whole page and will typically define the overall page size, i.e. width. Within the container <div> there are four other <div> which define the different sections of the page – *header*, *sidebar1*, *mainContent* and *footer*. Each of these <div> sections has its own CSS rules which will define such elements as their position and formatting. The beauty of this layout is its simplicity as all the formatting is contained within a separate CSS style sheet file.

The code shown above has been indented for clarity only – neither the browser nor Dreamweaver care whether the code is indented or not.

Just to demonstrate how to amend the rules within the style sheet file, we will change the header background colour and the font in the sidebar. This requires that we understand how to find the relevant CSS in order to change it! For a start, all the CSS is in the file *twoColFixLtHdr.css* and we should know where that is because we just saved it to disk. To save having to do a search we can just look in the CSS Styles panel and there is the file.

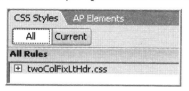

Figure 7.49 Dreamweaver's predefined CSS file showing in CSS Styles panel

Because the CSS Styles panel is context-sensitive and will show the current style details (when the **Current** button has been clicked) you might assume that simply clicking in Design view anywhere in the header area would bring up the relevant style information. Unfortunately, it doesn't and what we see is this:

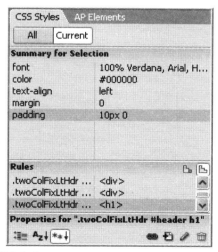

Figure 7.50 CSS Styles panel showing current style <h1>

In the Rules box, the entry containing <h1> is highlighted and below the box is a more explicit explanation – what we are looking at are the Properties for ".twoColFixLtHdr #header h1".

To select the correct style, we need to return to Design view. With the cursor still in the header area, look at the entries in the Status bar. These are in hierarchical order, i.e. **<body .twoColFixLtHdr>** is at the top level (the <body> tag representing the whole page), followed by **<div #container>** which is at a higher level than **<div #header>**; the latter defines the header area of the page of which the <h1> tag is a part.

```
<body.twoColFixLtHdr> <div#container> <div#header> <h1>
```

The current element is <h1> as we know from looking in the CSS Styles panel. In the Status bar, try clicking the next level up in the hierarchy, **<div #header>**, and you will see that Dreamweaver has highlighted the whole header area in Design view.

Figure 7.51 Design view with the <div#header> selected.

Now look in the CSS Styles panel.

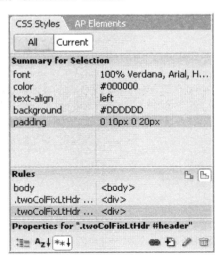

Figure 7.52 CSS Styles panel showing current style #header

We want to change the background, which is set to #DDDDDD.

1 Click the line containing background to highlight it then the **Edit Style** button at the base of the panel; the **CSS** dialog box opens at the page containing the highlighted attribute.

2 Change the **Background color** using the colour palette.

3 Click **Apply** to see the effect of your colour change before committing it and/or **OK** once you are happy with the change.

Having gone into lengthy detail about how to change one setting, it should now be much easier to change the font used in the sidebar. Click anywhere in it in Design view, then look in the Status bar – click the <p> tag and what do you see in the CSS Styles panel? Not a style for the <p> tag because one has not yet been defined. How do I know this? Because at the base of the CSS Styles panel is the text 'Properties for ".twoColFixLtHdr #sidebar1"'. If there is no <p> style, let's go up a level and choose **<div #sidebar1>** from the Status bar.

From the CSS Styles panel, highlight the font entry in the panel and click the **Edit Style** button. Change the font, click **OK** and the font for the whole page changes. Why is that? You might not have noticed that when you clicked on font, the text at the bottom of the panel changed to 'Properties for "body"'. The only font set for the page has been set at the highest level, for the <body> tag. Any changes will affect everything, which is not what we want.

What is needed is a custom class for the <p> tag within the sidebar only. So click anywhere on the text (not the header) in the sidebar again, and then in the CSS Styles panel click the **New CSS Rule** button; the resulting dialog box will look like this:

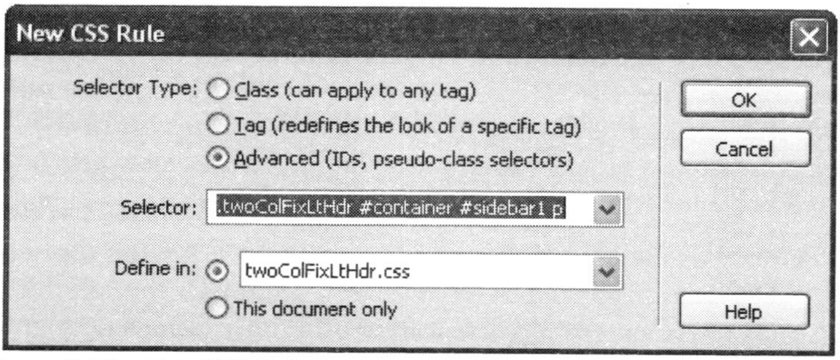

Figure 7.53   New CSS Rule for <p> tag

Note the hierarchy has been entered into the Selector box. Because **p** follows **#sidebar1**, the changes we are making to the <p> tag will only apply in the sidebar. Make sure **Define in** is set to make the changes to the existing CSS file. Click **OK**, choose a font, click **Apply** and you will see the sidebar font only will change this time. Click **OK**.

The CSS file *twoColFixLtHdr.css* will be opened by Dreamweaver and will need to be saved to preserve your changes.

From this short example, you can see that using predefined CSS layouts is slightly long-winded but not too difficult, though it does require a reasonable knowledge of CSS in order to make and understand changes. The best advice is to experiment.

Creating your own CSS layout

Having seen how to modify a predefined CSS page, and how a page is structured using <div>, we will now create one from scratch.

The structure of the page, as code, is shown below:

```
<body>
   <div id="container">
      <div id="header"></div>
      <div id="nav"></div>
      <div id="content"></div>
      <div id="footer"></div>
   </div>
</body>
```

As normal with pages which have been laid out using CSS, there is an overall page definition, which in this case is the ID selector called *container*. ID selectors are used here because it is intended that they will be used once only in this page. The rest of the ID selectors should be self-explanatory, but just to be clear the names have been added to the screenshot in Figure 7.54.

1   Create a new HTML page and select **Insert > Layout Options > Div Tag**. In the dialog box, enter 'container' (though this is an ID selector, you do not need to add the leading # sign) into the **ID** box and click **OK**.

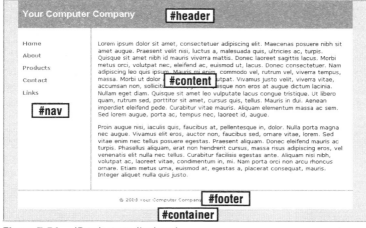

Figure 7.54 ID selectors displayed

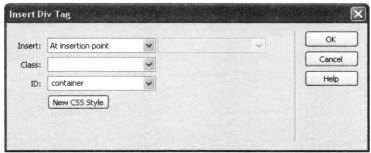

Figure 7.55 Insert Div Tag dialog box

In Split view, you will now see this:

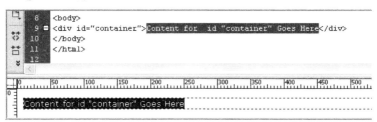

Figure 7.56 Code and Design views showing <div> tag added

2 The text added by this action in Design view is not needed – it is just there to act as a placeholder. So, without doing anything

else and with the text still selected, press [**Delete**] on your keyboard and what you are left with is just a dashed rectangle in Design view. The cursor should still be positioned within the rectangle – if it is not, make sure you place it there now.

The page code above shows that the ID selector *container* has the four other ID selectors nested within it, i.e. between the opening <div> and closing </div>. Therefore, these additional four selectors need to be added within the rectangle.

3   Repeat the insertion process you followed to add the first **ID Selector**, but this time the ID value should be *header*. Care is now needed to make sure that the remaining divs are correctly nested. To be sure, you need to work in Code view. Position the cursor in Code view as shown in the screenshot below.

```
8    <body>
9    <div id="container">Content for  id "container" Goes Here</div>
10   </body>
11   </html>                                          Add here
```

Figure 7.57   Position cursor before adding other divs

4   Add the ID selector *nav*. Position the cursor after the </div> tag of nav and insert ID selector *content*.

5   Finally, position the cursor after the </div> tag of content and insert ID selector *footer*. The code should (in fact must) look like this:

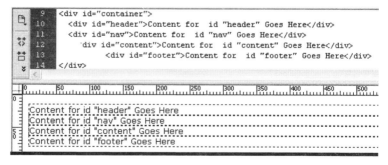

```
9    <div id="container">
10     <div id="header">Content for  id "header" Goes Here</div>
11     <div id="nav">Content for  id "nav" Goes Here</div>
12      div id="content">Content for  id "content" Goes Here</div>
13          <div id="footer">Content for  id "footer" Goes Here</div>
14   </div>
```

```
|0        |50       |100      |150      |200      |250      |300      |350      |400      |450      |500
0
  Content for id "header" Goes Here
  Content for id "nav" Goes Here
5 Content for id "content" Goes Here
0 Content for id "footer" Goes Here
```

Figure 7.58   Page structure complete

Don't worry about the code indentation in Code view – the important thing is that the opening and closing tags are correctly positioned. If they are not, your results will be unpredictable.

We have the page structure – now we need to define the CSS rules to be applied to each ID Selector. We will go through each one in turn after defining the rules for the <body> tag.

In each case below, the heading represents the tag or advanced name. You will need to create a new CSS rule for each – therefore, six new rules in total need to be added.

body

```
Category>Type
    Font - Verdana, Arial, Helvetica, sans-serif
    Size - 100%
    Color - #000000
Category>Background
    Background color - #ECE9D8
Category>Block
    Text align - center
Category>Box
    Margin - 0 pixels for all
    Padding - 0 pixels for all
```

Note: aligning the text in the centre will force the contents of the page to be centrally aligned.

#container

```
Category>Background
    Background color - #FFFFFF
Category>Block
    Text align - left
Category>Box
    Width - 760 pixels
    Margin - 0 auto 0 auto (for Top, Right,
    Bottom, Left)
```

Notes: the width defines the area available for the contents which are nested within *#container*. The auto setting for Right and Left means that, as the contents are centred but take up only 760 pixels, the space to left and right will automatically be controlled by the browser – this ensures equal, flexible margins on each side.

#header

```
Category>Background
    Background color - #9DACBF
```

#nav

```
Category>Box
    Float - left
    Width - 140 pixels
    Padding - 15 10 15 10 (for Top, Right,
    Bottom, Left)
```

#content

```
Category>Box
    Width - 140 pixels
    Padding - 15 (for each of Top, Right,
    Bottom, Left)
    Margin - 0 0 0 165 (for Top, Right,
    Bottom, Left)
Category>Border
    Left - solid, 1 pixel, #877D6C
```

Notes: setting the Left margin to 165 pixels takes account of the width of *#nav* (140 pixels + the *#nav* Left and Right Padding (10 + 10) + a few extra to avoid an overlap.

#footer

```
Category>Type
    Size - 80%
    Color - #736B5E
Category>Block
    Text align - center
Category>Box
    Padding - 5 (for each of Top, Right, Bottom,
    Left)
Category>Border
    Top - solid, 1 pixel, #877D6C
```

Without any content, the page should look something like this in Design view.

Figure 7.59 Page layout in Design view

As yet there is no content, just the placeholder text created by Dreamweaver. There are two other rules to be added, both custom classes, to format the page heading and also to fix the footer below the nav and content areas.

.title

```
Category>Type
    Font – Arial, Helvetica, sans-serif
    Size – 130%
    Weight - bold
    Color - #FFFFFF
Category>Box
    Padding  – 20 10 20 10 (Top, Right, Bottom,
    Left)
    Margin – 0 (for each of Top, Right, Bottom,
    Left)
```

.clearboth

```
Category>Type
    Size – 1 pixel
    Line height – 0 pixel
Category>Box
    Height – 0
    Clear - both
    Margin – 0 (for each of Top, Right, Bottom,
    Left)
```

Note: using **Clear** makes sure that the footer will sit below the nav and content areas.

Apply these custom classes to the page title and the footer text. The end result should now look like this:

This of course has only been an example and there are many possible variations on page layout. This example should have given you an insight into creating page layouts without the need to use predefined pages.

Summary

If you have followed all of the activities in this chapter, you should now be able to:

- Configure Dreamweaver to use CSS instead of HTML

- Create a style sheet from scratch or by exporting styles from a page

- Attach a style sheet to pages in your site

- Apply styles using the Properties panel

- Amend styles using the CSS Styles panel

- Create styles using each of the different selectors

- Create a page using a predefined template

- Amend the CSS rules in a predefined template

- Create a page and add CSS rules from scratch.

Exercises

1 Create a new HTML page and add a heading (Heading 1 format) and several paragraphs of text. Is it possible to create 3 different styles which relate to a paragraph, i.e. Tag, Class and Advanced? If so, what impact will each style have?

2 Is it possible to attach more than one style sheet to a page and, if so, what is the impact?

3 How would you detach a style sheet from a page?

4 How would you convert all text to upper case or start each word with a capital letter using CSS?

5 CSS and HTML are programming languages. True or false?

08

forms

In this chapter you will learn:

- how to add a form to a web page
- about form components
- how to configure form components
- about form validation
- about the process of form handling

The purpose of forms

Web pages of course can do much more than just display information. They are also a means of interacting with your visitors to determine a variety of things – their views on your site; further information they require from you; products they want to order. In each of these cases a form of some sort may be used to capture the required information.

What you do with that information will vary but generally speaking you will want to retain it for future use (in a database), check its validity (against a database) or notify your web administrator (probably you!) that a visitor request has been received. Working with a database is outside the scope of this book but it is not outside the scope of Dreamweaver. We will concentrate on the actual creation of the form and will also look at how we could receive a visitor's request for information in email format.

Forms may contain a wide variety of field types. You must consider the format you require the visitor to use as this will have implications when you come to validate the data. For example, the visitor's name should be alphabetic, the date of birth numeric or alphanumeric and so on.

You must also consider what information you actually need as visitors will be put off by requests for too much information or information they are not prepared to divulge. For example, don't ask for age unless there is a very good reason to do so, e.g. sending visitors to different areas of your site depending on age group.

Finally, forms need to be as user-friendly as you can make them, e.g. telling the visitor the format to use when inputting dates. There are also accessibility issues associated with forms as we will see.

What does a form contain?

You may be familiar with forms from using them in websites. But have you considered what elements make up a form?

A form is a distinct area within a page. It is defined in HTML by a <form> tag. A series of elements, or form controls, are available for us to use. Which ones you use depends on the information you are trying to obtain from the visitor.

♦ **Text field** – a single line box which may be used to capture short pieces of information, e.g. name.

♦ **Textarea** – for multiple lines of input, used for such things as feedback or comments, i.e. where the site owner wants to allow a reasonable amount of space for responses. Limits can be set to prevent the input of huge amounts of text.

♦ **Radio button** – a clickable graphic which is used to record the decision of a visitor. Radio buttons tend to be grouped and used to record the single response of a visitor to a question, e.g. 'Which age group are you in?' When selected, the graphic's central circle turns from empty to filled.

♦ **Checkbox** – a clickable graphic again used to record a decision. These are different from radio buttons in that they may be used to capture multiple responses, e.g. what methods can we use to contact you, with a possibility that the visitor might choose none, one or more.

♦ **List/menu** – the difference between a list and a menu, though created in the same way, is that the list is scrollable while the menu is a drop-down list. A list/menu is used to ask the visitor to select from a range of options, e.g. a colour from a choice of five. While the same choices could be represented with radio button selections, the list/menu is more economical of space.

♦ **Buttons** – data entered by the visitor must either be sent somewhere or captured in a database for later processing/response. For either of these events to occur, there must be a button of some sort which the visitor must click to send in their data. This is usually referred to as a submit button.

♦ **Hidden field** – as the name suggests the contents of a hidden field are not directly visible to the visitor. This is a useful form element if you wish to transfer data from the form to a background processing program or to a database. Virtually anything may be included, such as parameters required by the receiver of the form. Hidden fields are by no means secure and may be viewed simply by opening the source of the page.

♦ **Jump menu** – like a conventional menu with the difference that, after making a selection (or after clicking a button), the visitor is automatically transferred to another page.

- **File field** – this allows the visitor to upload files to your site and is used for such purposes as CV uploads to job search sites.

As you see, you have a considerable variety of options available to you when designing a form. Remember that adequate planning will ensure that you ask for, and therefore obtain, necessary information only. Visitors may be put off if your forms ask for too much information.

Creating a form

Let's start by creating a simple form which will ask visitors to choose their favourite pet and to submit their contact details.

The first point to make is that you must always add the form to the page before trying to add any components such as radio buttons. Select the **Forms** panel of the Insert toolbar.

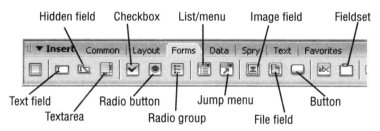

Figure 8.1 Forms toolbar

Before adding a form, first insert a heading for the page. Next position the cursor in Design view where the form is to be inserted and click the **Form** button in the toolbar (on the far left – hover over each icon to see the associated text).

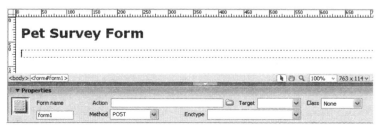

Figure 8.2 Heading and form inserted

The form is represented in Design view by a red dashed rectangle; in Properties you will see that the default name of *form1* has been applied to it and that the **Method** has been set to POST – these settings are important and we will deal with them shortly.

Everything that you do from now on, assuming it is form-related, must take place within the rectangle – if it does not, your form might appear in the browser but it will not work correctly. We have already established that the form should be user-friendly and, as a starting point we should at least provide it with a basic format – this will be done using a table.

What we are going to build is a simple form which will incorporate various form components, CSS styling and validation. The end result will look like this:

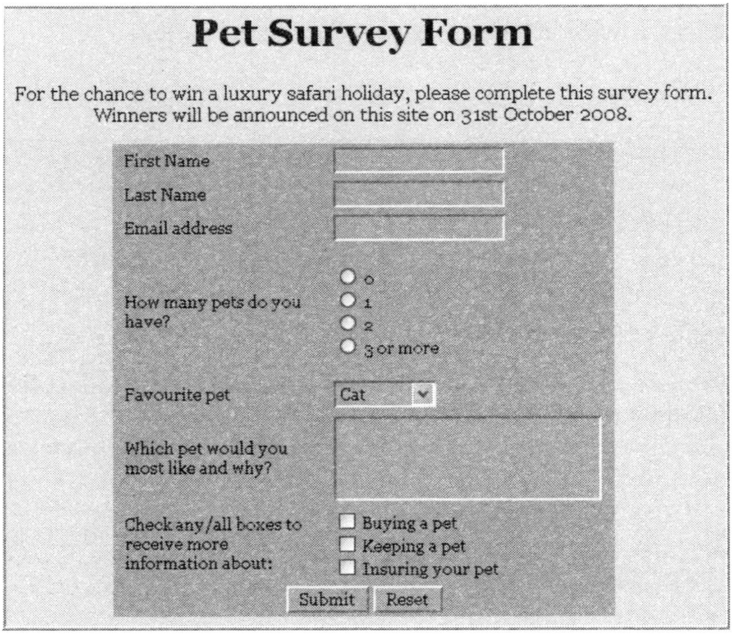

Figure 8.3   Survey form (complete)

As you can see there are a number of components used in this form – text fields to capture name and email, radio buttons for number of pets, menu for favourite pet, textarea to capture visitor free narrative, checkboxes for further information and buttons:

Submit to capture the form details and Reset to set the form back to its default settings in the event of the visitor making a mistake and wishing to re-input.

Within the form's dashed rectangle, position the cursor and add a table which has the following characteristics:

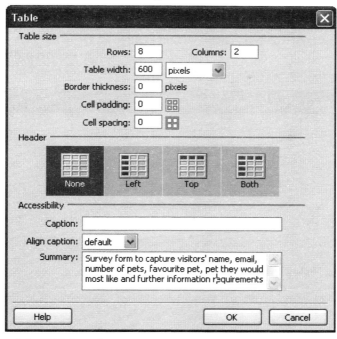

Figure 8.4 Table format

* Note the number of rows and columns.

* **Cell padding** will be set using CSS.

* Remember the **Accessibility Summary. Caption** could be used as an alternative to the heading we have already inserted.

* **Header** sets the selected rows and/or columns as table headings, i.e. they are assigned the HTML tag of <th> which is used for headings rather than <td> which is used for normal cells. Browsers will automatically embolden and centre the contents of <th> tags. If you are using a table for layout purposes then you are unlikely to use this setting.

The table columns must be sized after inserting the table or the browser will size the columns for you – 450 and 150 (pixels) for left and right respectively would be fine. In the left-hand column, insert the text you see in the screenshot above in Figure 8.3, e.g. First Name. Once all of the text has been added to the left column, position the cursor in the right-hand column of row 1 of the table.

To insert a text box, click the **Text Field** icon. Depending on your accessibility settings you may well see an **Input Tag Accessibility** dialog box appear every time you add a form component.

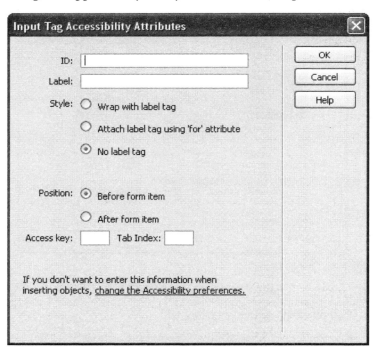

Figure 8.5 Form accessibility dialog box

* Into the **ID** field, type a meaningful name for the field, e.g. *first_name*. The name should not contain spaces.

* **Label** links descriptions with form elements and is useful for checkboxes and radio buttons; the text you enter here is displayed with the form element.

- If using Label, the best **Style** choice for accessibility is **Attach label tag using 'for' attribute**. Browsers will then allow this text to be clicked as well as the button, checkbox, etc.

- **Position** allows you to select whether the label precedes (*Before form item*) or follows (*After form item*) the element.

- **Access key** should hold a keystroke which will take the visitor to the field; this should be unique for this page and form.

- **Tab Index** is the number of tabs required to reach this field.

Click **OK** and you will now see a text box in the column. Look also at the Properties panel.

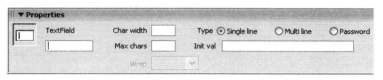

Figure 8.6 TextField properties

Immediately under the text **TextField** there is a box which will show the name you gave to the ID field in the dialog box (Figure 8.5). If you did not add a name then, do so now. The purpose of the name will become more apparent when we get to form validation. However, there is a general rule here – all form fields should be named.

There are other property settings we can set for the TextField such as the visible width of the text box (**Char width**) and the maximum number of characters that may be input by the visitor (**Max chars**). An initial value may be set for the field (**Init val**) though you would not usually set this for a name field. If it is intended that the TextField should accept a password, it may be configured so that passwords appear as a string of dots (**Password**). Be aware though that this does not in any way make the password secure – all it does is to stop someone seeing it on your screen.

Repeat the insertion of a text box for the second and third rows and name them respectively *last_name* and *email*.

For the fourth row we want to add a group of radio buttons using the **Radio Group** icon; you may also use the **Radio Button** icon but this requires a little more effort. Radio buttons should be used when a single response only is possible/expected – in this case, how many pets does the visitor have. They need to be grouped so that only one button in the group can be selected. This is achieved by naming each button identically, e.g. *number_pets*.

Click the **Radio Group** icon and the dialog box is displayed.

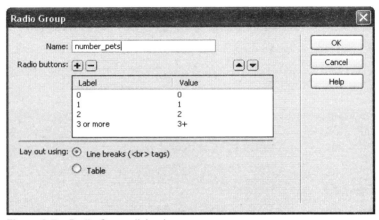

Figure 8.7 Radio Group dialog box

◆ Assign a **Name** to the group, in this case *number_pets*.

◆ Add **Label** and **Value** pairs – the Label is visible to the visitor, while the Value may be used for validation/storage.

◆ Finally, because the buttons are to be inserted in a table cell, from the buttons labelled **Lay out using** choose **Line breaks** (**
 tags**).

Click **OK** and the group will be added.

In the fifth row a list/menu will be added using the **List/Menu** icon. Unlike radio buttons, there is no need to make any amendments to the properties after insertion. However, you do have to add the items that you want to appear in the list.

Figure 8.8 List/Menu properties

You will see that for the group labelled **Type**, the **Menu** button is checked by default. If you choose **List** instead you then have the option to allow the visitor to select multiple items (using the **Allow multiple** checkbox) from a scrollable list. Otherwise both Menu and List options will operate as a drop-down list.

To add values for the drop-down menu, click the button labelled **List Values...** Two columns are displayed in the dialog box, **Item Label** and **Value**. The first is the text that will be visible to the visitor when using the menu; the second is a value you may wish to associate with the label for purposes of form processing. In this case both label and value will be the same because we will not be entering a value.

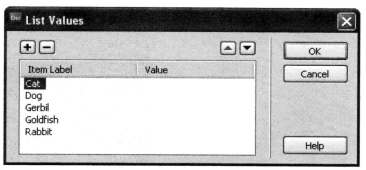

Figure 8.9   List Values dialog box

- To add an **Item Label,** use the + button and type in text.

- Use the − button to delete.

- To rearrange the labels (e.g. to put them in alphabetic order), use the up ▲ and down ▼ arrows.

- Click **OK** to insert the menu.

Note that, as with all other form components, you will not be able to view the drop-down menu in Design view. The contents may only be viewed in a browser.

In the sixth row we are inviting the visitor to type in free text into a textarea component. This may be inserted by clicking the **Textarea** icon. You can control the displayed size of the textarea.

Figure 8.10 Textarea properties

Char width sets the width of the box in characters and **Num lines** sets its depth in lines. You may type some text into **Init val** to guide the visitor as to what input is needed (e.g. 'Enter feedback here'). Leave the other attributes set to their default values.

In the next row, we will add three checkboxes using the Checkbox icon. Checkboxes do not behave in the same way as radio buttons – there are no restrictions on how many are selected. However, for the purposes of form validation, it makes sense to give each the same name but a different Checked value.

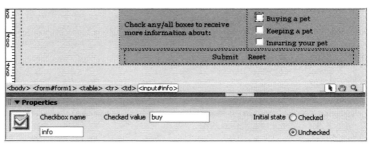

Figure 8.11 Checkbox properties

The properties of the first checkbox are shown above. The second would also be called **info** but would have a **Checked value** of, for example, **keep**.

In the final row, merge the two cells into one and add two buttons using the **Button** icon. By default, the button will be labelled **Submit** with the **Action** set to **Submit form**. To create the **Reset** button set the **Action** to **Reset form**. **Submit** will submit the form for processing when clicked. **Reset** will set it back to its default settings if the visitor wants to start inputting again from scratch.

You also have the option of using images instead of the standard buttons. Of course you need to have created an image. To insert it in the form, use the **Image Field** icon. You will be prompted

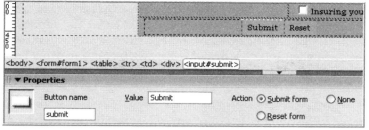

Figure 8.12 Button properties

to choose the image, then the **Accessibility** dialog box will be displayed for completion. The image will be added to the form – you need to make one change to convert the image into a **Submit** or **Reset** button.

Figure 8.13 Image Field properties

Make sure you change the name from **ImageField** (the default setting) to **Submit** or **Reset** (the name is set to **Submit** in the screenshot above). The image will now act like a standard button.

What we have not covered so far is what will happen to the form when the visitor clicks the **Submit** button. The short answer is nothing until we make some further changes. Let's go back to the form properties by clicking **<form#form1>** in the Design view Status bar, as shown in the Figure 8.12.

Figure 8.14 Form properties

Dreamweaver gives the form a name, in this case *form1*, which you can change; this is particularly advisable if you need to distinguish between different forms on the same page. **Method** is by default set to POST – do not change this. Post means that the contents of the form, when submitted, will be sent using the HTTP method Post.

We must complete the **Action** field, i.e. what happens when the form is submitted. This box will hold either the address of another web page or the name of a program which will process the form data. It is outside our scope to cover this in detail here, but one option is to use the FormMail program (see **http://www. scriptarchive.com/formmail.html**) which has been around for years but continues to be used and offered by hosting companies. In essence it transforms form data into an email. This means that the visitor can complete the form, click **Submit** and FormMail will strip out the data and send to you an email containing the actual data. Assuming the form contains a user email field, you may then reply via email to a query or feedback.

To use FormMail, you need to download it and install it in a folder in your site called *cgi-bin* (this is a standard name for storing programs like FormMail). Then add the following into the **Action** box: 'cgi-bin/FormMail.pl'. This can only be tested properly when working with a host or server which is set up to handle such programs correctly.

Figure 8.15 Action set for form

After installing FormMail you do need to make a minor change to its settings (see the *readme* file which comes with the program) to check that the email address to be used for sending on form data is a valid one. From the Dreamweaver and form perspective, this necessitates adding a hidden field to the form.

Hidden fields are used to transfer data with the form but the data is not input by the visitor nor can they see it (unless they look at the page source; remember the data is hidden, not secret). In this case, every time the user submits the form we want the email address that will receive the data to be included as well.

To create a hidden field, position the cursor in the form and click the **Hidden Field** icon.

If you are using FormMail you must change the name of the hidden field to *recipient*; the Value should be the email address which will receive the visitor's submitted data.

Figure 8.16   Hidden Field properties

After adding the hidden field, you will see a small gold icon in your form – this is only visible in Design view, not in the browser. To access the properties of the hidden field, click on the icon.

Formatting a form

We are now going to use CSS to add some style to the form. For the form to look as it does in Figure 8.3, we need to add styles as follows:

- body – choose a font and a background colour

- table – choose a text size and a background colour

- td – set padding between cell borders and content

- textarea, select, option, .input – choose a font, text size and a background colour

Each of the above is an HTML tag (with the exception of .input) so they may be defined using the **Tag** selector in the **New CSS Rule** dialog box; .input is defined using the **Advanced** not the **Class** selector (explanation below). Body affects the whole page, table affects the entire table while td applies to each and every cell within the table.

The final selector (textarea, select, option, .input) must be entered as an Advanced selector because of the use of commas. What this does is to make the defined styles apply to all textareas, all lists (which are created with the HTML <select> and <option> tags) with a custom class to be applied to text boxes only (not to radio buttons and checkboxes because this leads to differences in browser displays).

Your CSS might look something like this in Code view when you have added the rules:

```
6  <style type="text/css">
7  <!--
8  body {
9      font-family: Georgia, "Times New Roman", Times, serif;
10     background-color: #ECE9D8;
11 }
12 td {
13     padding: 3px 10px;
14 }
15 table {
16     background-color: #7B97E0;
17     font-size: small;
18 }
19 .input, textarea, option, select {
20     font-family: Georgia, "Times New Roman", Times, serif;
21     font-size: small;
22     background-color: #B1C3D9;
23 }
24 -->
25 </style>
```

Figure 8.17   Sample CSS to style table

Form validation

The final task is to apply some validation to the form. This means that we are going to enforce some rules on what the visitor may enter in the form fields. For example, we do not want the name fields to be left blank, and the address entered in the email field should be in a valid email format.

Dreamweaver contains some basic form validation functions which we will apply first. The first step is to select the form using the Status bar of Design view (see earlier in this chapter). Then the Behaviors panel needs to be opened, **Window > Behaviors**.

Behaviors, or to be more precise client-side behaviors, are pieces of Javascript code which Dreamweaver will insert into your web page. Each behavior carries out a particular task, in this case form validation. Javascript is a programming language, which is used to enhance the interactivity of web pages – in this case, to tell visitors when they have not input data in the correct format.

Because Javascript runs within your browser environment, it is deemed client-side as opposed to most other languages such as PHP which are server-side, i.e. they run on a remote server linked with the website you are accessing.

Chapter 9 deals in detail with Behaviors.

Click the + button to see the available options:

Figure 8.18 Behaviors options – If you do not see a list like this, or more options than shown here are greyed out, click Show Events For and select a later browser version

Assuming everything looks OK, click **Validate Form** and you will see the following dialog box.

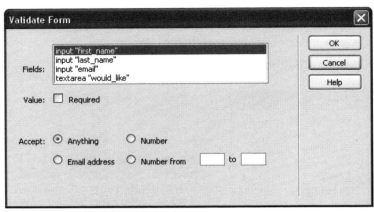

Figure 8.19 Validate Form dialog box

The **Fields** box will show some but not all of your form fields – it will not show radio buttons, checkboxes or lists. The reason for this is simplicity – this functionality is by no means comprehensive so if you are looking for more sophistication, another approach is needed. However, we will progress with this option for now.

The Fields box shows the text boxes and textarea which we defined earlier. Note that as well as showing the HTML tag (input and textarea), the display also shows the name of the field. Remember that I stressed earlier the need to assign a name to every form element – we are now starting to see why.

Click each field in turn to set the required validation. First, a field may be flagged with a **Value** of **Required,** i.e. the visitor must enter data in it. If the field is left blank, an error message will be displayed when the form is submitted. You may also select the acceptable content of a field using the **Accept** button (one option only may be selected as radio buttons are used!). The options should be self-explanatory – note that there may be other checks you would like to carry out such as ensuring names are only ever alphabetic; this cannot be achieved using the options here.

You do not need to click **OK** until you have finished setting options for each field.

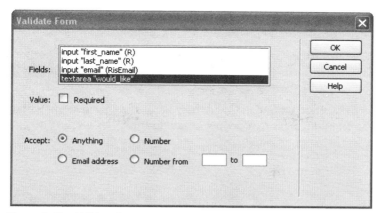

Figure 8.20 Validate Form options set

In the above example, the first two input fields are set to *Required* (R), the email field is *Required* and must be an Email address (RisEmail) while no input is required for the textarea.

When you click **OK**, your web page will change but the changes are to the code only not to the visible display. The way to see the messages that appear is to open your saved page in a browser. In this example, no data has been input before clicking **Submit**. The result is that a popup window displays the errors which result

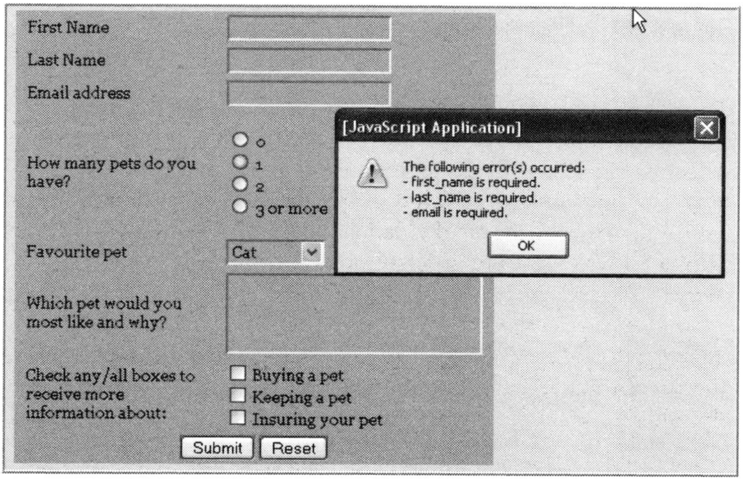

Figure 8.21 Validation example – missing mandatory fields

from validating the form – in this case three errors because we have not captured any data in the three mandatory fields.

Note that the error message popup has been moved for the purpose of making the display clearer. It would usually appear roughly in the centre of the page.

In the second example, mandatory fields have been supplied but the email field is not a proper email address.

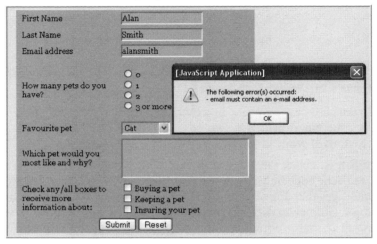

Figure 8.22   Validation example – invalid email address

If you wish to make changes to the validation you can open the dialog box again from the Behaviors panel. To see the dialog box entry first, select the form (from Design view's Status bar). You will then see in the Behaviors panel:

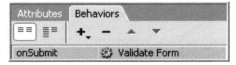

Figure 8.23   Validate form behavior

To edit the behavior, double-click **Validate Form**.

Note that the left-hand column must contain **onSubmit** (this is an event triggered by submission of the form) – if it contains any other value you must change it. To do so, click on the text

onSubmit and a drop-down arrow will appear; click the arrow, find **onSubmit** from the list of events and click it.

There is an alternative method of form validation which makes use of a Dreamweaver extension. Extensions are developed by a variety of people, including Adobe employees, and are intended to address specific tasks which the core product either does not do or only does in a limited way. Extensions may be free or they may have to be purchased, depending on their scope and complexity. Dreamweaver has, as do other Adobe products, a means of installing extensions – the Adobe Extension Manager.

First you shut down Dreamweaver as extensions only take effect when it is started. Download the extension from **http://www. adobe.com/cfusion/exchange/** – select Dreamweaver and then search for 'check form'. The one you want is Check Form by Jaro von Flocken. This had been downloaded, at the time of writing, 115,000+ times. After downloading, double-click the file (which has a .mxp extension) and the Adobe Extension Manager will start. Accept the disclaimer and the extension will be installed.

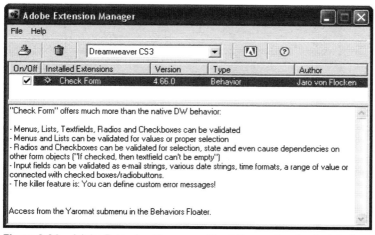

Figure 8.24   Adobe Extension Manager – Check Form extension installed

By selecting the extension you will see in the box below details of what this behavior will do. Bear in mind that extensions such as this one come with no support and are installed at your own risk. Having said that, community feedback would tend to identify poor quality extensions.

Start Dreamweaver and return to your page which includes the form. Select the form in Design view and open the Behaviors panel. This time you should see an option labelled **Yaromat**.

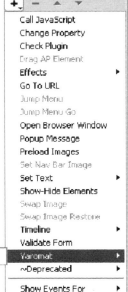

Figure 8.25 Behaviors panel with Yaromat showing

There is one option only – **Check Form**. Select this option and you will see the dialog box associated with this behavior.

The notable aspect of this extension is its ability to create custom error messages and to carry out a slightly more detailed validation of the form.

Note – before applying any validation using this behavior, do remove the Dreamweaver validation you created earlier. Open the Behaviors panel, click on the behavior and then hit [**Delete**].

As you can see, there are some additional validation options with this extension.

When you have finished click **OK** and a behavior will be added to the Behaviors panel.

Make sure the event is set to **onSubmit!**

The Check Form extension is by no means the answer for all form validation requirements. While it extends the default validation capabilities of Dreamweaver you will find as you become more

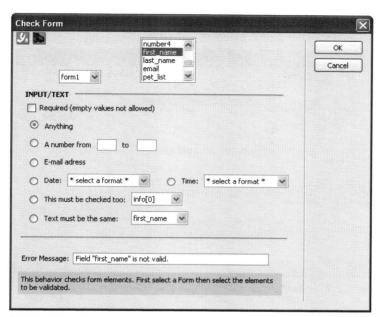

Figure 8.26 Check Form dialog box

familiar with forms that you may want to apply more stringent validation. To have validation matching your exact requirements there is really only one approach to take – to write your own Javascript code. This of course necessitates a huge learning process and, while beneficial, I would suggest concentrating on learning Dreamweaver first. As the old saying goes, learn to walk before you run!

However, do explore the other extensions available and remember that if there is something you wished Dreamweaver would do and it doesn't, then the chances are that someone has already written an extension to do it.

Jump menus

Jump menus present to the visitor a drop-down menu similar to the one we have seen above. The difference is that the list items are hyperlinks and, on selecting an item, the visitor is taken directly to another page/website (either immediately or after clicking a button).

Within the boundaries of a form, click the **Jump Menu** icon. This opens the **Insert Jump Menu** dialog box.

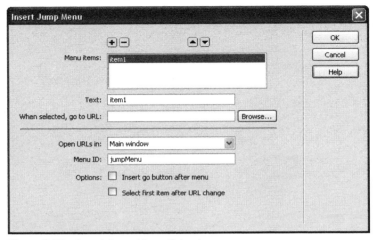

Figure 8.27   Insert Jump Menu dialog box

There are a couple of decisions you need to make before inserting your jump menu. First, do you want the visitor's selection to automatically trigger a switch to the associated URL or do you want the visitor to click a button after making their selection? Second, do you want the menu to display text at the head of the list such as 'Select one' to trigger visitor action?

In each case, enter your menu items by first clicking the **+** button. Type the link text into the **Text** box, then click **+** to add another and so on. For each entry, add the relative or absolute page address into the **When selected, go to URL** box, e.g. **products.html** (relative) or **http://www.ibm.com** (absolute). Once you have added all the menu items, you can look at the lower half of the dialog box.

By default, the pages accessed will open in the current browser window (**Open URLs in** will be set to *Main window*).

You may assign your own name to the menu if you wish, in **Menu ID**, or Dreamweaver will name it for you, e.g. *jumpMenu6*.

Finally choose whether or not to add a **Go** button by selecting or leaving blank **Insert go button after menu**; check the last checkbox,

Select first item after URL change, only if using a menu prompt (e.g. *Choose one*). Each of the examples that follows shows the dialog box together with the end result in a browser.

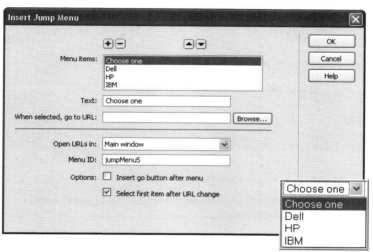

Figure 8.28 Menu prompt, no Go button. Visitor selects option and is transferred to the URL with no further action needed.

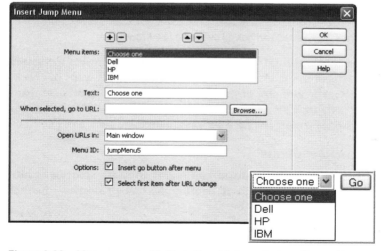

Figure 8.29 Menu prompt with Go button. Visitor selects option and is taken to the URL after clicking Go.

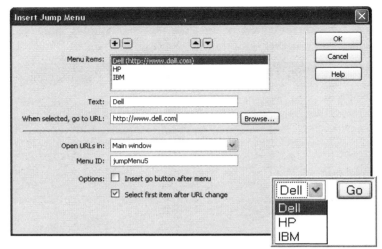

Figure 8.30 No menu prompt, Go button. Visitor selects option and is taken to the URL after clicking Go.

File upload

If you wish to incorporate file uploads into your page, use the **File Field** icon. This will add a text box and **Browse** button.

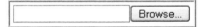

Figure 8.31 File upload box as displayed in a browser

A word of warning! While this component will present to visitors a means of uploading files, it does not include a means of checking the type and size of the files nor, more importantly, a means of specifying a storage location for the uploaded file. This needs additional coding, using a scripting language such as PHP.

Themed sections

If you have a lengthy form you might consider splitting it into 'themed' groups, e.g. user details, method of contact, further information. This is achieved using the **Fieldset** icon.

In Design view, select the area which you wish to place within a group (fieldset) and click the icon; in the **Fieldset** dialog box, add a **Legend** (this is the title of your group of form fields, e.g. *User Details*), click **OK** and the end result will look like this:

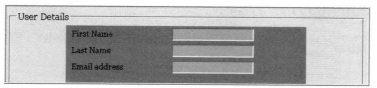

Figure 8.32   Fieldset example (partial)

If you are using a table to hold your form, trying to select a portion of it is unlikely to work and you will probably find that the whole form has been placed within a fieldset. Dreamweaver will not place a closing fieldset tag within the bounds of the table (because </fieldset> is not a valid tag to be placed between <table> and </table>). There is really only one option in this case – to create separate tables for each fieldset group.

Making your form more user-friendly

I am constantly amazed at the number of forms I encounter which require you to position the cursor in the first field before you may start entering data. There is a very simple piece of Javascript which you can add to your page to make sure that your visitor does not have to do this. Naturally, this comes with the caveat that, if the visitor has Javascript turned off (which is possible through the browser options) then this will not work; however, it won't do anything unpleasant either!

There are two things you need to know first:

◆   The name of your form

◆   The name of the first field in your form.

Both of these of course, you can find out by looking in Properties with the form and then the first field selected. Once you have the names, then the onload attribute and value below need to be added to your existing <body> tag.

```
<body onload="document.pet_survey.first_name.
focus();">
```

where **pet_survey** is the name of the form and **first_name** is the name of the first input field.

When the page is loaded in a browser the cursor should now automatically appear in the first field.

Summary

If you have followed all of the activities in this chapter, you should now be able to:

* Add a form to a web page and format it using CSS

* Make your forms more accessible

* Add a wide variety of form components and configure them to your requirements

* Install Dreamweaver extensions

* Validate the form using built-in functionality and an extension

* Locate other Dreamweaver extensions

* Describe the limitations of Dreamweaver with regards to validation.

Exercises

Create a form which looks like this one:

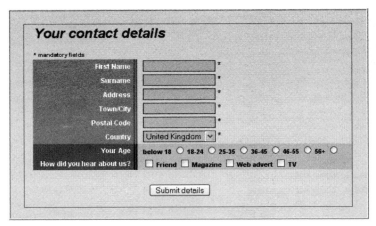

This will give you practice with all of the elements which go to make up a form. Use CSS for the form styling. Hints, together with the complete set of CSS rules, are in the Answers section.

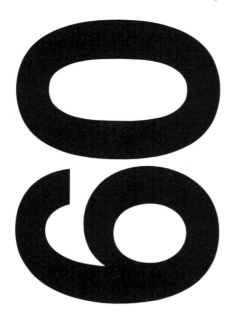

09

behaviors

In this chapter you will learn:

- how to add behaviors to a web page
- about behaviors and events
- how to amend and remove behaviors
- how to create simple animations

Introduction

Behaviors help to make your web pages more interactive and therefore improve their user-friendliness. They help bridge the gap between completely static pages and dynamic pages. We have already seen that behaviors have a panel of their own – **Window > Behaviors**. When you look at the options available, they may not mean very much to you at first. In this chapter we will look in more detail at some of them to help you understand their purpose and value.

As we saw in Chapter 8, behaviors may also be added by certain functions outside the behaviors panel, such as Jump Menus.

What is a behavior?

It is a piece of code written by Dreamweaver in the Javascript programming language and inserted into your page – don't worry about where it goes as Dreamweaver handles the insertion for you. Behaviours are event-driven, i.e. the Javascript code is triggered by the action of a visitor. Each behavior is a self-contained task, e.g. to create a popup message. The Javascript language itself is outside the scope of this book but if you are interested have a look at the W3 Schools Javascript tutorial at **http://www. w3schools.com/js/**.

These behaviors are also referred to as client-side behaviors to distinguish them from server(-side) behaviors which may also be created in Dreamweaver but are used primarily with databases.

Unlike many other programming languages, which require software to be installed on your site's server, Javascript does not require software installation as it is interpreted, or executed, by the visitor's browser. When the visitor opens your web page, their browser will display the page in accordance with the HTML; as the user 'interacts' with the page (and, by so doing, triggers 'events') the Javascript code will be executed by the browser. This is what is meant by client-side.

Why use behaviors?

To date all of the pages we have built, with the exception of the forms in the last chapter, have been static. That is, the page will look and behave in an identical way every time a visitor navigates to it. This is fine if we want to present information to visitors, but as you know web pages can provide much more, e.g. popup messages, showing/hiding page elements and, as we have seen, form validation.

Behaviours improve the interaction capabilities of your pages. The term 'interaction' means that the visitor has taken some action – for example, they might have moved the mouse over an image or piece of text, or they may have clicked a button. The range of visitor actions which can trigger a behavior is very wide – the actions are also termed events; hence the behaviors are 'event-driven'. It is important to note that behaviors and events are context-sensitive. For example, with a feedback form, you would not expect to, nor can you, trigger validation of the form's data by hovering the mouse over the form. Behaviours have associated valid events so do not try to create your own association as it is unlikely to work.

Examples of some of the more common events together with examples may be found in the W3 Schools tutorial at **http://www. w3schools.com/jsref/jsref_events.asp**.

Adding a behavior

We will look first at a simple example in order to explore the Behaviors panel functionality in detail.

Create a blank HTML page and, with the cursor positioned in Design view and the Behaviors panel open (**Window > Behaviors**), click the + button in the Behaviors panel menu and you will see the list of available behaviors displayed.

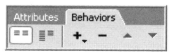

Figure 9.1 Behaviors panel menu

Figure 9.2 Behaviors listed – note that some behaviors are not available because they are dependent on selection of specific elements in Design view

Look first at the setting in **Show Events For** which allows you to create behaviors which will work in a variety of browser versions. The older the browser version the fewer behaviors that will be supported. There is no reason why you should not select IE 6.0 unless you have a very specific audience that you know use old browser versions.

Look also in **~Deprecated** as this lists behaviors which, in the fullness of time, Dreamweaver will drop from the list.

For demonstration purposes we will use the Popup Message behavior. The purpose of this is to display a message in a box when an event is triggered – in this case, a visitor opening this page.

Popup message

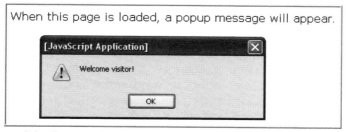

When this page is loaded, a popup message will appear.

[JavaScript Application] ☒

⚠ Welcome visitor!

OK

Figure 9.3 Extract from browser page showing text and popup message which appears when the page is opened/loaded

You have already opened a new HTML page so, with the cursor still in Design view, select **Popup Message** from the **Behaviors** drop-down list. In the dialog box, type the message which is to appear in the popup box and click **OK**. The Behaviors panel should now look like this:

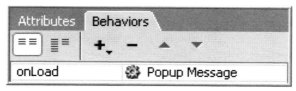

Attributes Behaviors

== ≣= ＋ ▬ ▲ ▼

onLoad   ⚙ Popup Message

Figure 9.4 Behaviors panel after adding popup message

There are two parts to the display in the Behaviors panel – the event, which in this case is **onLoad**, and the behavior, which is **Popup Message**. Look also in Code view and you should see:

```
15   <body onload="MM_popupMsg('Welcome visitor!')">
16   When this page is loaded, a popup message will appear.
17   </body>
```

Figure 9.5 Code generated by Dreamweaver (line 15)

Like an HTML attribute, Dreamweaver has added the Javascript command to the existing <body> tag. As <body> is in essence the whole page, when the page is loaded, or refreshed, the action in double quotes (MM_popupMsg('Welcome visitor!')) will be triggered. If you look further in Code view, you will find the code for MM_popupMsg.

If you wish to change the popup text, double-click the text 'Popup Message' in the Behaviors panel and you will see the original text. Make your changes and click **OK**.

If you click on **onLoad** in the Behaviors panel, a drop-down menu arrow will appear. Click this to see the events for this tag, <body>. You will see, for example, that one option is **onMouseOver**. This would make little sense though as every time the mouse was moved over the body of the page, the popup message would appear – this would be guaranteed to annoy any visitor!

Be aware that browsers can block popup messages like this, so it is not intended as an example to be used – the purpose was to demonstrate the means of setting up a behavior.

Let's look at some other examples.

Rollover images

Rollover images enable a number of different effects to be applied, from a simple change of image when the mouse is over an image to a more sophisticated disjointed effect where positioning the mouse over an image causes a change in another part of the page.

Starting with a simple rollover, first make sure you have two or more images in your *images* folder. They should be of a similar height and width so there are no strange visual effects resulting from a large image being replaced by a small one or vice versa.

This behavior is not directly available via the Behaviors panel. From the menu bar select **Insert > Image Objects > Rollover Image** and the following dialog box will appear:

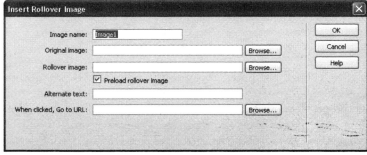

Figure 9.6 Insert Rollover Image dialog box

- Give the image a name, in **Image name**, or let Dreamweaver name it for you.

- The **Original image** is the one that will be displayed when the page loads.

- The **Rollover image** will be displayed when the mouse is positioned over the original image.

- Use the **Browse...** buttons to find your two images in the images folder.

- For accessibility purposes, enter some **Alternate text** to describe the images.

- A hyperlink may also be appended to the image/s by adding a page address in the **When clicked, Go to URL** box.

- Leave the **Preload rollover image** checkbox set – this ensures that, as soon as the page loads, the images will also load so there is no delay when the visitor invokes the rollover.

- Click **OK** and there should now be two entries showing in the Behaviors panel.

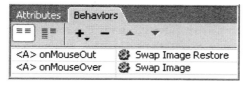

Figure 9.7 Behaviors panel showing rollover image actions

Swap Image swaps the rollover image with the original, triggered by the mouse being over the original image (**onMouseOver**); **Swap Image Restore**, which is triggered by the mouse being moved away from the image restores the original image (**onMouseOut**).

Try it.

Disjointed rollover

This is a variation of rollover images. Disjointed refers to the fact that when the mouse is over the original image, an image elsewhere on the page will change. In this example if the mouse is moved over the left-hand image, the right-hand image will change.

Figure 9.8 Disjointed rollover

Remember that images may contain text as well as photographs and illustrations. To create a disjointed rollover, first add two images in separate areas of the page and make sure each image has a name as this will make the swapping easier to implement.

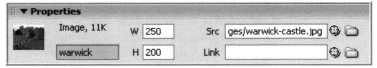

Figure 9.9 Image properties with name highlighted

The first image will trigger the disjointed rollover, which will be reflected by a change in the second. Select the first image by clicking the image in Design view. From the Behaviors panel select the **Swap Image** behavior and the dialog box will be displayed.

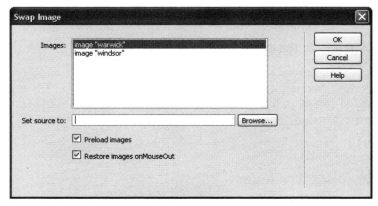

Figure 9.10 Swap Image dialog box

You should see now the advantage of naming your images. Select the second image and in the box **Set source to,** enter the location

of the image which will replace the original. Leave the checkboxes
Preload images and **Restore images onMouseOut** set.

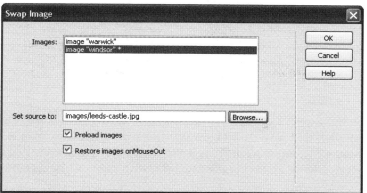

Figure 9.11 Completed dialog box

Note that the second image, which will be replaced when the
mouse is over the first, has an asterisk beside it. Click **OK** and
the relevant behaviors will be added to the Behaviors panel as in
Figure 9.7; note that the behaviors are attached to the first image
only as this is the one which triggers the events. Try it yourself.

To make changes to the set up, select the first image and double-
click the onMouseOver behavior **Swap Image**. This will result in
the **Swap Image** dialog box being displayed as above.

Disjointed rollover – a variation

You may have encountered sites
where, when moving the mouse
over a small image, a larger image
is shown below or alongside. It is a
useful technique when presenting
product images, allowing the visitor
to mouse over images of interest to
see a larger copy. This is achieved
using a disjointed rollover.

Figure 9.12 Disjointed rollover to
display thumbnails and larger images

When the visitor moves the mouse over any of the small images in the first row, the equivalent larger version will be displayed in the second row.

When the page loads, the second row may be filled with a blank image or you could choose to display the large version of the first image automatically. We will start with a blank image.

In order to align the images exactly, the method used here for presenting the images will be described in detail.

In the *images* folder I have three images of castles – each has an original size of width 251 pixels and height 200 pixels. You will need something similar. We will also need a blank image, created in Fireworks or any other image editor, with the same dimensions.

Create a table with two rows and one column, with a width of 100% and cellspacing and cellpadding each set to 1 pixel. Into the first row, add all three images and give them dimensions of 80 × 80 (this is not of course an exact reduction of the original image but it will do for the purposes of this exercise). Make sure each image is assigned a name and the centre image should have its H Space attribute set to 5 pixels (this will help to space the images correctly).

In the second row add the blank image and give this image a name as well. Now select each of the smaller images in turn and add a **Swap Image** behavior. An example with using first thumbnail image (named leedsthumb) follows:

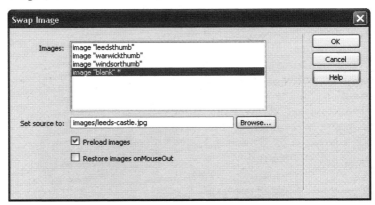

Figure 9.13   Swap Image dialog box completed

Note that the images have each been named '…thumb' just to make identification easier. The image which will be affected in every case is the blank image which will be replaced by the larger version of the selected thumbnail. Note also that the checkbox to **Restore images onMouseOut** has been unchecked – this means that the castle image will remain in the second row until another thumbnail is activated. If you set this checkbox, moving the mouse away would restore the blank image.

As we are dealing with *leedsthumb*, we select the blank image in the **Swap Image** dialog box and choose the larger version of the image in **Set source to**. Click **OK** and repeat for the other '…thumb' images, selecting the appropriate larger image for each.

If you wish to start with an actual image rather than a blank, place a full size image in the second row. If you want to revert back to this initial image when the mouse is moved away, just check the **Restore images onMouseOut** checkbox.

Try it yourself. If you get into difficulties, delete any behaviors you have added and start again.

Show-hide elements

In this example the element is an additional piece of text in a page which we can show or hide according to visitor actions. The purpose of this text is to provide more information about a topic mentioned in the main text. Of course a similar effect can be achieved by using a link to open a new window, though this would require another web page. The beauty of this solution is that all of the text is contained within a single page.

Figure 9.14   Initial page – note instructions to visitor in original text

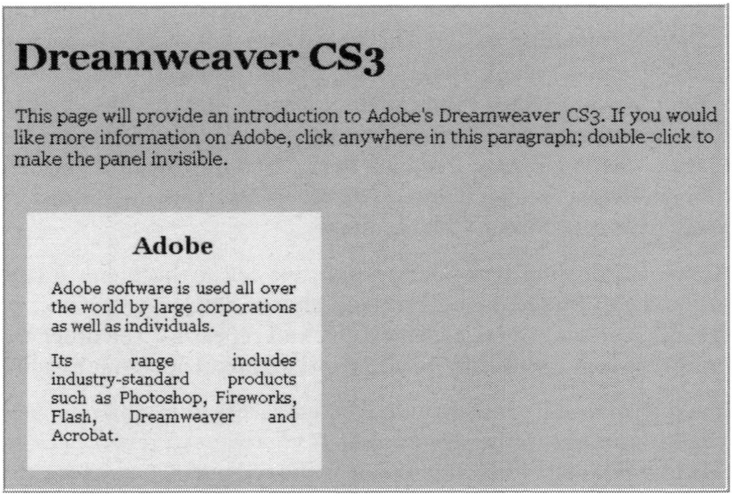

Dreamweaver CS3

This page will provide an introduction to Adobe's Dreamweaver CS3. If you would like more information on Adobe, click anywhere in this paragraph; double-click to make the panel invisible.

Adobe

Adobe software is used all over the world by large corporations as well as individuals.

Its range includes industry-standard products such as Photoshop, Fireworks, Flash, Dreamweaver and Acrobat.

Figure 9.15   Visitor has clicked original text to view additional information on Adobe (displayed in box below text)

If the visitor now double-clicks the original text, the box will disappear. Let's look at how this is done.

First create a new page and add a heading and a paragraph of text. Now add what Dreamweaver used to call a 'layer' in older versions of the program (because Netscape supported a tag for overlapping content called <layer>) and now calls an AP Div. AP stands for Absolutely Positioned and Div refers to the use of an HTML <div> tag which is a means of providing structure to a web page.

AP Div and a standard <div> tag

We saw in Chapter 7 that an HTML <div> tag may be inserted into a page to create structure. When an AP Div is inserted an HTML <div> tag is also used. So are they the same thing? In short, no. The AP Div is always absolutely positioned, hence the AP. A standard <div> may be positioned in any way. AP Divs are also manoeuvrable within Design view, which a standard <div> is not and AP Divs are automatically allocated a Z-index attribute to facilitate stacking while a standard <div> is not.

Select **Insert > Layout Objects > AP Div** and a box like the one shown in Figure 9.16 will appear in Design view.

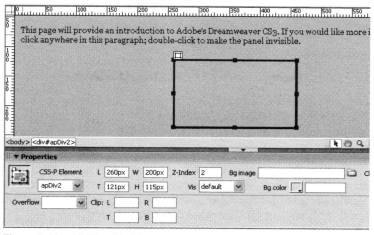

Figure 9.16   AP Div added to page

The AP Div above has been selected to show its properties in the Properties panel. Note that it may be moved by hovering anywhere over the border until you see the cursor change to a multi-arrow format – now you can hold the left mouse button down and drag the AP Div anywhere on the page. You may also change the initial shape by using the resize handles shown. As already mentioned the AP stands for absolutely positioned which means that, once placed, the AP Div will stay in place irrespective of other page elements – this has good and bad points as we will see.

Other methods of changing the AP Div position

You may have a specific need to size and/or position the AP Div precisely. One method is to type the values into the L (Left), T (Top), W (Width) or H (Height) boxes in **Properties**. L and T set the box position relative to the left and top browser borders, while W and H of course set the width and height of the box.

While selected as in Figure 9.16, you may also use [**Shift**] and the Up, Down, Left or Right keys in order to change the position by 10 pixels at a time up, down, left or right.

Finally, you may wish to design your page layout based on a grid. To see the grid, **View > Grid > Show Grid**. You may choose the size of the grid squares and, to make positioning easier, you can set Snap to Grid (**View > Grid > Snap to Grid**). When you move your AP Div near to the grid lines, Dreamweaver will align it automatically for you.

Enter some text into the AP Div and format it as normal.

Default attributes for an AP Div may be set in Preferences – **Edit > Preferences...** and then click **AP Elements**. You may set the default Visibility, Width, Height, Background color and Background image.

With the AP Div still selected, look in the Properties panel for an attribute called **Vis** which stands for visibility – this defines essentially whether the AP Div is visible or hidden when the page loads. You should set this value to hidden in this case.

The Overflow value is also important as this setting controls what happens if the content of the AP Div is larger than the defined box size. You have a choice to make the extra content visible or hidden (i.e. truncated) or to add scroll bars in all circumstances (scroll) or only when needed (auto). Clip may also be used to show only selected parts of the content of the AP Div if required.

Z-index is a value set by Dreamweaver which is used when stacking AP Div elements. If you open **Window > AP Elements** you will see all AP Div settings for this page. In this case there is only one, with the name **adobe**; the closed eye icon in the left-hand column indicates that this element is hidden. The Z setting is 1 as this is the only element. If there were more and there was a requirement to stack elements, then the Z setting may be changed (the higher the number, the higher in the stacking hierarchy); you would also need to uncheck **Prevent overlaps** which, as the name suggests, prevents you overlaying one AP Div on another.

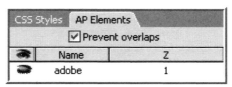

Figure 9.17 AP Elements panel

Having added the AP Div, which will be hidden when the page loads, we want to give the visitor the means to display the box on request. This is achieved using the Show-Hide Elements behavior. Some form of trigger is needed to show and hide the box; I have chosen to show with a click and hide again with a double-click.

Two behaviors are therefore needed. They need to be added to the paragraph of text, so click anywhere in the paragraph in Design view and select the **Show-Hide Elements** behavior from the **Behaviors** panel.

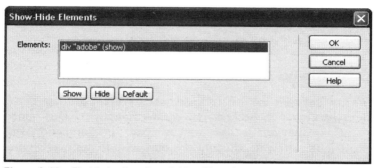

Figure 9.18 First behavior after clicking Show button

Repeat and add a second behavior – again, select the **Show-Hide Elements** behavior.

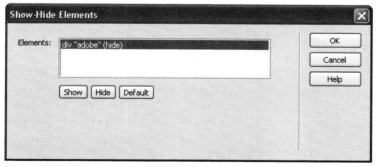

Figure 9.19 Second behavior after clicking Hide button

The Behaviors panel should now something look like Figure 9.20. Make sure that the events are sensible (i.e. based on actions such as clicking or moving the mouse) and that they match the action you asked the visitor to take.

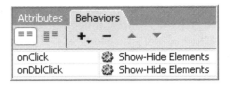

Figure 9.20 Behaviors panel after adding show and hide behaviors

Unfortunately, the Behaviors panel does not show the specific action relating to an event – you have to double-click **Show-Hide Elements** to re-open the dialog box.

Now test the page and the additional box should be shown and hidden depending on the actions you take.

Overlapping AP Elements

We saw in Figure 9.17 that the checkbox **Prevent overlaps** in the Behaviors panel is checked. This means that any AP Divs added to the page may not overlap, even by a pixel. In conjunction with the Z-index attribute, though, you may wish to use overlapping to achieve a required effect.

If you add a second AP Div to the page and uncheck **Prevent overlaps**, then you can stack (overlap) the AP Divs and set the stacking order by amending the Z-index. In the AP Elements panel we can also set the visibility of each. Let's look at an example.

In this example, a background AP Div is overlaid with three other AP Divs.

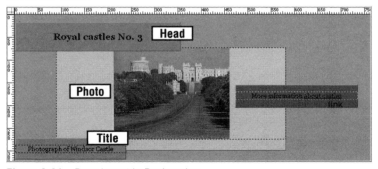

Figure 9.21 Page layout in Design view

Each section has been labelled in Figure 9.21 with its id – head, photo, link and title. The idea is that the central AP Div containing the photograph will be partially overlaid by each of the other AP Divs, with the end result in a browser looking like this:

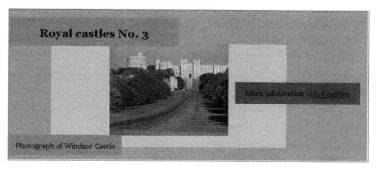

Figure 9.22 Page layout in browser view

The steps to follow are:

1 **Insert > Layout Objects > AP Div** and enter the name *photo* in Properties panel.

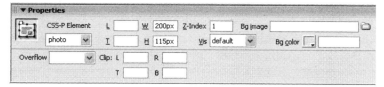

Figure 9.23 Name photo entered

2 Resize and position the AP Div as required.

3 Make sure that **Prevent overlaps** is unchecked in the AP Elements panel.

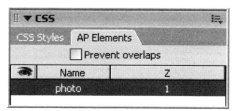

Figure 9.24 Overlapping of AP Divs now possible

Note that photo has automatically been assigned a Z-index value of 1.

4 Add three more AP Divs and give them names of head, link and title respectively.

5 Move the three AP Divs so that they slightly overlap *photo*. You might also try setting **Prevent overlaps** to see what happens when you try and overlap with this option set.

6 The setting of **Vis** (derived from the default setting of Visibility in Preferences) will determine what is shown in the visibility column of the AP Elements panel, which is headed with the eye icon.

   Blank – indicates the default setting

   👁 – visible

   👁 – hidden

   To change the set value, click in the column beside the named element whose visibility attribute you wish to change.

7 Add content to each of the AP Divs, save and display in a browser.

To change the stacking order, you would need to change the Z-index. For example, if the idea was that *photo* should overlay *head*, then the Z-index for *photo* would need to be amended to a higher value than that for *head*.

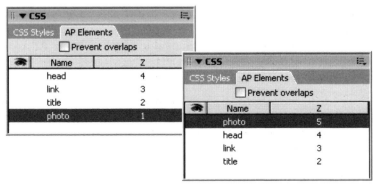

Figure 9.25 Z-index for photo – before and after

To change the Z-index value, click the value in the Z column and enter a new value.

Draggable elements

Another feature of the AP Div is that, when a Drag AP Element behavior is added to the page, the div can be dragged at will by the visitor – within limits defined by you. Again, the AP Div may also be configured to be displayed or hidden, depending on visitor choice.

The starting point is to add an AP Div as described earlier.

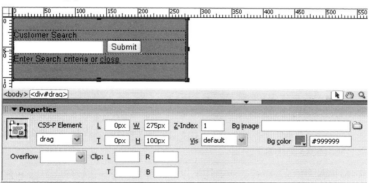

Figure 9.26 AP Div added

The contents of the AP Div, to which I have assigned the name *drag*, are not particularly important – I have added a table (100% width setting) which contains a form allowing users to enter search terms. The word **close** is a hyperlink which will be used to hide the AP Div; initially, it needs a value of # in the Link property (this creates a link but the # is effectively a dummy value; clicking on the link will not open a new page).

The behavior Drag AP Element needs to be added to the page rather than to the AP Div. To do this select the <body> tag from the Status bar of Design view and, in the Behaviors panel, select **Drag AP Element**. The event that triggers the behavior is onLoad – this means when the page loads, the page being defined by the <body> tag. Open the page in a browser and the AP Div should be draggable (hold the button down on the AP Div and move the mouse around the page; release the button to stop dragging).

The next step is to add a behavior to the hyperlink identified by the word **close** – this will, when clicked, hide the AP Div.

1 Select **close** in Design view and add the behavior **Change Property**. A dialog box will be displayed:

Figure 9.27 Change Property dialog box

2 The AP Div uses a <div> tag, so **Type of element** should be set to DIV.

3 The **Element ID** contains the name of the AP Div which we defined earlier.

4 Click the **Property** button labelled **Enter** and add *style.visibility*.

5 Add *hidden* in the **New value** box.

6 Click **OK** to create the behavior.

7 In the Behaviors panel, the event for this behavior should be set to **onClick**.

Open the page in a browser and the close link should, when clicked, now hide the AP Div. Of course, once it is hidden, we need to have a means of showing it again. Add some text below the AP Div in Design view e.g. 'Show search box', select the text and add a # in the Link box. With the text still selected, add a Change Property behavior, this time with *visible* in the New value box. Again, make sure that the event is set to onClick.

Test again and, after hiding the AP Div, you should see it again after clicking the link you have just added.

As a final step, we will amend the Drag AP Element behavior to change the scope of the movement from unconstrained (the default setting) to constrained, i.e. we will dictate exactly where on the page the AP Div may be moved. You may have noticed that there are no limits to where the AP Div may be dragged.

First select the <body> tag from the Status bar of Design view and double-click the behavior in the Behaviors panel.

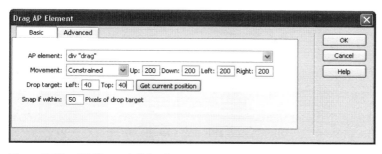

Figure 9.28 AP Element dialog box

• Change **Movement** to *Constrained* and the boxes labelled **Up, Down, Left** and **Right** will appear; these boxes allow you to define the scope of movement within the page, e.g. if you want to allow movement **Down** and **Right** for 200 pixels only, set **Up** and **Left** to 0 and **Down** and **Right** to 200.

• **Drop target** defines the location of the AP Div when the mouse is released, assuming that you have defined a **Snap if within** value (in the above example, if the mouse is within 50 pixels of the Drop target coordinates when released, the AP Div will automatically be positioned using the drop coordinates).

• Click **OK** once you have added your movement properties.

Now try dragging the AP Div and you will find that it may not be moved outside the defined movement area.

Animation

AP Divs may also be animated (by which I mean moved without user intervention) to a certain extent by using Dreamweaver's Timelines functionality. Let's start by looking at the Timelines window; it is opened by selecting **Window > Timelines** and will usually be displayed below the Properties panel.

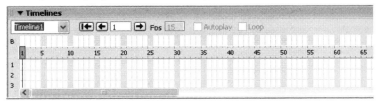

Figure 9.29 Timelines window

An animation might consist of moving an image from one part of the page to another when the page loads. It contains keyframes which, in the example we will see below, define the start and end positions of the image. The animation occupies a number of frames and frames are processed at so many per second – the larger the number of frames per second, the smoother the animation.

Let's look in detail at the Timelines window.

* Dreamweaver assigns a name to the timeline by default, *Timelinen* (where *n* is a number) – you may change this if you wish by overwriting the name. On the same line, the box shown containing the number 1 indicates the current frame – this will change as you move from frame to frame.

* **Fps** sets the speed at which the animation is played and stands for frames per second – by default, an animation will extend to 15 frames, so an Fps setting of 15 would see this run for 1 second while an Fps of 5 would extend it to 3 seconds.

* **Autoplay** means that the timeline can be set to play automatically, normally when the page loads – this should be set for the examples that follow.

* **Loop** allows the timeline to repeat automatically.

* The row with the letter B at its left will indicate the presence of behaviors when added to a frame.

- Below that, the red/orange rectangle is the playback indicator; it can be moved with the mouse to simulate an animation.

- The rows with numbers on the left, hold page elements which have been animated. These may be dragged into the row.

To give you an idea, a simple animation might do something like this; it is easier to demonstrate looking at Design view.

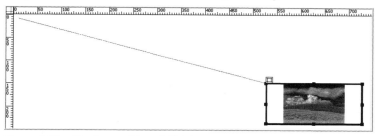

Figure 9.30 Starting position of AP Div – line is displayed only when the animation has been created

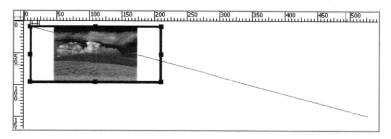

Figure 9.31 End position of AP Div, with line indicating animation path

As you can see, the path that the element will take is marked by a single line. So, how is it done?

First, I added an AP Div in Design view and, within it, inserted an image. Next, I decided that I wanted the image to move from a location on the right hand side of the page to the top left when the page loads. The positioning could be precise but I was not too bothered for the purposes of this demo.

When you add an AP Div, Dreamweaver automatically assigns it a name, something like *apDivn* (where *n* is a number) – you can change this in the Properties panel if you wish.

1   Select the AP Div (so it shows resize handles) and position it where you want it to be when the animation starts.

2   Now drag the AP Div using the mouse into the Timelines panel, which will now look like this:

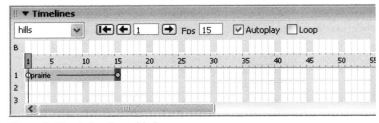

Figure 9.32   Animation added

I renamed my AP Div as *prairie* and the Timeline as *hills*. By default the timeline will be 15 frames in length and will start and end with a keyframe, the O symbol at frames 1 and 15. The animation length may be altered by dragging the end keyframe to the right. In this simple case, the first keyframe will indicate the starting position of the AP Div, while the second keyframe will specify the end position.

3   With the AP Div still at the start point, click the cursor in the second keyframe.

4   Drag the AP Div to where you want it to appear at the end of the animation. You will now see a line displayed in Design view which indicates the path the animation will follow. That is all you need to do.

5   Save your file and test in a browser.

If you want your animation to take a more complex path than a straight line, select the AP Div as above and then click **Modify > Timeline > Record Path of AP Element**. You may then drag the AP Div anywhere on the page – when you have reached your chosen end point for the animation, simply release the mouse button and your path will have been automatically recorded in the Timelines panel.

We have looked at moving an AP Div within the boundaries of the visible screen, but can we also move it off screen? The answer is yes, although this cannot be done by dragging with the mouse.

When selected, you will see that the AP Div's coordinates include Top and Left. These may be changed to negative values e.g. by setting Left to –50 the position will be 50 pixels to the left of the visible screen area (and also the browser).

You might also wonder whether it is possible to have multiple AP Divs animated? Again the answer is yes. You may either run them consecutively or simultaneously, depending on their position in the Timeline. To create a consecutive animation, drag the AP Div onto the same row as the existing animation. To create a simultaneous animation, drop the AP Div onto the row below the existing animation.

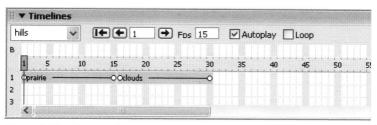

Figure 9.33   Consecutive animation

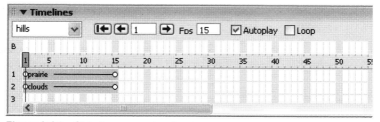

Figure 9.34   Simultaneous animation

Controlling the animation

So far, the animations have been triggered automatically, where Autoplay is checked. This tells Dreamweaver to adds a behavior to the <body> tag of onload= "MM_timelinePlay('hills')"; you can also view the behavior in the Behaviors panel by selecting the <body> tag in the Dreamweaver Status bar and opening the Behaviors panel. Double-click the behavior (Play Timeline) and you will see this dialog box:

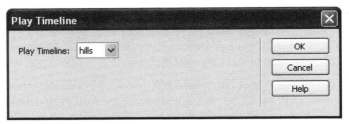

Figure 9.35   Play Timeline dialog box

From the drop-down menu, you may select the timeline to play – assuming there is more than one.

Where a timeline is automatically started, the visitor has no control over it. To allow the visitor to control the animation we can add some hyperlinks to the page. These will allow the visitor to play, pause or stop the animation. We will leave Autoplay set, though of course you could equally well unset it if you wish the visitor to be in complete control.

In the same page as the animation, add a link. The link text will be 'Play' and the **Link** value in Properties will be set to '#' (you will recall that this enables the text as a link but does not open a new page). Select the text and, in the Behaviors panel, select the behavior **Timeline > Play Timeline** and you will see the same dialog box as in Figure 9.35. Select the timeline and click **OK**.

In the Behaviors panel you will see the behavior and event. Change the event to whatever you consider appropriate, e.g. onClick is a good choice for a link.

If you have Autoplay set, the animation will already have completed and the AP Div will be in its final position. Playing the timeline again will therefore have no effect. The timeline needs to be reset to its start position before playing.

With the text 'Play' selected, add another behavior, **Timeline > Go To Timeline Frame**.

By default, the Go to Frame setting will be 1 which takes the animation back to the start. You may also set a Loop value if you wish the animation to repeat a number of times. Click **OK**.

A second behavior has now been added to the Behaviors panel – the event should be set to the same value as the first, e.g. onClick

Figure 9.36 Go To Timeline Frame dialog box

as the behaviors will be triggered consecutively. We must first put the behaviors in the right order because if left unchanged the Play command will be run before the Go To command – naturally, this would not work correctly. Select the **Go To Timeline Frame** behavior and, using the **Move event value up** ▲ icon, rearrange the events into the correct order.

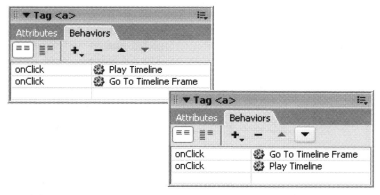

Figure 9.37 Behaviour order before (incorrect) and after (correct) order change

When positioning your link, be careful to ensure that the AP Div in its final position does not overlap the link text or this will affect the operation of the link itself.

Depending on the content and length of the animation, allowing the visitor to pause it may make sense. Add another link with the text 'Pause' and add to it the behavior **Timeline > Stop Timeline**. A dialog box will appear asking you to select either ** **ALL TIMELINES** ** (the default) or an individual timeline from the drop-down menu. As we have one timeline only, we will accept the default setting. Again, make sure the event is set to a suitable value such as onClick. Test by clicking the link while the animation is running – it should pause!

Alternatively, you may want to allow the visitor to stop the animation altogether, i.e. move the animation to the last frame. Add a link with the text 'Stop', add to it the behavior **Timeline > Go To Timeline Frame** – and in the **Go to Frame** box, enter the last frame number (the one which holds the keyframe). Add the behavior **Timeline > Stop Timeline**. When the link is clicked the animation will be advanced to the last frame and then stopped.

When an animation is paused you may wish to restart it. Add a link with the text 'Restart' and add to it the behavior **Timeline > Start Timeline**. When clicked the animation will resume at the point it reached when Pause was activated.

Finally, if the animation is intended to be shown before another page of the site is displayed, a behavior **Go to URL** may be added to trigger automatically the opening of a new page. This could be added whenever the animation completes but we will also add a link to allow the animation to be skipped entirely. Add a link with the text 'Skip animation' and add to it the behavior **Go to URL** with a valid page URL added in the **URL** box. When the link is clicked, a new page should now be opened in the browser without waiting for the animation to complete.

Open new browser window

This behavior gives you the facility to open a new window based on a visitor action, e.g. mouse click. You can specify the size and appearance of the window.

Add some text to a new page, e.g.

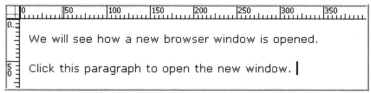

Figure 9.38   Sample text for new browser window behavior

The idea is to make the second paragraph clickable and to open a new browser window on top of the current window. This could be used for a variety of purposes such as additional Help or more information related to a topic on the page.

In Design view, click anywhere on the second paragraph and add the behavior **Open Browser Window**. You are presented with a number of options.

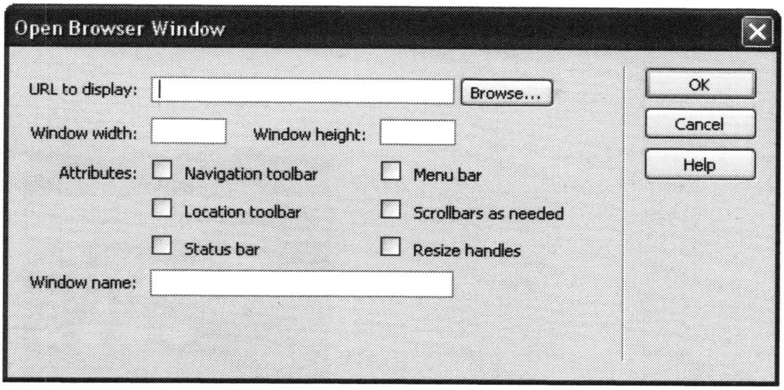

Figure 9.39   Open Browser Window dialog box

+ In **URL to display**, enter the address of the page to be opened.

+ **Window width** and **Window height** should be specified in pixels (no need to add px, just a value like 200 will do).

+ The **Attributes** control the appearance of the browser window itself, e.g. if you want to see the browser's menu bar, tick **Menu bar**. If you do not check any, none of the specified attributes will appear. Try them out to see what each one does.

For reasons unknown, the dialog box does not allow you to specify the page location of the new window, i.e. the distance from the top and left of the browser window. If you don't set these values then the browser will position the new window arbitrarily. Here is an example of how to change the left and top settings by adding some code in Code view.

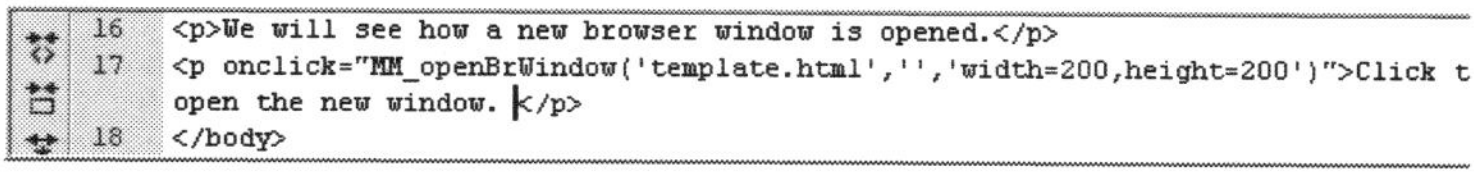

```
16    <p>We will see how a new browser window is opened.</p>
17    <p onclick="MM_openBrWindow('template.html','','width=200,height=200')">Click t
      open the new window. </p>
18    </body>
```

Figure 9.40   New browser window with no left and top settings

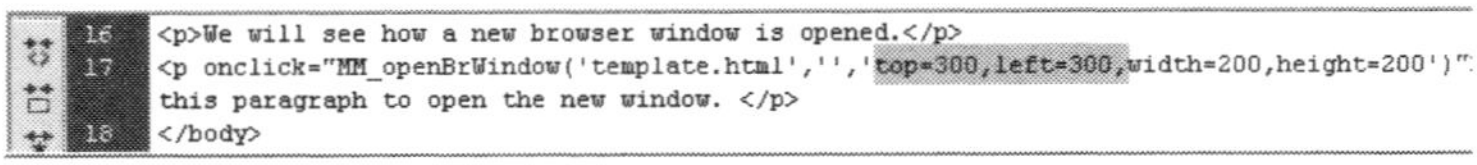

```
16  <p>We will see how a new browser window is opened.</p>
17  <p onclick="MM_openBrWindow('template.html','','top=300,left=300,width=200,height=200')">
    this paragraph to open the new window. </p>
18  </body>
```

Figure 9.41   New browser window with left and top settings

In Figure 9.41, the highlighted code was inserted to control the new window's position. If you do this, be careful and make sure you create code as in the above example.

Figure 9.42   New window positioned in browser

Status bar message

In the browser Status bar, you are probably used to seeing **Done** when a page loads. Using behaviors you can customize the text that appears in the Status bar.

Figure 9.43   Status bar changed to hold custom text

Care needs to be taken that the behavior is attached to a suitable event. In this case, attaching it to the <body> tag with the onLoad event would be fine – when the page loads, the text 'Pet survey form' would appear. This should be done in the same way as we created the popup message. The behavior to select is **Set Text of Status Bar** which is in the Set Text group. All you need to do is to add suitable text, click **OK** and make sure the event is set correctly and the behavior is attached to the <body> tag. Note that Dreamweaver will warn you that this feature is not universally supported by browsers, so you may wish to use it with caution.

Text field text

Using a similar method to the one above, you can specify text to appear in a form text field. This could be to prompt visitors to use the correct field format when tabbing through a form. When tabbing into a text field, the text is highlighted enabling the visitor to read it and then easily delete it using a single [Delete].

The text should be activated by the event onFocus which is triggered by the visitor tabbing into the field.

Spry effects

These were introduced with Dreamweaver CS3 and allow a number of effects to be applied, namely appear/fade and grow/shrink. Spry is a means of including Ajax (Asynchronous Javascript And XML) features into your pages; it consists primarily of Javascript files which Dreamweaver will prompt you to include in your site. Ajax uses existing technologies to create more interactive applications. Though the Spry files are supplied with Dreamweaver, Spry is an evolving technology so you may wish to obtain and install the latest files (go to **http://labs.adobe.com/technologies/spry/home. html**; there is a download link on this page).

As and when you add Spry functionality to your site, the necessary files will be copied to your site folder. If we look at one of the effects (appear/fade), this will become more apparent. First add a paragraph of text to a standard HTML page, select it and, from the Behaviors panel, select **Effects > Appear/Fade**.

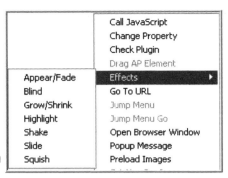

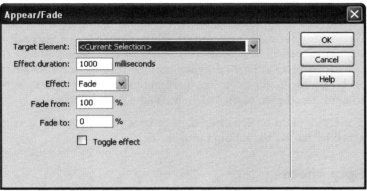

Figure 9.44 Behaviors menu

Figure 9.45 Appear/Fade dialog box

In the dialog box you can select the effect, the time duration (**Effect duration**) as well as the level of fading (**Fade from** and **Fade to**) and whether the mouse may be used to toggle the effect on or off (**Toggle effect**). When you save your page, you will see a prompt box appear, like the one in Figure 9.46.

Dreamweaver has identified the fact that you have added Spry functionality to the page but do not yet have the relevant Javascript file/s included in your site. This is a reminder that the file/s have been copied and will need to be uploaded to the remote server when your site goes live. Dreamweaver will automatically create a folder in your site called SpryAssets to hold this (look in the Files panel), and any subsequent, Spry files. This prompt will not appear again if you add more effects.

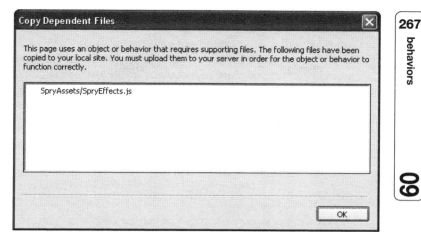

Figure 9.46 Prompt to copy relevant Spry files to your site

Try it and you will see the paragraph of text fade. This is a simple example of Ajax – a technique which combines JavaScript and XML.

Try the other effects as well to see what is available.

We have covered many of Dreamweaver's behaviors in this chapter. Some have not been covered because they are deprecated and/or because do not work in every browser.

Summary

If you have followed all of the activities in this chapter, you should now be able to:

♦ Add a range of Dreamweaver behaviors to your web page – rollover image, disjointed rollover, show-hide elements, popup message, new browser window, Status bar message, text field message, special text effects using Spry

♦ Link suitable events to each behavior

♦ Amend and remove behaviors

♦ Create draggable elements

♦ Create animations using the timelines functionality.

Exercises

1   You may well have encountered web pages where, when you hover over a piece of text (which usually stands out from the surrounding text because of its colour or because it may have something like a dotted line below it), you then see some further information appear in a rectangular box. An example is shown below:

Information about Dreamweaver CS3

In this section, we will look at site creation. We will then focus on creating individual pages.

> Creating a site will always take place before pages are created. A site contains everything - images, text, forms, stylesheets etc.

The visitor has moved the mouse over the text 'site creation', which is underlined with dots, and the additional information then pops up.

Just to confuse the issue, this is not a behavior in the sense that Javascript is not created by Dreamweaver. I have included it here as it is based on moving the mouse over selected text.

Because you will not find anything in the Behaviors panel, here are some hints:

+ First create a custom style for border bottom only

+ Now apply the style to your choice of text

+ Finally add a title attribute with the value set to the text you wish to appear in the rectangular box (this may only be done in Code view).

Save and test and you see a similar effect to the example above.

2   You can use a behavior called **Set Nav Bar Image** to create a navigation bar which uses images rather than just text (but remember that an image may also contain text as well as drawings, photos, etc.). Try it.

templates

In this chapter you will learn:

- about the importance of templates
- about the different components of a template
- how to create and edit templates
- how to create and add library items

Introduction

Templates provide a very important and time-saving tool for the web designer/developer. A template provides an identical design for each page, thus removing the need to copy elements from page to page. The template is split into editable and non-editable areas so that if you are working in a team environment, for example, the page design may be 'locked down' and edited only by the designers and content added only by the administrators.

The huge advantage with using templates is in the decreased time required for maintenance. Imagine you have a site of 50 pages and you need to alter the navigation bar – either you have to make the change to each of the 50 pages or, if you are using templates, you make a single change to the base template and every associated page is updated automatically. Not only do you save time but you also lower the risks associated with making any change – the chances of making a mistake when changing 50 individual pages is significantly higher than when changing only one.

Template components

A template is not a web page in the sense that you have become accustomed to. Though it is part of your site it is not a page that the visitor will ever see. It will be stored by default in a folder called *Templates* and does not even need to be uploaded to the remote server when going live.

The template must contain at least one editable region; it would not be a very useful tool if we were unable to make any changes at all! It is also possible to specify attributes which may be changed, e.g. background colour, so that pages, while having a standard appearance may be customized so that they are not identical.

The file suffix for a template is .dwt (Dreamweaver template). The .dwt file is, despite the suffix, actually a valid HTML file.

Creating a template

When creating a template you have a choice of methods – either create the template from an existing HTML page or from scratch.

Creating a template from scratch is very straightforward, in fact just like creating any new file.

1 Click **File > New...** then select **HTML template** as the **Page Type** in the **New Document** dialog box. You may then work in either Code or Design view as you would do in a normal HTML page. However, when you come to save the page, you will be prompted to save it as a template.

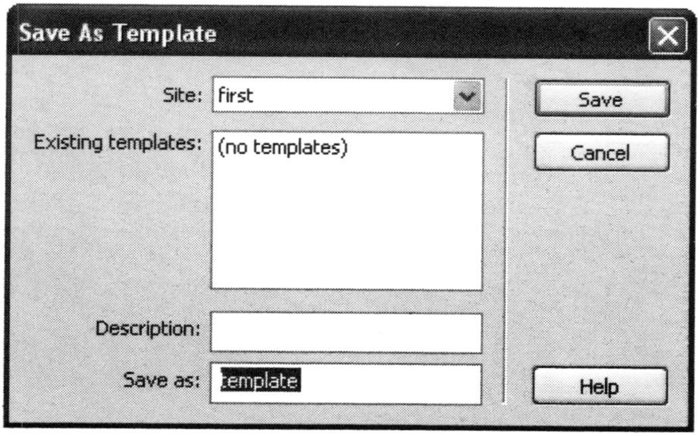

```
Save As Template                                          X

           Site: first              v           [  Save  ]

Existing templates: (no templates)              [ Cancel ]




    Description:

     Save as: template                           [  Help  ]
```

Figure 10.1   Save As Template dialog box

2 Your site name will appear in the **Site** drop-down menu and, before any templates have been created for this site, **Existing templates** will show (**no templates**).

3 Choose a name for your template, enter it in the **Save as** box and click **OK**.

The template will automatically be saved in a folder within your site, which Dreamweaver will create, called *Templates*. Unless otherwise specified, all subsequently created templates will also be saved in this folder as well.

Let's assume that we are starting with a completely new site. Before launching into full-scale development, we need some idea of what the pages will look like and what they will contain. Developing a mock-up of a page is a good starting point; this allows you to experiment with layout and appearance and, if necessary, seek design approval before continuing. Once agreed, the draft page may be used as a template for all other site pages.

We will revert to the page we were working with in Chapter 6, which is a dummy site for a computer company. Let's assume that the page as shown in Figure 10.2 is deemed suitable for the rest of the site.

Figure 10.2   Page layout to be used as template

We can convert this standard HTML page into a template very simply. Select **File > Save as Template…** and save the file just as if you had started from a HTML template, as earlier.

If your page contains links, as this one does, after clicking **Save** you will be prompted to update the links.

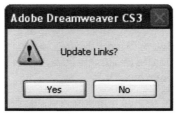

Figure 10.3   Update Links prompt

The links point to pages in the same folder, the site's root folder. When you save the page as a template in the *Templates* folder, the links need to be updated to reflect the fact that the pages referenced are in a higher level folder. Click **Yes**.

Note that when the file has been saved, the file name has been changed from *file_name.html* to *file_name.dwt*. The template may now be used to create all other pages in this site.

Editable regions

Before we start using the template, we need to add at least one editable region to it. In this case, the editable region will be the main content area. There are a number of possible approaches here; the one we will take is to create two regions within the contents area, one for the header (set to Home Page in Figure 10.2) and another for the remaining text.

1   First, select the header text only in Design view and then **Insert > Template Objects > Editable Region** – a dialog box will appear, asking for a region name; call it *heading*.

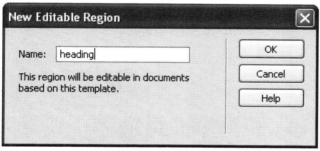

Figure 10.4   New Editable Region dialog box

2   Give the region a meaningful name or Dreamweaver will call it something like *EditRegion1*. Click **OK**.

Select one of the paragraphs and repeat the above actions, this time naming the region *text*. Delete the other text on the page – you do not need it. You may either leave the existing text in the heading and text regions or delete it; it does not matter as both regions will be updated every time a new page is created and edited.

If you are interested, have a look in Code view and you will see that Dreamweaver has added entries relating to the regions created, e.g.

```
<!-- TemplateBeginEditable name="heading" -->
<!-- TemplateEndEditable -->
```

These entries are in the form of comments so they are ignored by browsers and have meaning only for Dreamweaver. In pages created from the template, content will be added between the TemplateBeginEditable and TemplateEndEditable tags.

CSS

When creating the dummy page which formed our template, we will assume that CSS has been added to a separate style sheet. If it has not, we should do this now – CSS maintenance is much more straightforward if all the rules are within a single style sheet rather than embedded in separate pages.

1   Select all CSS rules in the CSS Styles panel – click on the first rule (**body** in this example) and then select the other rules using **[Shift] + [Down]**.

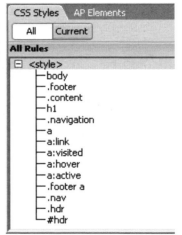

Figure 10.5   CSS Styles panel

2   With all of the rules selected, right-click over them and click **Move CSS rules…**

3   You will be prompted to add the rules to an existing style sheet or to create a new one – we will create a new one.

4   When prompted to create and save the style sheet, make sure you place it in a folder called *stylesheets* (create one if it does not already exist).

The selected rules will be added to the style sheet and removed from the template. Dreamweaver will automatically attach the style sheet to the template.

Note that the rules may be changed in pages created from the template as the rules are not part of it.

If you leave the CSS rules in the template, then pages created from the template may not alter them, although additional rules may be added to the individual pages.

Creating pages from a template

Now we can create a page from this template. You can do this by selecting **File > New > Page From Template** which shows all templates for the current site; select the one you wish to use and click **OK**. An alternative, which we will use, is to make use of the Assets panel. To access it, select **Window > Assets**.

Figure 10.6 Assets panel

The purpose of this panel is to gather into one place all elements which make up your site (other than the pages themselves).

On the far left-hand side, click on each icon to see site images, links, library items, etc. Click on the icon second from bottom to see all the templates for the site.

To apply a template to a page, right-click on the template and choose **New from Template**.

A new page is created which shows, in the top-right hand corner of Design view, the name of the template from which this page was created.

Figure 10.7 Part of Design view showing name of template (primary) used to create this page

You will notice when moving around this page that the cursor will change to the ⊘ symbol when hovering over areas which were not declared as editable regions. As you may have guessed, this symbol indicates that the cursor is over a non-editable region. You cannot change anything other than add content to the editable regions heading and text. In this way, control is maintained over the overall page appearance.

Create a couple of pages from the template and add headings and some text to each. Save the pages. We will need them later.

Changing a template

This is when the advantage of using templates becomes most apparent. Let's assume that we need to add another page which must be referenced in the navigation bar. Add it to the template.

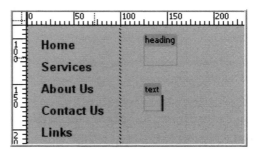

Figure 10.8 A new link, Services, has been added in the navigation bar of the template

When you save the template, this dialog box will appear.

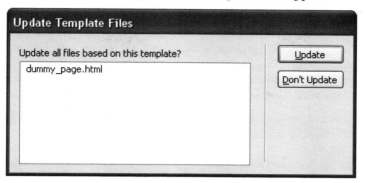

Figure 10.9 Template changed and saved

In this case there is only one file created from the template. Click **Update** to apply the link change to *dummy_page.html*.

Dreamweaver will now apply the updates to the associated pages and will report back when complete.

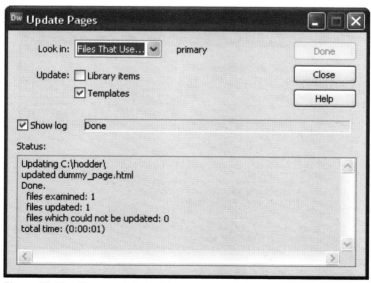

Figure 10.10 Pages updated – this message confirms the number of pages updated, in this case only one, but there could have been 500 pages updated, so you can appreciate the power of this functionality

Changing an attribute

There may be a circumstance where you would like to be able to change some of the attributes of a page, for example, background colour. Using our template, which uses a combination of CSS and tables to control the layout and appearance, let's assume that we want to be able to change the background colour of the main content area whenever a new page is created from the template.

In this example, a table has been used to lay out the page. The main contents are contained within a cell. First we need to add a background colour attribute to the cell (<td>) without changing any others in the table. Click anywhere in the cell in Design view and, from the Properties panel, choose a background colour using the Bg colour palette. If we leave things like this then the only effect will be that associated pages will take this colour when the template is saved.

We need to make the bgcolor attribute of the <td> tag editable.

1   With the cursor in the main cell in Design view, click **Modify > Templates > Make Attribute Editable...**

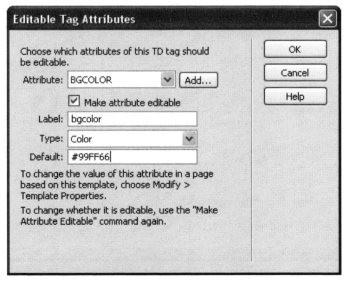

Figure 10.11   Editable Tag Attributes dialog box

2 In the dialog box, from the **Attribute** drop-down list, which will show attributes added to the selected tag only, select **BGCOLOR**.

3 Check **Make attribute editable** and the remaining boxes will be populated – you may need to adjust the **Type** selection to make sure that in this case it is set to **Color** as #99FF66 is a colour.

4 Click **OK**, save the template and update associated pages. Open any page created from the template and select **Modify > Template Properties...**

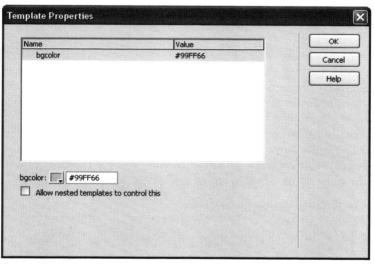

Figure 10.12 Template Properties dialog box

Listed will be all attributes which can be amended on this page – there is one only here, bgcolor.

Use the colour palette to change the cell background colour.

Other template features

We have concentrated on the main features of templates which are the ones you are most likely to use. As well as making maintenance and updates much easier and safer for individual website developers, templates are also designed for collaborative working, i.e.

where there may be a team of people working on different aspects of a site. As we have seen with the previous section 'Changing an attribute', template functionality also supports features which aid collaborative working.

Repeating region

This can be useful for listing multiple items, e.g. if you wanted to display a list of products for sale. The code inserted into the page provides a means of managing the entries that have been added to the page created from the template.

Remember that a repeating region must contain at least one editable region or you will be unable to add anything! Let's look at an example.

In my template, I will add a repeating region which I will call *products*. Start by positioning the cursor and click **Insert > Template Objects > Repeating Region**. Dreamweaver will display the name of the region in the displayed box; this may be removed. Now click inside the repeating region and add an editable region – **Insert > Template Objects > Editable Region**. You might also wish to insert a line break after the editable region to force all new entries to begin on a new line – position the cursor in the repeat region to the right of the editable region and press **[Shift]+[Enter]**.

The template will look like this:

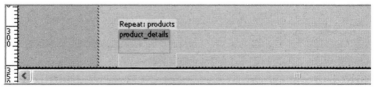

Figure 10.13   Editable region inside repeating region

The repeating region is named *products* and the editable region *product_details*. Save the template and create a page from it.

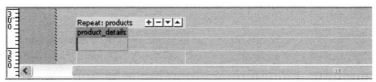

Figure 10.14   New page created, showing repeating region

There is a menu bar in the repeating region header. This allows you to add, delete, move up or move down individual items. Your data is entered into the *product_details* editable region; when you wish to add another item, click the **+** button. To delete an item, click in the region then click the **–** button. To move an item up or down, click in the relevant box and use the appropriate button.

Repeating table

Start by positioning the cursor in your template and click **Insert > Template Objects > Repeating Table**. A dialog box will be displayed, asking you to define the table's properties.

Insert Repeating Table

Rows: 2	Cell padding: 0		OK
Columns: 3	Cell spacing: 0		Cancel
Width: 75	Percent		Help
Border: 3			

Repeat rows of the table:

Starting row: 2   Ending row: 2

Region name: product_list

Figure 10.15 Insert Repeating Table dialog box

Let's assume that we want to define an initial table of two rows and three columns, where the first row will be non-repeating (column headings) and the second row will be repeating (content). The first few fields are familiar to you from the chapter on tables.

You need to decide which rows will repeat; we want the second row only to repeat so **Starting row** is set to 2 and as there are only two rows, so is **Ending row**. The inserted region looks like this:

Repeat: product_list

EditRegion6   EditRegion7   EditRegion8

Figure 10.16 Repeating table added to template

As the Border value has been set to 3, you can clearly see the table outline. Note that the second row only has repeat information over it; the first row is essentially just a normal table row. If you wish the column headings to be locked, which they are by default, enter the values in the template. To make the column headings editable, you would need to insert an editable region into each cell of the row. Save the template and create a new page from it.

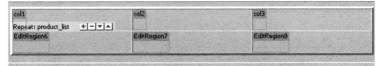

Figure 10.17 New page created, showing Repeating table

If, as in the above example, the column headings are editable, enter appropriate values in the editable regions labelled *col1*, *col2* and *col3*. Add data to each of the cells in the second row and then, as for the Repeating region, click the + button to add another row.

Optional region

If your pages will have different sections depending on the context, then you may well need to install one or more optional regions. This avoids the need to have different templates for different page types. When working with pages created from the template, you may ignore or use any available optional regions.

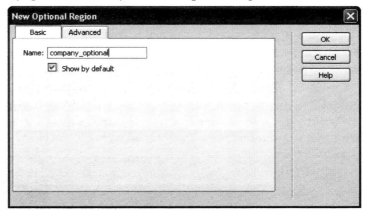

Figure 10.18 New Optional Region dialog box (basic)

Start by positioning the cursor in your template and then click **Insert > Template Objects > Optional Region**. A dialog box will be displayed – enter a meaningful **Name** for the region and decide whether it should be visible or hidden in pages created from the template by checking or unchecking **Show by default**.

Click **OK** to insert the optional region. Its contents may be either locked or editable; like the repeating region, you must insert at least one editable region in order to add content.

When a page is created from the template, select **Modify > Template Properties...** to include or exclude optional regions.

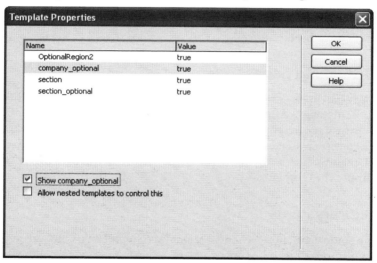

Figure 10.19 Template Properties showing optional regions

If the **Value** is set to *true* then the optional region will be available for use in the page; however, click on the region Name and uncheck **Show [optional_region_name]** to set the Value to *false* – the region will now be hidden.

Editable optional region

The alternative to the optional region where you wish to make the entire contents of the region editable (rather than having both locked and editable regions) is to insert an editable optional region.

Start by positioning the cursor in your template and click **Insert > Template Objects > Editable Optional Region**. The same dialog box is displayed as for an optional region. When inserted though you will notice that an editable region has already been inserted. No other input is possible so you cannot add any standardized text that you might wish to appear on every page.

Detaching pages from templates

It is possible to uncouple a page and its template. In the page created from the template, select **Modify > Templates > Detach from Template** and you will see that the text at the top right of Design view indicating the page has been created from a template will have been removed.

Attaching pages to templates

You can apply a template to an existing page by selecting **Modify > Templates > Apply Template to Page...** Depending on the layout of the page and the template, this may or may not be successful. Experience suggests that this is best avoided as it is likely that Dreamweaver will meet what it calls inconsistencies in trying to apply the template.

Library items

In some ways, library items are similar to templates. Once created and inserted into a page or pages, any subsequent amendments to the library item will be rolled out to all the pages containing that item. Library items can be virtually anything, e.g. images, text, Flash. A good example of usage is a copyright message in a page footer. Every year you want to update the date; rather than update every page individually, you simply update the library item, save it and the pages are updated automatically.

Library items are very easy to create as we will see now. In the footer of our page we have a copyright message:

    © C S & T 2007 - 2008

Select the whole message and then select **Modify > Library > Add Object to Library**.

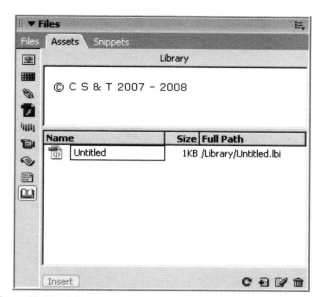

Figure 10.20 Library item added

The item will, if you do not change it, have a name of *Untitled*. Dreamweaver highlights the name when creating an item so you can simply type in the name, e.g. *copyright*.

Note also that the item will be created in a folder called *Library* which Dreamweaver sets up. It will have a file suffix of .lbi.

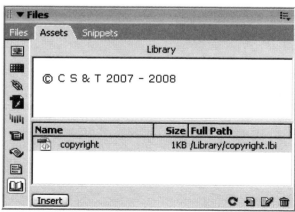

Figure 10.21 Insert library item

To add the library item to other pages, open the page and position the cursor at the point the item is to be inserted.

After positioning the cursor where the library item is to be inserted, select the item in the Assets panel and click the **Insert** button.

To make changes to the library item, double-click its name in the Assets panel and Dreamweaver will open it for editing. Make your changes and save the item. Like the template functionality, you will be presented with a prompt listing the pages including your item and asking whether or not you wish to update the pages.

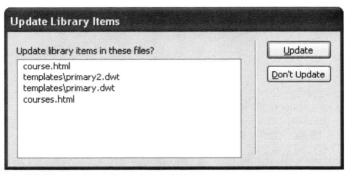

Figure 10.22   Update Library Items dialog box

On selecting **Update**, the pages will be updated and Dreamweaver will display a message, similar to Figure 10.10 showing the number of pages updated.

Removing a library item from a page

If you wish to make a specific change to a library item that is applicable to a particular page, you can detach the library item by selecting it and, in the Properties panel, clicking **Detach from original**.

You will then see a warning message stating that changes to the original library item will no longer apply to this page if you proceed. Click **OK** and the library item now appears as standard editable content, in this case text, in your page.

Figure 10.23 Library item selected

The **Recreate** button will do just what it suggests – create a library item, overwriting an existing one if present. **Open** will open the item for editing.

Summary

If you have followed all of the activities in this chapter, you should now be able to:

* Create templates

* Make additions or changes to a template

* Add editable, repeat and optional regions to a template

* Configure attributes for amendment in pages created from a template

* Detach a page from a template

* Create and add library items.

Exercises

1 If you have not already done so, I suggest that now is the time to create a template. Think about the site that you are going to produce, or are already in the process of producing, and create a template page to be used for rolling out all your other pages. In the long run, it will save you huge amounts of time and effort.

2 It is possible that the colours you choose to use in your page might clash with the default colours used to display editable regions. This could result in the editable regions being partially

or wholly invisible, not a good state of affairs! It is worthwhile knowing how to change the colours, so try to find out now. Hint – looking in Preferences (**Edit > Preferences**) would be an excellent starting point; I won't say any more.

Spry

In this chapter you will learn:

- how to select and create a Spry panel

- about Spry validation

- how to implement a multi-level Spry menu bar

- about the usage of XML

- how to create an interactive web page using Spry and XML data

Introduction

Spry represents a significant addition to Dreamweaver CS3. Each version of Dreamweaver has introduced functionality to make the life of web designers and developers easier and has also ensured that the product keeps pace with current technologies. Spry fits both of these criteria.

Dreamweaver's Spry functionality gives you the means to make pages more interactive by creating features such as menu bars and panels quickly and easily. The technology used is essentially Javascript, which you do not need to know in order to use Spry. If you would like more information about Spry, start here – **http://labs.adobe.com/technologies/spry/.**

Spry widgets

What is a Spry widget? Dreamweaver uses the term 'widget' to describe the code added to your page when selecting a Spry component. This code is made up of HTML (structure), CSS (format) and Javascript (behavior). Widget may be taken to mean an element of a page with which the visitor interacts – an example might be the Spry menu bar which enables quick and easy creation of a multi-level navigation system.

As we saw in Chapter 9, use of Spry functionality requires that supporting files (CSS and Javascript) are copied into the site and then uploaded to the remote server. We also saw some of the Spry effects (e.g. appear/fade) that may be added via the Behaviors panel.

Spry panels

There are three types of panel – tabbed, collapsible and accordion. Their purpose is to enable the presentation of information in considerably less space than would be needed for a conventional contents page.

The tabbed panel presents a panel headed by a number of tabs – the visitor selects a tab and information relevant to it is displayed. In terms of space, this is an economical way of presenting information.

The collapsible panel allows presentation of information in two formats: closed (showing the panel title only) or open (showing in addition, related text, images, etc.). The panel state of open or closed is controlled by the visitor.

The accordion panel is a variation on the tabbed panel. Rather than have a series of tabs at the head of a panel, the accordion format sets out the information in rows – the row becomes visible when the heading is selected.

Figure 11.1   Tabbed panel with two tabs

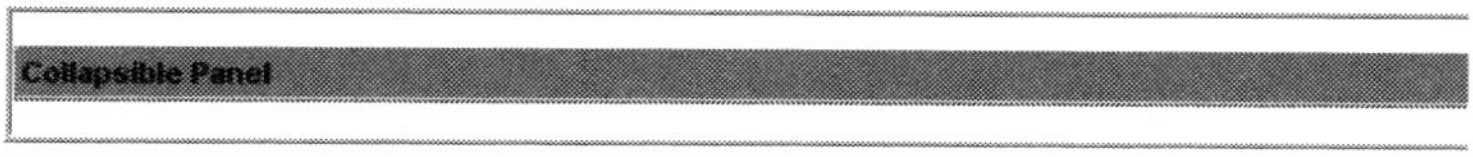

Figure 11.2   Collapsible panel – closed

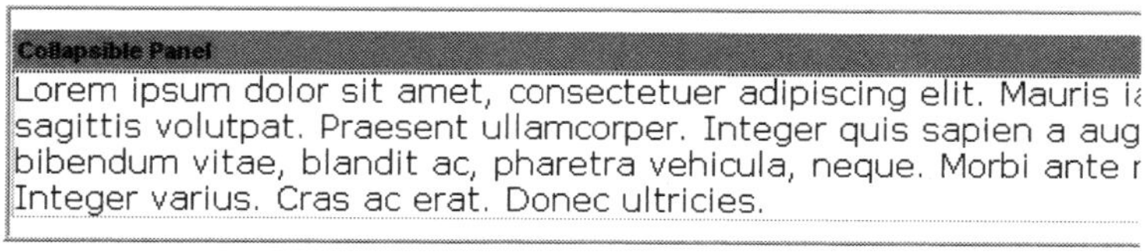

Figure 11.3   Collapsible panel – open

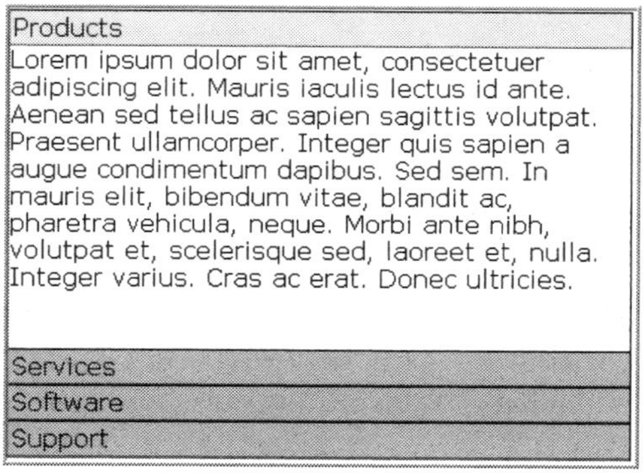

Figure 11.4   Accordion panel – first entry showing by default

In each case shown above, the visitor clicks the tab or heading to reveal or hide related information.

Let's look in turn at how each of these panels is created. In all cases, note that when creating a panel, Dreamweaver will allocate a default name to the panel, e.g. *TabbedPanels1*. By all means change this to a more suitable name; this would be particularly worthwhile if you have more than one of the same type of panel in the same page.

Tabbed panel

1 Position the cursor in Design view at the point you wish to insert the tabbed panel.

2 Open the Spry tab of the **Insert** toolbar.

Tabbed   Collapsible
Accordion

Figure 11.5 Spry section of Insert toolbar

3 Click on the Spry Tabbed Panels icon and Dreamweaver will insert a tabbed panel, as seen below.

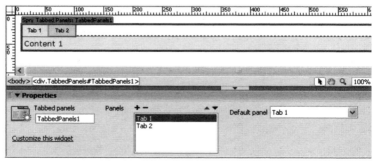

Figure 11.6 Tabbed panel as inserted by Dreamweaver

Naturally you will want to customise this so you will need to decide how many tabs you want – we will set up three which I will label 'Products', 'Services' and 'Software'.

Dreamweaver has created two tabs which are labelled *Tab 1* and *Tab 2* – these need to be changed to *Products* and *Services*. The easiest way to do this is to select the text in Design view and overtype the new values.

To add the third tab, click the + icon above the tab names in the Properties panel. Dreamweaver will add a tab called *Tab 3* which we need to change in Design view, to *Software*. Use the ▲ and ▼ icons in Properties to change the order of the tabs (if you wish).

Now the content must be added for each panel, which is also done in Design view. Dreamweaver has added some dummy content. The first panel's text will be displayed in Design view – replace this with your new text. When you want to amend the content for another panel, hover over the relevant tab until you see the eye icon (as in Figure 11.7) then click the eye to reveal the associated text. Again, overtype with your new text.

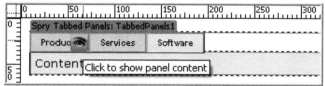

Figure 11.7   Eye icon showing

Save your file and you will be prompted with the message shown in Figure 11.8.

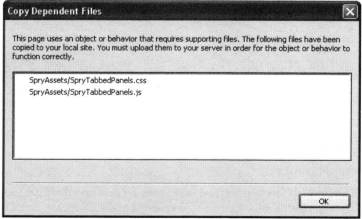

Figure 11.8   Spry files copied to site

The relevant Spry files to support the tabbed panel behavior have been added to your site in a folder called SpryAssets. This is an information message – you do not need to do anything other than click **OK**.

Test your page in a browser by tabbing through the panels.

If you want to change the appearance of the panel, look in the CSS Styles panel and you will see a set of rules which have been created under the name of the style sheet, SpryTabbedPanels.css.

Collapsing panel

Follow the same initial instructions as for the tabbed panel but this time click the icon labelled **Spry Collapsible Panel**.

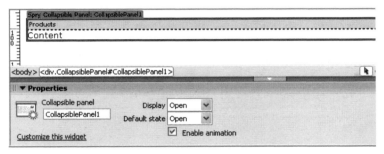

Figure 11.9 Collapsible panel as inserted by Dreamweaver

One panel only may be configured – if you need more, you should use the Accordion panel. Changing the panel title and the panel contents is done in the same way as for the tabbed panel.

The panel will by default be open when displayed in Design view – this is controlled by the attribute **Display** in the Properties panel. Also by default the panel will be open when the page is opened in a browser – this is controlled by the attribute **Default state**. The checkbox **Enable animation** will, when selected, make the transition from open to closed smooth; if deselected, the transition will be quicker. You need to try both settings to see what I mean!

When you save the page you will again be prompted with a message relating to the copying of Javascript and CSS files. Click **OK** to acknowledge the prompt.

Accordion panel

Again, follow the same process as before, this time clicking the icon labelled **Spry Accordion**.

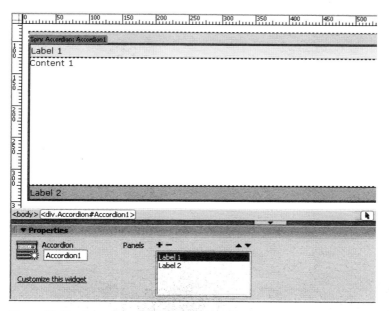

Figure 11.10 Accordion panel as inserted by Dreamweaver

By default, two panels are created. More may be added, and the panel titles changed, using the same techniques as were used above for the tabbed panel.

When you save the page you will again be prompted with a message relating to the copying of Javascript and CSS files. Click **OK** to acknowledge the prompt.

Spry validation

We saw when looking at forms that before the input data is collected for processing it must be validated, i.e. checked to ensure that the format is as we expect. We also noted that Dreamweaver's built-in validation was fairly basic though it may be supplemented either by an extension or hand-written Javascript code.

Spry validation provides additional validation without the need for extensions or writing code. It covers four form fields – text field, textarea, checkbox and select (list/menu). We will see that the validation is somewhat different from that which we saw in Chapter 8 (Forms).

Text field

The text field, in common with all form fields, must be placed within the bounds of a form. So before adding a Spry validation field, first add a form to your page.

The main difference when using Spry validation is that we select the text field from the Spry toolbar rather than from the 'traditional' Forms panel. Position the cursor within your form and click at the point where the text field is intended to go; click the **Spry Validation Text Field** icon to insert the field. As before, you will be prompted to input accessibility information.

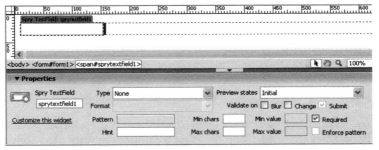

Figure 11.11 Spry validation text field as inserted by Dreamweaver

Note the Spry heading that appears over the text box.

- To see the Spry attributes for this field in the Properties panel, hover above the field until the Spry title shows then click it.

- To see the standard text field attributes, click anywhere in the text field itself.

The Spry attributes differ considerably from those of a conventional text field. The one attribute that is in common is the name field to which Dreamweaver assigns a value of *sprytextfield1* – feel free to change it to a more meaningful name.

Let's look at the attributes in detail.

Type allows you to apply a format to a field. We will choose *Phone Number* as an example. To the right of this field, **Preview states** allows for up to four conditions:

- ♦ **Initial** – when the page is opened or reloaded
- ♦ **Valid** – the data entered is in the correct format
- ♦ **Invalid Format** – the data is not in the correct format
- ♦ **Required** – data must be keyed into this field (only available when the Required checkbox is set).

Let's take a look at this field in its various states in a browser.

Telephone number | 12345-123456

Figure 11.12 Initial Text field when page loads, showing a Hint (see page 298) with the required data format

Telephone number | 01892-232425

Figure 11.13 Valid – Form successfully validated on Blur (see page 298)

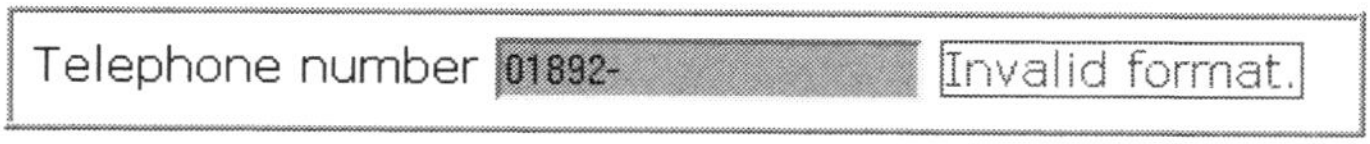

Telephone number | 01892- | Invalid format.

Figure 11.14 Invalid Format – Form has been submitted but the data format is incorrect

Telephone number | 12345-123456 | A value is required.

Figure 11.15 Required – Form has been submitted but no data has been entered to replace the Hint

Now let's go back to Dreamweaver. As you select each condition in turn, note how the field appears in Design view. The example below shows the field as it would appear in a browser if the visitor submitted data in an invalid format – note there is also a message which will appear alongside the field ('Invalid format' in this case); the message may be edited if you wish by simply overtyping Dreamweaver's default message.

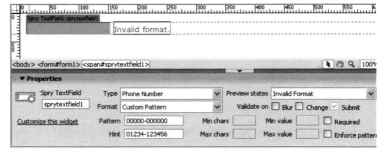

Figure 11.16 Spry validation text field showing Invalid Format state

Depending on the **Type**, there may well also be a range of **Format** settings. As an example, there are none if the Type is *Integer*, while if set to *Phone Number* there are two options. The Format you choose dictates the data the visitor may input – if they do not use the correct format the message 'Invalid format' will be displayed.

To explore more of the attributes, I have chosen a **Format** of *Custom Pattern* which allows us to choose the format of the phone number. To the right of this menu, we may select when the validation is applied by clicking one of the **Validate on** options – by default, it will be applied when the form is submitted but you may also want to notify the visitor immediately of any problems by checking **Blur** (validate when the visitor tabs out of this field) or **Change** (validate when the field content changes i.e. as the visitor types, the data will be checked character by character).

Because I have chosen the Format of Custom Pattern, the **Pattern** box becomes accessible; into this, I may type the format of the data which I require the visitor to use. In this example, 12345-123456 would be an acceptable phone number but 1234-123456 would not (because the latter has only 4 digits before the hyphen, not the required 5 digits). Immediately below, and to help the visitor understand the required format, the **Hint** field can hold an example; when the visitor moves the cursor into this field, the hint will automatically disappear.

The attributes **Min chars, Max chars, Min value** and **Max value** apply to Formats such as Integer. We may specify the minimum/ maximum size of the data as well as the minimum/maximum value, e.g. 2 and 4 to limit the number of digits; and 10 and 4999 to represent the minimum and maximum values allowed. These would render 5 or 10000 invalid in respect of size, while 9 or 5000 would similarly be invalid with regards to value.

Further to the right, the checkbox **Required** means that, when set, data must be entered into the field and, if left blank, the default message 'A value is required' will be displayed.

Finally, **Enforce pattern** will help to guide the visitor. For example when keying a phone number, after typing the first 5 digits, a hyphen will automatically be inserted.

As pointed out above, each of the states has its own style, in terms of the text field background colour and the font and colour of any message. These may be changed to fit in with your overall page design if required.

Textarea

Now select the icon **Spry Validation Textarea** 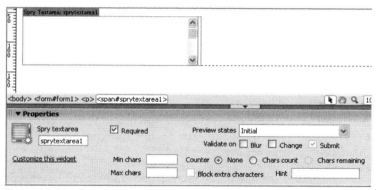.

Figure 11.17 Spry validation textarea as inserted by Dreamweaver

There are some similarities between the textarea and text field – there is a **Required** checkbox, **Preview states** (but no Invalid Format, as a textarea is designed for free format input with the only restriction being on the amount of data), options for when to validate the data and a setting for **Min chars** and **Max chars**.

Counter controls whether or not there is a visible display of either the number of characters input or the number remaining (the latter may only be set when Max chars has been set). This would be used when you want to control the amount of information entered by the visitor. A simple figure is displayed.

The radio button **Block extra characters** will, when set, physically prevent the visitor keying in more characters than are defined in Max chars. If not set, and there is a value in Max chars which has been exceeded, a message indicating that the maximum has been exceeded is displayed.

Hint may be used to give an indication if you are using character counting. Again, any hint message will disappear as soon as the cursor enters the textarea field.

Select

Select the icon **Spry Validation Select** .

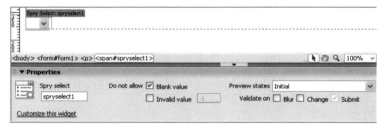

Figure 11.18 Spry validation select as inserted by Dreamweaver

Before adding the validation, you should first add values to the list/menu – click the list/menu box displayed in Design view and then click the **List Values…** button in the Properties panel; follow the instructions as set out on page 217.

Now select the Spry select field. The content you have added to your list/menu will enable you to decide which attributes need to be set. We will start with a simple list like this:

Figure 11.19 Simple list/menu

With this type of list/menu (where every entry is a valid choice) you want the visitor to make a selection; if they do not, a message should be displayed. This is achieved by using the default settings but with **Do not allow Blank value** unchecked.The reason to uncheck this is because, in its simplest form, your list/menu entries will not have values. (Remember that, if you do not supply a value, the value will be assumed to be the same as the label.)

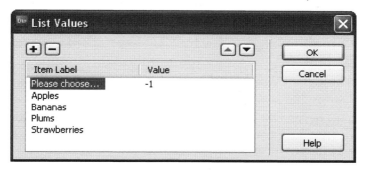

Figure 11.20 List/menu values

The **Item Label** is what the visitor sees in the drop-down list. If you do specify one, the **Value** is a hidden equivalent of the label, e.g. each of the fruits could be assigned numbers, 1, 2, 3, etc.

You may want to add to your list/menu, some text asking the visitor to choose an item, as in the above example. The text **Please choose...** is of course not a valid item; it is there just to prompt the user. To avoid the visitor choosing this item, a value of –1 has been added in the **Value** column.

Look back at the Spry attributes and you will see **Do not allow Invalid value**; check this and the box alongside containing –1 will become usable. You can choose a value to use but –1 is as good as any. With this box checked, any items in your list/menu which have Value set to –1 will not be treated as a valid option and, if selected, an appropriate message will be displayed when the form is validated.

Similarly, if your list/menu did use the Value column, you could check the **Blank value** checkbox which would disallow any items with no associated value. In that case, your list values might look like this.

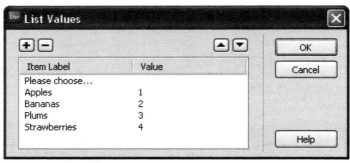

Figure 11.21 List Values

This variation illustrates the use of values with non-selectable items having no value.

Remember that the purpose of Value is associated with validation and determining what the visitor selected. The Value is never visible to the visitor.

Checkbox

Select the icon **Spry Validation Checkbox** .

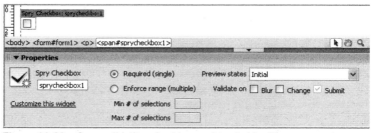

Figure 11.22 Spry validation checkbox as inserted by Dreamweaver

Checkboxes may be used either singly or in groups. Starting with a single checkbox, Dreamweaver by default sets the attribute **Required (single)**, i.e. the visitor has to click the box. Interestingly, Dreamweaver does not appear to allow a single checkbox to be optional, so I would suggest only using this when either you want to force use of the checkbox or you have a number in a group. To force use of a single checkbox you do not need to do anything after adding it – the default settings will be adequate.

Adding several checkboxes so that they are validated by Spry is slightly tricky. All of the checkboxes need to be within the same HTML tag, <span>, which Dreamweaver uses when a checkbox is inserted. If you try and add more checkboxes in Design view, they will either not be part of the same group of checkboxes (necessary for range validation) or you will see an error message.

Follow these instructions carefully. Insert the first checkbox as above.

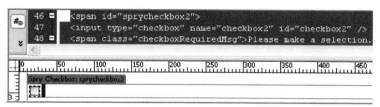

Figure 11.23 Checkbox inserted showing code (in Code view) and outline (in Design view)

All of the checkboxes must be grouped so that they show within the boundary in Design view. However, if you simply try to insert another checkbox alongside the first, Dreamweaver will display a message saying that you cannot do this. What you need to do is duplicate the line in Code view. Here's how.

In the example above, click on the line number to select line 47, then copy it (right-click and **Copy**). Insert a new line using **[Enter]** and select **Paste**. Add as many checkboxes as you need. Each one will have identical details, so we will need to edit them.

Select each checkbox in turn in Design view and make sure each has a unique Checked value. Also, remember to include some text indicating its purpose.

Because all of the checkboxes have been grouped together, they can be treated as a single entity. That is, we can add validation to make sure at least one is selected or to enforce selection of a number of checkboxes. This is done using the properties **Enforce range (multiple)**, **Min # of selections** and **Max # of selections** shown below. Remember that these are properties of the Spry validation checkbox so make sure you select it first.

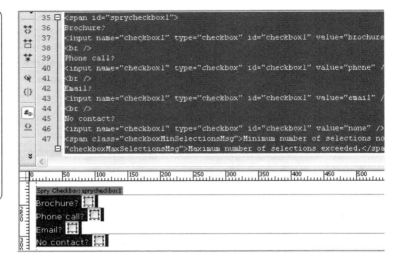

```
35 ⊟ <span id="sprycheckbox1">
36    Brochure?
37    <input name="checkbox1" type="checkbox" id="checkbox1" value="brochure
38    <br />
39    Phone call?
40    <input name="checkbox1" type="checkbox" id="checkbox1" value="phone" /
41    <br />
42    Email?
43    <input name="checkbox1" type="checkbox" id="checkbox1" value="email" /
44    <br />
45    No contact?
46    <input name="checkbox1" type="checkbox" id="checkbox1" value="none" />
47    <span class="checkboxMinSelectionsMsg">Minimum number of selections no
   ⊟    "checkboxMaxSelectionsMsg">Maximum number of selections exceeded.</spa
```

Figure 11.24 Completed multiple checkboxes

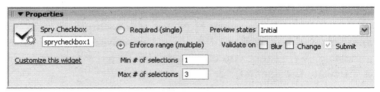

Figure 11.25 Multiple checkbox properties

With the above settings, from the choice of four available checkboxes, the visitor must select at least one; the maximum number they may select is three. If their number of selections is not in this range, an error message will be displayed in the browser.

Try out your form. Remember – the key to successful validation of multiple checkboxes is to ensure they are all similarly named and are all within a single <span> tag.

Spry Menu Bar

There are a number of ways in which menu (or navigation) bars may be created; Dreamweaver CS3 has introduced a Spry method of creation which is both simple and straightforward to implement.

Let's assume that we want to create a navigation bar like this.

Figure 11.26 Spry menu bar (example)

Points to note are that the menu bar is horizontal, has five main links (Home, Services, Products, About Us and Contact Us) and that Services and Products have further sub-menus.

To start the process, click the **Spry Menu Bar** icon 🔣. You will be asked to select the layout.

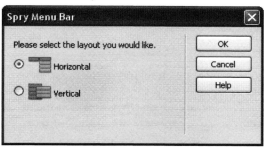

Figure 11.27 Spry menu bar layout

For this example, choose **Horizontal**. By default, Dreamweaver will insert a menu bar in Design view that looks like this:

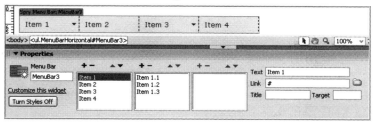

Figure 11.28 Default menu bar

To change the menu bar text, and to add additional items and/or sub-menus, you must work in Properties. For example, to change 'Item 1' to 'Home', amend the entry in **Text** and hit [Enter]; your change will be displayed in Design view.

To remove default sub-menu items, click on *Item 1.1* and then select the – button above; repeat for the other two entries and you should now have your first entry set to *Home* with no sub-menu.

To add new sub-menus and items, first select the top-level entry in the left-hand box, e.g. *Item 2*. Then click the **+** button above the middle box to add an entry – you will have to change the Text value as Dreamweaver will automatically give it a name of *Item 2.1*, etc.

You may also add a third menu layer by utilizing the third box.

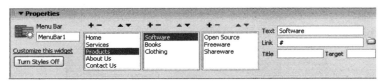

Figure 11.29 Three-level menu bar

In the above example, which relates to the menu shown in Figure 11.26, *Products* represents the top-level navigation link; *Software*, *Books* and *Clothing* are in the *Products* sub-menu, and *Open Source*, *Freeware* and *Shareware* are in the *Software* sub-menu.

The **Link** property will in all cases hold the address (either relative or absolute) of the page you are linking to. Use the **Title** property to give an indication to the user where the link will take them. Finally, use **Target** if you wish to open the link in a specific window rather than the default which is the current window, e.g. *_blank* will open the target link in a new window.

Displaying data

To improve the interactivity of your page, Dreamweaver's Spry functionality includes a means of displaying data derived from an XML data set.

For further information about XML, try the W3 Schools tutorial at **http://www.w3schools.com/xml/**.

XML (or eXtensible Markup Language) is, in common with HTML, a computer language. The great difference between the two is that HTML describes to a browser how a web page should be displayed. XML does not have anything to do with the appearance of web pages – it is a means of describing data.

To demonstrate the capabilities of this functionality, we will add to our computer services site, a page which will show training course summaries which, when clicked, will show more detail for the relevant course.

XML reads **data sets** – collections of related information, e.g. products for sale. Before we can work with this, therefore, we need an XML data set. To create an XML data set, **File > New...** then from the **New Document** dialog box, with **Blank Page** selected in the left-hand column, choose **XML** from Page Type and click **Create**. Dreamweaver will open the new XML data set. Save the file as *courses.xml*, ideally in a new folder called *xml*.

Figure 11.30 New XML data set saved as courses.xml

XML is in a sense, freeform because you define the data using tags of your own choosing. On the other hand, XML does enforce strict rules of usage. You will see what I mean as we proceed.

Here is the finished product which we will work towards. Note that I have added a link to this new page (*Courses*) in the left-hand navigation bar (by amending the template – see Chapter 10 if you need a reminder about templates).

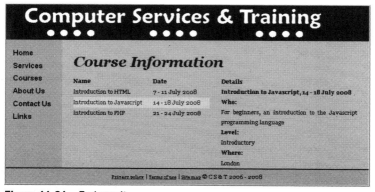

Figure 11.31 End result

The idea of this page is to show a list of course titles on the left-hand side and, when the visitor hovers over a title, further details will be shown on the right-hand side. In the example above, the visitor has hovered over the 'Introduction to Javascript' title.

Let's now focus on the XML data set. The data needs to be added by hand and we need to be careful how we do it. You need to add a root element, something which all XML files require – in this case I have called it 'courses'.

```
1  <?xml version="1.0" encoding="utf-8"?>
2  <courses>
3
4  </courses>
```

Figure 11.32   Root element added

Note the format of the opening and closing tags, <courses> and </courses>. These look like HTML tags but both tags must be present, they must be in lower case and they must be properly nested (e.g. text is correctly nested but text is not because the ordering of opening and closing tags has not been correctly followed). XML is not forgiving of these types of errors.

```
1  <?xml version="1.0" encoding="utf-8"?>
2  <courses>
3
4      <course>
5          <name>Introduction to HTML</name>
6          <date>7 - 11 July 2008</date>
7          <venue>London</venue>
8          <level>Introductory</level>
9          <description>For beginners, an introduction to
   Markup Language</description>
10     </course>
11     <course>
12         <name>Introduction to Javascript</name>
13         <date>14 - 18 July 2008</date>
14         <venue>London</venue>
15         <level>Introductory</level>
16         <description>For beginners, an introduction to
   description>
17     </course>
18
19 </courses>
```

Figure 11.33   Data added to XML data set

I have left a line gap between the opening and closing tags of the root element, as this is where the course descriptions which will be displayed in the page are to be added. You create the tag names yourself, so you do not need to use the same ones as mine. Figure 11.33 has an example showing the first and second entries.

Each course has its own <course> and </course> start and end tags. Within these tags are the details of each course, each of which comprises an opening tag, data and a closing tag – name, date, venue, level and description. Whatever tag names you use, remember to observe the nesting shown above.

Save your file and we are now ready to construct the courses page that the visitor will see. Create a new page from your template and I will assume that you have a heading area and a text or content area. Add a heading and then position the cursor in the content area.

We need two separate content areas, one for the summary of courses and the other for the details. To achieve this, I will use the <div> tag. Before I start I know that the overall width of the content area is 700 pixels, but this is reduced because I have used padding on the left and right of 25 pixels each, so I have in reality 650 pixels to work with.

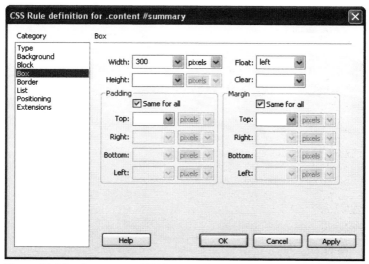

Figure 11.34   #summary – Width set to 300 pixels and Float to left

We need to style the two areas we will be adding so I have created the following CSS styles – *#summary*, *#details* and *.hov* (two ID selectors and a custom class).

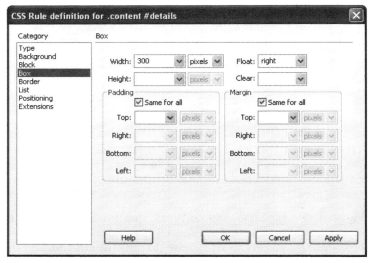

Figure 11.35   #details – Width set to 300 pixels and Float to right

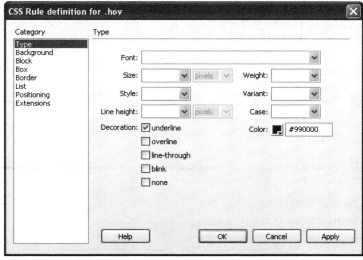

Figure 11.36   .hov – Color set to a shade of red and Decoration set to underline

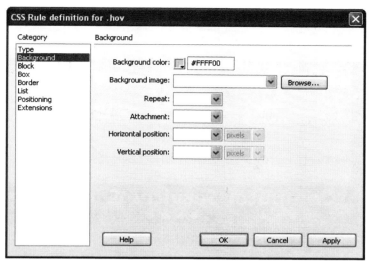

Figure 11.37 .hov – Background color set to yellow

It makes the following steps easier if we have the CSS in place beforehand. Position the cursor within the contents editable region and select, from the **Layout** panel of the **Insert** toolbar, **Insert Div Tag** 📰.

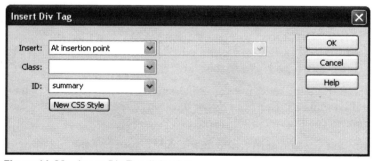

Figure 11.38 Insert Div Tag dialog box

As you have just created an ID selector called summary, type 'summary' into the **ID** box.

In Design view, position the cursor in Code view after the </div> which has just been added. Repeat the process above to insert a <div> tag but this time type 'details' into the **ID** box of the **Insert Div Tag** dialog box.

Position cursor here

```
126  <!-- InstanceBeginEditable name="text" -->
127  <div id="summary">Content for id "summary" Goes Here</div>
128  <!-- InstanceEndEditable --></td>
```

Summary div with dummy text

Figure 11.39 First div added; position cursor before adding second

Figure 11.40 Both divs now added

With the structure of the page complete, we now need to add the Spry functionality. Make sure that the Spry panel is open in the toolbar (see Figure 11.5, page 292). Now click the **Spry XML Data Set** icon to open the **Spry XML Data Set** dialog box (Figure 11.41). Before we can add data to the page we must first tell Dreamweaver where that data is held.

Give the data set a meaningful name in **Data Set name**. I have called mine *ds_Course* – *ds* for data set, *Course* because the data relates to courses.

Browse for and select your file in **XML source** – the file must be an XML file and it should be within your site.

Click **Get schema** and the box labelled **Row element** will be populated.

Click **course** – not **courses** as this is the root element. The data that repeats in the file is the row here called 'course'. You may well have named your tags differently but the principle remains the same – don't select the root element; do select the row.

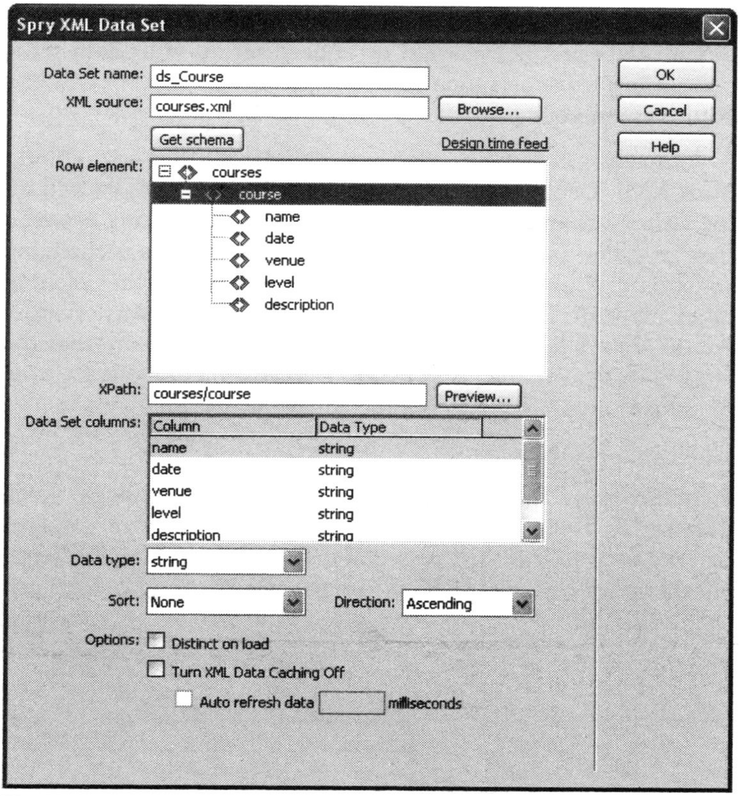

Figure 11.41 Spry XML Data Set dialog box

Xpath should now display a two-part entry – *courses/course* in this case. The first part is the root element, the second part the row. To see the data that will be extracted for use in your page, click the **Preview...** button.

If your data will always have a certain format, e.g. if it will always contain a number, then you may change the default **Data type** from *string* using the drop-down menu. This may help with validation or sorting. If the data is to be sorted then you may choose which field will be used to sort from the **Sort** drop-down menu. You may additionally choose the sort order using the **Direction** drop-down menu – *Ascending* (a-z or 0-9 order) or *Descending* (z-a or 9–0 order).

Set **Distinct on load** to eliminate any possible duplicate columns in your data set. This should be unnecessary if your data set is created correctly and validated before use, i.e. it should be checked before use in your page.

If your data set is being constantly updated, then you should **Turn XML Data Caching Off**. By default, the data is cached on the visitor's computer to save constant requests passing between their machine and your server. However, if your data is changing constantly, you would want to select this option so that caching takes place on the hosting server instead. In this way, visitors would always have access to the latest data. To ensure that the latest data is available, select *Auto refresh data* and enter a time in milliseconds.

Finally, click **OK** to create the data set.

Switch to view the bindings panel (**Window > Bindings**) – the data set *ds_Course* has been added but note that the contents may be used in this web page only. To use the same data set in another page, you would have to repeat the process we have just followed.

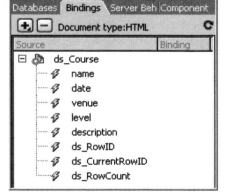

Figure 11.42 Bindings panel – displayed here are the field or tag names in the XML file courses.xml. The last three fields, prefixed ds_ are used by Dreamweaver to process the data set contents.

Back in Design view, select the text in the first div, 'Content for id "summary" Goes Here'; see Figure 11.39. This text will be replaced as it is acting as a placeholder only. With the text selected, click the **Spry Region** icon and the resulting dialog box will identify the data set which you have just created (if you have more than one data set defined for this page, you need to select the one to work with from the **Spry Data Set** drop-down menu).

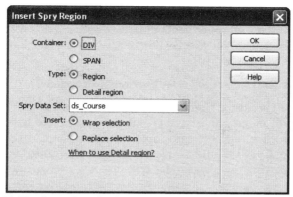

Figure 11.43 Insert Spry Region dialog box

By default, the DIV and Region buttons will be selected as will the Spry Data Set. In this case, all you need to do is click **OK**.

You will not see any great difference in Design view at this stage (other than another border around the div area) though code has been added if you look in Code view.

As we need to display course summary data, we will insert a table. With the text still selected, click the **Spry Table** icon 🔣.

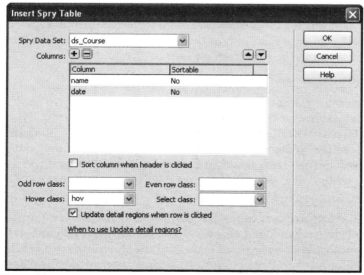

Figure 11.44 Insert Spry Table dialog box

As this section of the page will display course summaries (name and date) only, all other fields initially displayed under **Column** have been deleted by selecting the entry and using the – button to delete.

In **Hover class**, select the class previously defined.

Click the checkbox **Update detail regions when row is clicked** which will make our summary entries behave like hyperlinks; when we click one, the associated details of the course will be displayed. Click **OK** and a table of entries will be added in Design view (replacing the placeholder text that was there originally).

Figure 11.45 Data table added to summary area

You may well want to make adjustments to the table size – the easiest way is to click anywhere in the table and then click <table> in Design view's Status bar; this will give you access to the table attributes in the Properties panel.

We need to add the details to the right-hand div.

Select the placeholder text and add another Spry Region. This time make sure that you select the button **Detail region** (from Type). You may now drag the fields from the **Bindings** panel into Design view; the names will appear in curly brackets, {}, as they did in the summary area. You may also wish to add additional text as I have done (e.g. **Where**) and space the data using line breaks. The final version in Design view looks like Figure 11.46.

All that remains is to test the page. Save it, open it in a browser and select individual courses from the left-hand column – the row should be highlighted because of the application of a custom class (.hov) and every time you click a row, the details on the right should change.

Figure 11.46 Design view – after all modifications

The advantage of this functionality is that the page does not need to be refreshed so there are no delays or interruption to the visitor's usage of your site.

Summary

If you have followed all of the activities in this chapter, you should now be able to:

* Describe the additional Spry functionality that has been added to Dreamweaver CS3

* Select and implement a suitable panel type

* Validate certain form elements using Spry

* Add a Spry menu bar to your page/s

* Create a simple XML data set

* Create a connection to an XML data set

* Use an XML data set to provide interactive pages.

Exercises

1 Create a vertical menu bar as specified below where each column represents a menu level, e.g. click **Contact** and there will
   be two further choices, **Office Locations** or **Jobs.** Click **Office
   Locations** and there will be two further menu choices:

Level 1	Level 2	Level 3
Home		
About	Board of Directors	
	Management Team	
	News	
Services	Consultancy	
	Support Services	Contact
		Login
Contact	Office Locations	US
		Europe
	Jobs	
Links		

   Finally, adjust the font size of the text in the menu bar from
   its default 100% to 80%.

2 Create a page for your own website containing a panel (type
   of your choosing) to present the services you are offering. The
   page should be based on the template created in Chapter 10.
   Amend the default colours and font of whichever panel type
   you choose to match those used in your template.

3 Design and create an XML data set which will display details
   of books for sale. When the visitor clicks a title, further details
   of the books will be displayed – Author, Publication Date,
   Price and Contents Summary. Create a page to display this
   book information.

going live

In this chapter you will learn:

- how to remove spelling mistakes
- how to check your hyperlinks
- about browser compatibility
- how to check for accessibility
- how to amend your site definition prior to uploading
- how to upload your site
- how to synchronize your local and remote site folders

Preparing your site

There are a number of steps that you can take before going live which will improve the usability of your site and the impression given to visitors. These are the most important:

- Checking your spelling throughout
- Ensuring there are no broken links
- Checking for browser compatibility issues
- Running an accessibility check.

Checking spelling

Spell checking is vitally important, as nothing looks less professional than spelling mistakes. Spell checks are run on individual pages so it's quicker to run them as you proceed rather than waiting until your site is finished. The check is against the text in the page code, so do not be surprised to see messages indicating an error when the actual text does not appear in Design view (e.g. mistakes in error messages, which are event-driven).

Open the page and select **Text > Check Spelling** or press [**Shift**] + [**F7**]. Any errors found will be displayed like this:

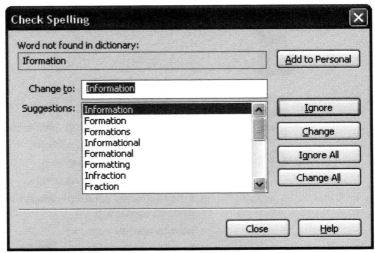

Figure 12.1 Check Spelling dialog box

When all errors have been corrected and/or when the whole page has been checked, Dreamweaver will display a message indicating that the check is complete.

Note that the check ignores HTML tags and attributes.

Broken links

Broken links (which are simply links which do not work) within your site represent another serious error if left uncorrected. What impression will visitors get of your site if they click a link and they see an error message or blank page? To check for broken links, open the Results panel (**Window > Results**) and select the **Link Checker** tab.

Dreamweaver will automatically select broken links and you should then click the green arrow on the far left ; this will present you with three options – choose **Check Links for Entire Current Local Site**.

Click to see the options

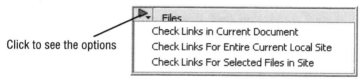

Figure 12.2   Menu options for broken links

In the example shown below, one page in the site has been identified with a broken link. The reason in this case is that *cgi-bin/FormMail.pl* does not exist.

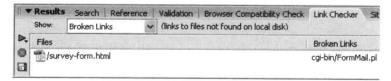

Figure 12.3   Sample results from link check

How do you correct a broken link? Depending on the cause, you might correct the spelling, change the link to reflect the correct file location or delete the link altogether. In each case, you must edit the page which contains the link – identified above in the column labelled **Files**.

Browser compatibility

Browser compatibility is a significant issue for all web designers, because different browsers do not always interpret your code in exactly the same way. This is a huge issue and one that cannot be covered in detail here. In the Results panel, click the **Browser Compatibility Check** tab and then select **Check Browser Compatibility** after clicking the left-hand side green arrow.

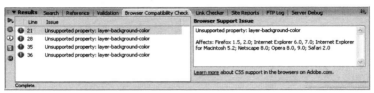

Figure 12.4   Example of failed browser compatibility check

In the above example, Dreamweaver has identified a CSS property, **layer-background-color** which is not supported by the browsers listed in the right-hand box (all of them in fact!). What action would you take? In this case, this is a redundant CSS rule which may simply be removed from Code view. What will the impact of this be? As the rule is unsupported by all browsers (see the Browser Support Issue box), it would not actually cause any problems as it would be ignored by them all in any case. You may also use the link **Learn more** which will take you to Adobe's CSS Advisor pages. It is impossible to say what action you should take in all circumstances but the best advice is this – do not ignore any errors, investigate them fully so that you understand the cause and probable implications of doing nothing and take action only when you understand why you are doing so.

At the very least, if you do not take any action, make sure you test your page with a number of browsers to determine the impact of the highlighted issue.

If you have a specific requirement to change the default target browser settings, select the option **Settings...** after clicking the green arrow and you can adjust browser versions using the dialog box shown in Figure 12.5.

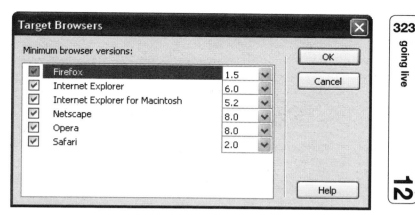

Figure 12.5 Target Browsers list

Use the drop-down menus to change versions from the defaults as shown.

Accessibility

As you added to your pages (particularly images and form elements) you were prompted to improve accessibility by adding, for example, text to describe images. It is worth running a check before going live just to make sure that nothing has escaped and also to identify any other areas which might need revision. Click the **Site Reports** tab and then click the green arrow (there is one option only) to see the dialog box shown in Figure 12.6.

Don't be too alarmed if a large number of messages is produced – many of them will be warnings, indicated by a '?'. Concentrate on the errors which are flagged with a red 'X'.

In Figure 12.7, the report has identified a table with a fixed rather than relative width. Click the **More Info** icon ⓘ to see a more detailed explanation of the issue and why it has been highlighted.

Of course in this instance you may well wish to retain the fixed table width, so you will not make any changes. Overall though it is worth considering the items flagged as errors because it will give you a better idea of accessibility issues generally and will perhaps prove beneficial to your future developments.

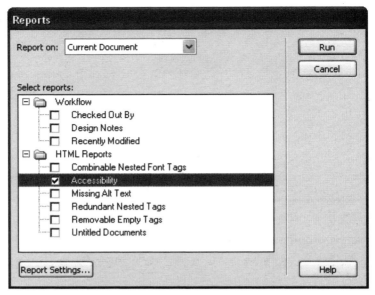

Figure 12.6 Reports dialog box – check Accessibility and then click Run

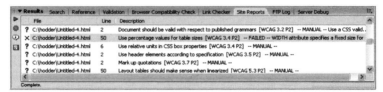

Figure 12.7 Sample output from Accessibility check

Amending the site definition

We have now carried out a number of useful checks to ensure our site is ready for upload to the Web. I will assume you have a web host (see **http://en.wikipedia.org/wiki/Web_hosting_service** for more information on what this means) and a domain name (see **http://en.wikipedia.org/wiki/Domain_name,** again for more information). If you do not have a contract with a provider yet, you may well want to consider doing so now. Typing in 'hosting provider' to a search engine such as Google UK will return many thousands of results as this is a highly competitive market.

How do you select a provider from the thousands in operation? Even if you have a recommendation from a friend or colleague, you still need to know how to determine a host's suitability – there are many articles on the Web which may help, e.g. **http://malektips. com/choosing_a_web_hosting_provider_help_and_tips.html**.

Once you have a contract, the host will tell you where to place your files. They have to be uploaded from your computer to the host's computer using FTP (File Transfer Protocol), a standard means of moving files between computers. Dreamweaver incorporates the necessary FTP functionality so there is no need to look elsewhere. We simply need to alter the site definition to include the remote host details and then we can 'go live'.

Let's return to the site definition. Open the Site Definition window and on the Advanced tab select the Category of **Remote Info**. Select **FTP** from the **Access** drop-down menu.

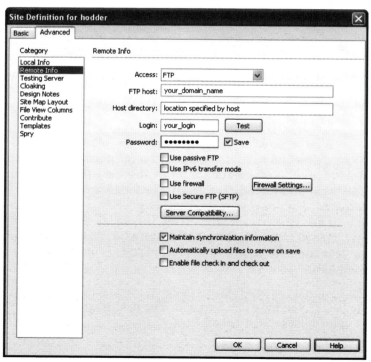

Figure 12.8   Host information required in site definition

Much of the information required to complete this page of information is supplied by your hosting company. Their requirements may well differ from those set out below.

* **FTP host** – typically, this is your domain name without the protocol (http://) or the www.

* **Host directory** – the usual destination for your site files will be the root directory, represented by a forward slash, /.

* **Login** and **Password** – as supplied by the hosting company.

Make sure the **Save** checkbox is set (so you do not have to enter your password every time you connect via FTP) then click the **Test** button – this will determine whether the details you have entered so far are correct. If they are, you will see a message stating that a connection has been made; if they are incorrect, you will see a message indicating failure but not which part of the information is wrong – you need to check and double-check what you have entered to make sure it is the same as supplied.

One possible problem area if the connection fails is your firewall settings. By default, firewalls may prevent programs such as Dreamweaver having direct access to the Internet. Check your firewall settings and adjust them to allow Dreamweaver to have this level of access. If all else fails, you may need to contact your hosting company.

There is no need to change the settings of any of the other checkboxes unless you have a specific reason for doing so. **Maintain synchronization information** is set by default – this will ensure your local and remote files are synchronized automatically. In particular, be careful with the checkbox labelled **Automatically upload files to server on save** – if set, this will do exactly what it says, upload files to the Internet as soon as you have saved them on your computer; as you can imagine, this is not necessarily a good idea!

Once you have successfully tested the connection, click **OK** to save the details you have just keyed in. The next stage is to transfer, or upload, files to the remote host.

Uploading the site

This is a very straightforward process and, as always with Dreamweaver, may be done in a variety of ways. This is one way – with the **Files** panel open, click on the site name at the top of the panel.

Figure 12.9 Files panel set for transfer of whole site

The first entry, **Site – hodder (C:\hodder)**, in the Files panel has been selected.

Note that **Local view** is showing in the right-hand drop-down menu. This is important as, if set to another value, the results will be highly unpredictable!

Click the **Put File(s)** icon ⬆; because you have selected the site name, Dreamweaver assumes you want to transfer all of the site files but, before proceeding, you will be asked to confirm this.

Figure 12.10 Prompt to transfer all site files

You will see the prompt, Figure 12.10, when you ask Dreamweaver to transfer the complete site. Click **OK** to start the transfer.

Depending on the number and size of files to be transferred as well as the speed of your connection, you may well see a dialog box showing the progress of the transfer. Once all files have been transferred, there is no on-screen notification of completion. If you are really interested, then select **FTP Log** in the Results panel to see the details of the FTP activity.

Of course, you may also transfer individual files or folders by following the same steps as above.

Checking the uploaded site

How do you know your files have been transferred? The simplest way is to change from **Local view** to **Remote view** in the Files panel. Remote view, as the name suggests, will show the files on the remote server, i.e. the hosting provider's machine.

Figure 12.11   Remote view showing files on the hosting provider's server

An alternative method is to click the **Expand to show local and remote sites** icon . The resulting display will be split into two halves. Typically the left-hand panel will look like the screenshot in Figure 12.12 at first.

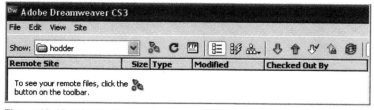

Figure 12.12   Initial state of Remote view

Click the icon 🔌 in the toolbar to connect – it is a common mistake to click the icon alongside the text; this will not work! You will now see the local and remote views side by side as here:

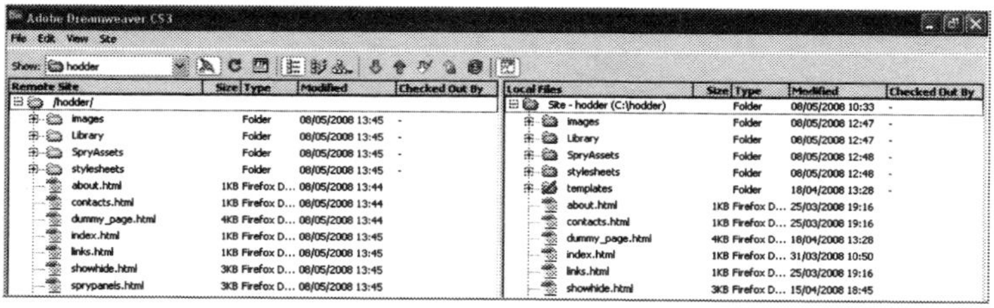

Figure 12.13   Alternative file transfer method – the expanded file view

As you can see, the remote files are shown on the left and the local files on the right. Transfers are done in the same way as using the **Files** panel – select the site, folder or file in the right-hand window and click the **Put File(s)** icon. The advantage of this approach is that you can see both sets of files on one screen.

The *templates* folder does not appear in the Remote Site files list because it has been cloaked. Cloaking a file or folder in your Local Site means that it will not be transferred to the Remote Site. There are some files in your site which may have no relevance to the operation of your site on the host's server, an obvious example being *templates*. This does not need to be uploaded because the files within it are used for page development only. They are not referenced when a page is requested by a visitor to your site.

Once the files have been successfully transferred, you should of course test your site to ensure everything works as it did on your own computer. Once you have done this, you are well and truly live. Well done!

Figure 12.14 Setting cloaking

To set Cloaking, right-click on the folder or file and select **Cloaking** then **Cloak**. By default, cloaking should be enabled; if it is not, click **Settings...** and check **Enable cloaking**.

Be careful what you cloak – it may affect the operation of your site if you cloak required files!

Retrieving files

It is highly likely that your site will change after the initial upload as a result of typical issues such as visitor feedback and/or the need for additional functionality. Care is required because you need to make sure that the pages you change are the ones that were originally uploaded. If months have elapsed since the original upload, it is quite possible that you may have changed some of the local files while experimenting with ideas or new techniques.

The best way forward with your new changes is to get the relevant pages from your host's computer to your local computer. This is done by reversing the steps to upload – instead of **Put File(s)**, you use the **Get File(s)** icon .

Now you can work on the specific page or pages and, once you have finished testing, upload again.

Synchronizing folders

With a very small site, making sure that the local and remote folders are synchronized (i.e. the right files have been transferred to the remote site) is very straightforward – a simple visual check would be sufficient. This approach will not work when dealing with larger sites. Fortunately Dreamweaver provides a means of synchronization so you do not have to trawl through lists of files and dates to determine which files to update, or to remove, etc.

To determine whether local files are more up to date than those on the remote server, select **Edit > Select Newer Local** from the Files panel menu.

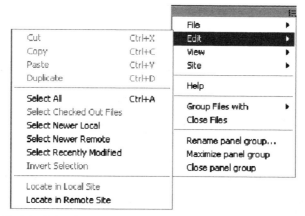

Figure 12.15 Select Newer Local and Select Newer Remote options are accessed from the Files panel.

Dreamweaver will compare local and remote and will highlight any files that are newer in the **Files** panel.

Figure 12.16 Newer local files highlighted in the Files panel

To synchronize with the remote site, simply click the **Put** arrow as the files have already selected. All newer local versions will be transferred to the remote site.

To see if there are files on the remote server which are more up to date, select **Edit > Select Newer Remote** and Dreamweaver will highlight the newer files; this time, though, the Files panel display is the Remote view not Local view – be careful when transferring files; use **Get File(s)** to transfer from remote to local!

A more advanced method is to use the synchronize command. Select **Site > Synchronize Sitewide...** and you will see this dialog box.

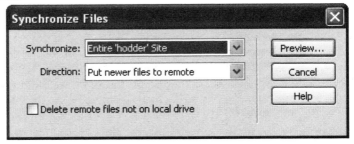

Figure 12.17 Synchronize Files dialog box

You may select from the **Synchronize** menu either the current site or **Selected Local Files Only** – the latter requires that you first select a file or files in the Files panel.

Depending on the outcome of this activity, you may then select the Direction for any subsequent actions taken – **Put newer files to remote** (send), **Get newer files from remote** (receive) or **Get and Put newer files** (send and receive).

A useful action is **Delete remote files not on local drive** which will initiate a 'tidy up', if you have (perhaps for testing purposes) previously moved files to the remote site which you subsequently deleted from the local folder.

Whichever option you select, click the **Preview...** button because Dreamweaver will not take any action without you first seeing the possible impact of the requested action.

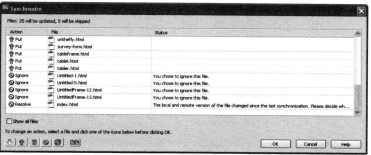

Figure 12.18 Synchronize preview

Having selected **Put newer files to remote**, the screenshot shows files in different states. There is also a summary which here shows that 25 files will be updated and five will be skipped.

Files marked with an Action of **Put** are newer on the local system and have been identified for upload to the remote system; the files marked **Ignore** have been manually set using the toolbar at the base of the dialog box (click on a filename then on the **Ignore selected files during this synchronization** button) – as these are just dummy test files I do not want to upload them; finally the file marked **Resolve** requires some investigative action as both local and remote versions have changed since the last synchronization so you need to decide which one is correct.

The buttons at the base of the dialog box allow you to change the Action selected by Dreamweaver if you wish (and, more importantly, if you know what you are doing and why).

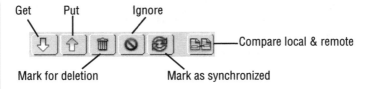

Figure 12.19 Synchronize buttons

Select the file(s) and click a button to change the Action.

The **Compare local and remote** action requires that you have a file compare program and it is defined in Preferences (**Edit > Preferences...** then select from the Category list **File Compare**).

Click **OK** and the selected action will be performed for each file. The result of the synchronization is shown below; only five files remain. I have now determined that the file *index.html* should be copied from the local to the remote system; therefore, I have manually changed the **Action** to **Put** using the button.

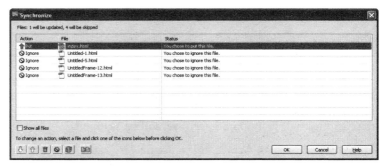

Figure 12.20 Post-synchronization preview

If **OK** is clicked, the file will be copied to the remote system and the only difference between the two will be the files I chose to Ignore.

To check the synchronization details for individual files, right-click the filename in the **Files** panel and select **Display Synchronize Information** (Figure 12.21).

As you can see, Dreamweaver's synchronize functionality is a powerful means of maintaining local and remote file versions.

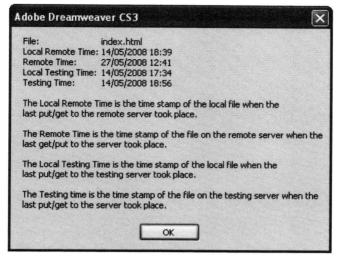

Figure 12.21 Synchronize details for the file index.html.

Summary

If you have followed all of the activities in this chapter, you should now be able to:

- Prepare your site by eliminating annoying mistakes (certainly to the visitor so ultimately to you as well!) such as spelling errors and broken links

- Determine whether your site may have browser compatibility issues prior to release

- Make sure your site is as accessible as Dreamweaver can make it

- Amend your site definition to include your hosting provider's details

- Upload your site to the server and check that the upload has been successful

- Prevent files or folders from being uploaded by cloaking

- Keep your local and remote site folders synchronized.

appendices

A: Useful resources

Some of these resources have been mentioned in the course of the book, but I wanted to bring them all together into one section.

As you will probably be aware, there are likely to be hundreds of sites which provide information on the topics listed below. There is a danger in listing too many resources – you would probably find the list overwhelming and not use any of the sites at all. I have therefore restricted the list to what I consider to be the most useful sites that I use. They are not in a significant order, just the order I happened to write them in.

Of course, don't forget Dreamweaver's excellent built-in Help facility as well.

1 The Dreamweaver section of Adobe's website provides you with a wealth of materials, as you might expect. Start at this address:

   http://www.adobe.com/products/dreamweaver/

   and you have access to tutorials, articles, extensions, documentation, resolutions of product problems. All levels of user are catered for so don't imagine that it is only for advanced users.

2 W3 Schools provides fantastic, user-friendly and detailed introductions to a wide variety of web technologies including HTML, XHTML, CSS, Javascript and XML. There are even quizzes to test your knowledge. Start here:

   http://www.w3schools.com/

and select the technology which interests you from the left-hand navigation bar.

3 As the developer of web standards and guidelines, the World Wide Web Consortium (W3C) provides essential documentation relating to, amongst many others, HTML, CSS, Accessibility and XML. Start here:

http://www.w3.org/

and select a topic from the right-hand navigation bar.

4 You might be interested to learn that the W3C also provides validators for HTML and CSS at:

http://validator.w3.org/ (HTML)

http://jigsaw.w3.org/css-validator/ (CSS)

A validator checks your code (which is either written by Dreamweaver or by you) to determine whether it matches the language rules established by the W3C. While it is not essential to use these tools, you can, if your code passes either or both validation process, add a logo to your site indicating compliance with one or both. This has the benefit of advertising your adherence to standards and perhaps encouraging others to go down the same path.

5 Web Page Design for Designers hosts a wide variety of useful links to information about the use of colour, CSS layouts, typography and accessibility at:

http://www.wpdfd.com/resources/

6 Webmonkey is useful for all levels of web developers and designers, containing as it does tutorials, code snippets and reference material; the address is:

http://www.webmonkey.com/

7 Although the site design is quirky to say the least (for reasons justified by the author), Jakob Nielsen's site at:

http://www.useit.com/

is an invaluable resource for usability issues. Usability is vitally important for anyone creating a website.

8 An excellent online CSS reference manual has recently been released by SitePoint at:

   http://reference.sitepoint.com/css

   You might also wish to subscribe to one or more of their newsletters. These are informative and represent the latest developments in all aspects of web development, from marketing to technology.

9 Once you become more familiar with CSS, you might find some of these sites inspiring:

   http://www.alistapart.com/ (A List Apart)

   http://www.csszengarden.com/ (CSS Zen Garden)

   http://meyerweb.com/eric/css/ (Eric Meyer)

10 As a final point, don't discount the written word. I have found over the years that the magazine .net provides consistently good articles and forums for all web-related topics. I have not yet found an equivalent or one that even comes close. The web address is:

   http://www.netmag.co.uk/

B: What next?

This book has concentrated on the essential functionality you need to get a site up and running. The emphasis has been on static pages – a term which was defined early in the book, meaning pages that do not change between one visitor's viewing and another's. Even the use of behaviors and Spry do not make your pages dynamic; they become more interactive, but still the fundamental page content is the same for each visitor.

At some stage you will almost certainly want to, or be asked to, build a site containing dynamic pages. The transition to dynamic pages can be made using Dreamweaver as it contains a great deal of functionality to help you build a dynamic site. You do need other software though:

* **Web server** – receives, and responds to, requests for web pages e.g. Apache, IIS

* **Database** – repository of permanently stored, changing data e.g. MySQL, SQL Server

* **Application interface** – handles database requests and inserts data into HTML pages e.g. PHP, ASP .NET

Depending on the specific requirements of your site, these may be sourced from a range of different places, some commercial and some open source. A comprehensive, easy-to-install package called XAMPP is available from the Apache Friends site at **http://www.apachefriends.org/en/xampp-windows.html**. This would provide you with all of the additional software you need (Apache, MySQL and PHP).

Dreamweaver has some useful explanations under 'Preparing to build dynamic sites' in the main Help file. Other sections deal with how to go about creating dynamic pages.

Building dynamic pages can be a highly complex activity, requiring hand coding, but the simpler requirements such as displaying data can be easily achieved using Dreamweaver.

Once you have mastered the contents of this book, why not try dynamic pages?

Good luck!

C: Answers to exercises

Chapter 2

1 If you had problems with this exercise, you should review the section of this chapter relating to file creation. In summary, what you need to do is make sure that the site name appears in the Files panel window then click **File > New...** After each file is created it will be given a name of *Untitled* followed by a number; make sure you save the file (**File > Save**) and give it a meaningful name. When you have finished, all of the files created will appear in the Files panel.

Other ways to create files:

♦ In the Files panel, right-click and select **New File** – the file will automatically be named *untitled.html*, *untitled2.html*, etc. To change the name, right click on the file name and select **Edit > Rename** – type in a new meaningful name, making sure you retain the suffix *.html*. If you lose it, you will not be able to display the page in a browser.

♦ Use the shortcut **[Ctrl]+[N]** (Windows) or **[Command]+[N]** (Mac).

2 Look at the **Edit** menu. The Windows shortcut is **[Ctrl]+[U]**; for Macs, **[Command]+[U]**.

3 Use your search engine to find browsers – examples are Firefox, Internet Explorer, Opera, Safari. Make sure that you download the right version for your operating system!

4 In the browser header – look at the header when you open a page in the browser. If you have no page title defined, you will see 'Untitled Document' – this should never happen!

5 Look at the **File** menu. The Windows shortcut is **[Ctrl]+[S]**; for Macs, **[Command]+[S]**.

Chapter 3

1 To start and end the document you normally need <html> and </html>. XHTML documents have a DOCTYPE statement which precedes the <html> tag. There are then two main

sections, head and body which are defined by the \<head\> and \<body\> tags, and their respective closing tags \</head\> and \</body\>. Within the \<head\> area, you should also have a title tag \<title\> together with a meaningful page title and a closing tag \</title\>.

2   An attribute modifies the default behavior of a tag. An example is the paragraph tag \<p\> which by default aligns all paragraph contents on the left of the page. An attribute is used, e.g. align="center", to modify this behavior.

3   This is not valid XHTML. There are several problems – the tag names should always be lower case; opening tags should always have a matching closing tag; attribute values must always be in quotes. The code should look like this:

```
<p align="center">This is a paragraph</p>
<p>So is this</p>
```

This is now valid XHTML.

4   The \<font\> tag is deprecated, which means that at some stage in the future it will be dropped from the HTML language specification. When this might be is impossible to say, but in the meantime use should be made of CSS for all font-related settings. There are other deprecated tags, such as \<center\> which centres content, which is likely to be the only one other than \<font\> that you are likely to come across. See HTML Goodies at **http://www.htmlgoodies.com/tutorials/html_401/html4-ref/article.php/3460291** for more details.

5   These tags embolden and italicise the text that follows them. You may come across the alternatives \<b\> and \<i\> respectively. Dreamweaver can use either – see **Edit > Preferences…** and then choose **Category** of **General**; there is a checkbox which controls usage of one set or the other. It is recommended to stick with \<strong\> and \<em\>. In reality, \<strong\> and \<b\> are not for exactly the same purpose though the browser will interpret them in the same way; this is also true of \<em\> and \<i\>.

6   There is no purpose because aligning text on the left is the paragraph tag's default behavior.

Chapter 4

1 Look at the document window Status bar and you will see the page size followed by an estimated download time, e.g. 10K/1 sec. You can adjust the default download speed through **Edit > Preferences > Status Bar** and clicking the drop-down list of pre-configured speeds. Remember that not everyone uses broadband yet!

2 A bit of a trick question as the answer is not in Dreamweaver. While you can amend the size of images in Dreamweaver, the only way to resize them correctly is using an image editor such as Fireworks or Photoshop. Increasing the size of your image using Dreamweaver alone may result in distortion.

3 **Align.** You first must select the image and then the option you want from the **Align** drop-down menu.

4 **Alt.** The Alt attribute should always be set by you for this purpose. To ensure you do so, check that the accessibility options are selected (**Edit > Preferences > Accessibility**) – if they are you have no excuse for ignoring the prompts!

5 As always with Dreamweaver there are many ways in which to achieve the same result. Here are four methods: using the image icon in the Common toolbar; use the menu bar (**Insert > Image**); use a shortcut ([Ctrl]+[Alt]+[I]); drag and drop. The last option means that you can literally drag the image from the Files panel and drop it onto the page.

6 The correct answer is d. Note that b will have no impact on the underlying file size.

Chapter 5

1 **Link.** Always make sure that you have first selected the text which is to become the link.

2 **#toc.** The leading # is important; if you omit it, the link will not work.

3 Go to the Link box, highlight the link text and delete it. Remember to hit [Enter] after deletion or Dreamweaver may not carry out the change.

4 Select the image and use the **Align Center** icon in the Properties panel.

5 The image will be returned to its original setting, i.e. the height and width used when it was created. Using this option means you do not need to remember the original size.

Chapter 6

1 False – you can do both.

2 Justify does not work at the paragraph level, so you need to apply justification at the cell or row level. Select either and then click the **Justify** icon in the Properties panel.

3 The hint probably gave this away. In the **Layout** panel of the **Insert** toolbar is the **Expanded** button. Position the mouse anywhere in the table and click this. Work on the table becomes much easier, particularly the selection of rows and columns.

4 This is HTML code for a non-breaking space. In a table, its presence stops individual cells from collapsing which could adversely affect its appearance when displayed in a browser.

5 In Standard view you can set border and background image properties, as well as row and column properties; in Layout view you have the option to create fixed or autostretch cells as well as the height.

6 The former gives you more control over the placement (before or after the current selection) and allows the insertion of multiple rows or columns. The latter inserts a single column to the left of, or a row above, the current selection. To add a single row or column and choose where it is inserted, you could also use **Insert > Table Objects** and select from Insert Row Above/ Below, Insert Column to The Left/ to The Right.

Chapter 7

1 Yes this is possible. Tag would redefine the HTML <p> tag. Class could be called .p and Advanced could be similarly named, #p. Tag would automatically apply to any instance of the <p> tag in the page. Class and Advanced (ID) would

only apply if 'attached' to the paragraph. If you attach Class or Advanced, the styles defined will override similar styles in the Tag definition. Do not attach both a Class and Advanced definition to the same page element (if you do, Advanced will take precedence) – one or the other, depending on whether or not they are to be reused in the page, is sufficient.

2   Yes, it is possible to add multiple style sheets to a page. The impact is not dissimilar to the previous question – the order (reversed) in which they are added determines the precedence of application. Precedence is determined by proximity to the page element, so in-line styles would take precedence over in-page which would therefore take precedence over style sheets. Let's take an example where a page contains a rule for the <p> tag in three places.

```
p {color: blue; }
```

defined in attached style sheet

```
<style type="text/css">
```

defined within <head> tags

```
p {color: green; }
</style>
<p style="color: red;">What colour am I?</p>
```

What colour would the text within the <p> tags be? Answer – red; reason – this definition is nearest to the page element. Remove the in-line style and the colour would be green. Finally, if only the style sheet defines a rule for the <p> tag, the text would be blue.

If two or more style sheets are attached to the page which define the colour of a <p> tag, then the colour will be applied in the order in which the style sheets appear in the code. The last definition will take precedence.

3   Click on the style sheet name in the CSS Styles panel and then click the Dustbin symbol at the base of the panel which will unlink the style sheet. (Note that the file is not deleted.)

4   Amend an existing rule or create one and in **Category Type** set the **Case rule** to uppercase or capitalize respectively.

5 False. Programming languages have, for example, the ability to determine text values in a field, make decisions based on that value and store the data in a database (among many thousands of other functions); CSS and HTML are able to create forms and define an input box into which data may be entered but they are unable to do anything with the data.

Chapter 8

Listed in Figure C.1 is the content of the style sheet file used for the form. By all means experiment with the CSS as this is an excellent way of seeing how it works.

The **ID Selector #holder** contains all of the page contents.

The form is contained within a 2-column table, 550 pixels wide. The first column is 175 pixels wide and the second 375 pixels wide.

Remember that, with a Class or Advanced (ID Selector), you decide where to add the rules. The following statements give an indication of where to add the rules, either to the <tr> or the <td> tag.

The Class used to define the mandatory rows (attached to <tr> tag) is **.required.**

The Class used to define the labels (First Name, etc., attached to <td> tag) is **.lbl.**

The Class used to define all of the form controls (text fields, radio buttons, etc., attached to <td> tag) is **.inp.**

Specific ID Selectors are also applied to the radio buttons (#radio_buttons), checkboxes (#checkboxes) and submit button (#submit_button) attached to <td> tags.

Chapter 9

1 Let's look at each of the requirements in turn:

Custom class

I created a class called .ul; its only rule is as shown in the screenshot in Figure C.2

```
1    /* ********************  PAGE LAYOUT  ******************** */
2
3    body {
4         font-family: Arial, Helvetica, sans-serif;
5         padding: 15px;
6         background: #DAE6EF; }
7
8    /* ********************  CONTAINER  ******************** */
9
10   #holder {
11        width: 550px;
12        padding-left: 15px;
13        border: 1px solid #666666;}
14
15   /* ********************  HEADING  ******************** */
16
17   h1 {font-size: 150%;
18        font-style: italic;}
19
20   /* ********************  TABLE  ******************** */
21
22   td {padding: 2px;}
23
24   .required .lbl {
25        background: #999999;
26        border-right: 6px double #666666;
27        color: #FFFFFF; }
28   .lbl {
29        background: #666666;
30        border-right: 6px double black;
31        font-size: 12px;
32        font-weight: bold;
33        text-align: right;
34        padding-right: 5px;
35        color: #FFFFFF; }
36   .inp {padding-left: 10px;
37        font-size: 2ems; }
38
39   /* ********************  FORM ELEMENTS  ******************** */
40
41   .select {width: 125px;
42        background: #CCCCCC;
43        border: 1px solid black; }
44   #radio_buttons {font-size: 11px;
45        font-weight: bold;
46        text-align: left;
47        background-color:#CCCCCC; }
48   #checkboxes {font-size: 11px;
49        font-weight: bold;
50        text-align: left;
51        background-color:#CCCCCC; }
52   #submit_button {padding-left: 200px; }
```

Figure C.1   The style sheet file used for the form

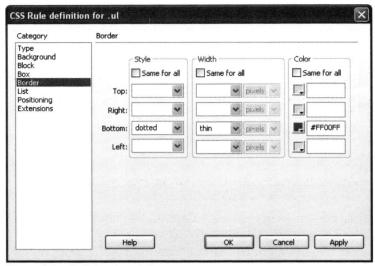

Figure C.2 Defining the .ul class

Apply class

Select the text in Design view and apply the custom class ul from the Style drop-down menu in the Properties panel.

Look in Code view and you will see that the selected text is now contained within <span> tags. The actual tag will read <span class="ul">.

Add title

This has to be done in Code view. Position the cursor after 'class="ul"' in the <span> tag. Enter a space and then start typing 'title' – Dreamweaver's attribute helper should be displayed as soon as you have typed the initial letter 't'. Select by double-clicking, then enter your required text between the double quotes.

The end result should look something like this in Code view:

```
<span title="Creating a site will always take
place before pages are created. A site contains
everything - images, text, forms, style sheets
etc." class="ul">site creation.</span>
```

Save it and open it in a browser. Hover over the marked text and you should now see the additional text which you added to the title attribute.

2   Before doing anything else, you need to have your images prepared. As there are four link states, you need (ideally) four versions of the image – they should certainly all be the same size. In theory, of course, you could get away with a single image but by doing this you would lose the link effects.

Let's assume we have four images then. Mine looks like this. The other three versions are the same with the exception of the background colour. You would need to create these images in Fireworks or Photoshop.

First, insert what Dreamweaver calls your Up image (this corresponds with the Link state, i.e. unvisited). With the image still selected, go to the Behaviors panel and select **Set Nav Bar Image**. You will see this dialog box:

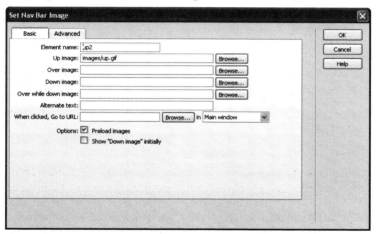

Dreamweaver assigns an Element name, which you may change, and adds the name of the inserted image to the **Up image** box. Add other details as required and some Alternate text for accessibility purposes. Finally, add the details of the link page in **When clicked, Go to URL**. Click **OK** to finish.

Three behaviors will have been added to the Behaviors panel if you have configured four images.

Save it and test in a browser. The number of images you have used will dictate the behaviour of the navigation link.

Chapter 10

1 There is no answer! If you have not created a template yet, there is no time like the present. If you are having trouble, then look back through this chapter. This is a really important topic so don't ignore it.

2 If you have not managed to find the relevant colour palette, go to Preferences, choose the **Category** of **Highlighting** and you will see the palette alongside the label **Editable regions**.

Chapter 11

1 Your final menu bar might look something like this in Design view:

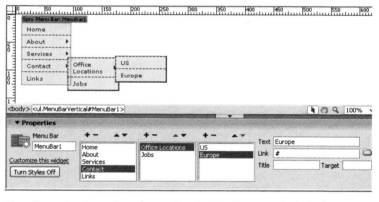

To adjust the font size, go to the CSS Styles panel with the menu bar selected and click font-size in the Properties for "ul.Menu-BarVertical" panel. You can then amend the percentage to 80.

If you are really stuck, and your end result looks significantly different, compare your code with mine (Figure C.3).

2 Figure C.4 shows a sample page. I have chosen to use a tabbed panel with colours blending with those of the template.

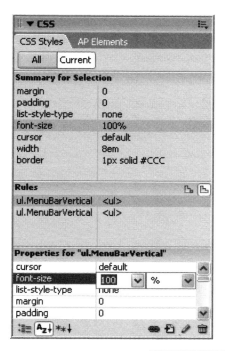

CSS Styles

Browser view

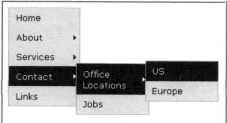

You will undoubtedly want to change the colours from the default grey so let's look at how this is done. After adding the tabbed panel in Design view, simply click in one of the tabs and, in the Properties panel, change the background colour using the Bg colour palette. This does not affect the background colour of the currently active tab. In the example, the Consultancy tab is active as this is the default panel when the page loads. You can do exactly the same with the contents area – simply click anywhere in the contents area and again change the background colour using the Bg palette.

```
11   <ul id="MenuBar1" class="MenuBarVertical">
12     <li><a href="#">Home</a>        </li>
13     <li><a href="#" class="MenuBarItemSubmenu">About</a>
14       <ul>
15         <li><a href="#">Board of Directors</a></li>
16         <li><a href="#">Management Team</a></li>
17         <li><a href="#">News</a></li>
18       </ul>
19     </li>
20     <li><a class="MenuBarItemSubmenu" href="#">Services</a>
21       <ul>
22         <li><a href="#">Consultancy</a>        </li>
23         <li><a href="#" class="MenuBarItemSubmenu">Support Services</a>
24           <ul>
25             <li><a href="#">Contact</a></li>
26             <li><a href="#">Login</a></li>
27           </ul>
28         </li>
29       </ul>
30     </li>
31     <li><a href="#" class="MenuBarItemSubmenu">Contact</a>
32       <ul>
33         <li><a href="#" class="MenuBarItemSubmenu">Office Locations</a>
34           <ul>
35             <li><a href="#">US</a></li>
36             <li><a href="#">Europe</a></li>
37           </ul>
38         </li>
39         <li><a href="#">Jobs</a></li>
40       </ul>
41     </li>
42     <li><a href="#">Links</a></li>
43   </ul>
```

Figure C.3 CSS code for a menu bar

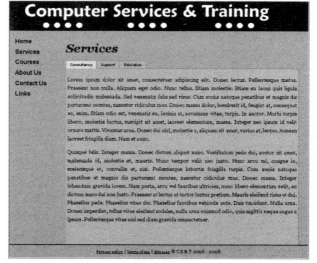

Figure C.4 Sample page

3 The XML data set structure would look like this if you followed the specified requirements (the tag names are of course of your own choosing):

```
1   <?xml version="1.0" encoding="utf-8"?>
2   <books>
3       <book>
4           <title>Napoleon's Retreat from Moscow 1812</title>
5           <author>S. J. Greene</author>
6           <publication>1998</publication>
7           <price>£27.50</price>
8           <precis>Lorem ipsum dolor sit amet, consectetuer adipiscing elit.</precis>
9       </book>
10      <book>
11          <title>Radicalism in England, 1790 - 1832</title>
12          <author>P. Ratcliff</author>
13          <publication>2002</publication>
14          <price>£17.95</price>
15          <precis>Mauris iaculis lectus id ante. Aenean sed tellus ac sapien sagittis volutpat.
    Praesent ullamcorper.</precis>
16      </book>
17  </books>
```

Remember that you need a root element; in this case mine is called <books>. The details of each book are defined within the opening and closing <book> tags – this is in fact, a row. I saved my file as *books.xml*.

Create a new HTML page and add the XML file you have created as a new data set.

When displayed in the browser, my page looks like this (with a hover class added):

Title		Description
'Orator' Hunt and Peterloo	Author:	J. C. Williams
Life of Napoleon	Date of Publication:	1987
Napoleon's Retreat from Moscow 1812	Price:	£15
Radicalism in England, 1790 - 1832	Summary:	Lorem ipsum dolor sit amet, consectetuer adipiscing elit. Mauris iaculis lectus id ante. Aenean sed tellus ac sapien sagittis volutpat. Praesent ullamcorper. Integer quis sapien a augue condimentum dapibus. Sed sem. In mauris elit, bibendum vitae, blandit ac, pharetra vehicula, neque. Morbi ante nibh, volutpat et, scelerisque sed, laoreet et, nulla. Integer varius. Cras ac erat. Donec ultricies.
William Cobbett: From Plough to Parliament		

To get this, I followed these steps after creating the data set:

1 Insert a div and in the dialog box, enter an ID of *title*.

2 Create an ID selector called *#title* (in the CSS Styles panel, click the **New CSS Rule** icon) with the following settings:

   Font: Georgia

   Size: small

   Width: 300 pixels

   Float: left

3 Insert another div with an ID of *details*.

4 Create an ID selector called *#details* with these settings:

> Font: Georgia
>
> Size: small
>
> Width: 500 pixels
>
> Float: left
>
> Margin Left: 50 pixels

Make sure that the two sets of <div> tags are not nested. They should look like this in Code view:

```
 8   <body>
 9   <div id="title">Content for  id "title" Goes Here</div>
10   <div id="details">Content for  id "details" Goes Here</div>
11   </body>
```

5 Select the text 'Content for id "title" Goes Here' in Design view and insert a Spry region then a Spry table (deleting all fields except *title* (my XML tag for the book title) and make sure **Update detail regions when row is clicked** is selected). This resulted in a 1-column, 2-row table being displayed in Design view.

6 Change the width of the table to match the div width, 300 pixels, by clicking <table> in the Status bar below Design view (it should be already selected as it has just been added) and entering a **W** value of 300.

7 Select the text 'Content for id "details" Goes Here' in Design view and insert a Spry region, this time making sure I select the **Detail region** under **Type**.

8 Still with the text selected, insert a table with 5 rows and columns and a width of 500 pixels (to match the div width).

9 Add a heading 'Description' after merging the cells in the first row.

10 Add text in column 1 of rows 2–5 as labels for the content which will appear in column 2 of these rows.

11 Drag the fields from the **Bindings** panel into column 2.

12 Align the tables in the two divs by ensuring they each have the same CellPad, CellSpace and Border settings (5, 0 and 0 respectively).

index

absolute links **107–8**
accessibility
    and colour **72**
    and forms **213, 214**
    and images **77–9**
    checking **323–4**
accordion panels (Spry) **291, 295**
ActiveX controls **94**
Adobe Extension Manager **227**
advanced rule definition (CSS)
    172–6
advanced selector (CSS) **155,
    157–9**
Ajax **265**
alternate text (images) **79**
anchor links **108–11**
animation **256–62**
AP Div elements **246**
    animating **256–9**
    dragging **253–5**
    overlapping **250–3**
    showing/hiding **247–50**
AP Elements panel **248**
appear/fade effect (Spry) **265–7**
Apple Safari browser **7**
applets, adding **92**
assets **23, 25, 26**
attributes (HTML) **46**
    format **47, 51**
autostretch (table column) **145–7**

background colour **47, 61–2**

behaviors **236**
    benefits **237**
    deprecated **238**
    example of adding **237–40**
    for form validation **222–7**
Behaviors panel **237, 239–40**
<body> tag **47**
box model of CSS **186**

 tag **67, 139**
broken links, checking for **321**
Browse in Bridge (CS3) **36**
browsers
    and plug-ins **94**
    compatibility checking **322–3**
    differences between **6, 42**
    for site testing **6–7, 42**
    preview preference **40–2**
Browsershots **7**
buttons in forms **210, 218–19**

Cascading Style Sheets *see* CSS
cell spacing and padding **131–4**
Check Form extension **227–9**
checkboxes (forms) **210, 218**
    Spry-validated variant **302–4**
class rule definition (CSS) **168–70**
class selector (CSS) **155, 156**
Clear (CSS Box property) **185**
cloaking files **329, 330**
Code view of page **33, 34**
    direct coding in **53–5**
    linkage with Design view **50–1**

Coder layout of workspace **15**
collapsible panels (Spry) **291, 294**
colour
  usage **72**
  web-safe **73–4**
colour palette **68–9**
Commands function **97–8**
Common toolbar **76**
copyright message (library item)
    284–5
CSS **151**
  advantages **151, 153–4**
  and Dreamweaver **161**
  and predefined pages
      193–200
  generated code **62–3, 69**
  methods of applying **159–61**
  overview **151–3**
  page creation with **200–6**
  resources **339**
  syntax **153–9**
  validator for **338**
  versions **152**
CSS rules **153**
  defining new **163–5**
  order of definition **174**
  precedence **171–2**
  property catalogue **180–90**
CSS Styles panel **163, 165–8,
    170–1**
custom class *see* class selector

data sets, display of XML **306–17**
decoration of text (CSS) **174, 182**
deprecated
  Dreamweaver behaviors **238**
  HTML tags **52, 123**
Design Notes **37**
Design view of page **33, 34**
  linkage with Code view **50–1**
Designer layout of workspace
    15–16
disjointed rollover (behavior)
    241–4
<div> tag **195, 246**

docked and undocked **13, 20**
document window **14**
dragging elements (behavior)
      250–3
Dreamweaver
  Adobe resources for **337**
  alternatives to **4–5**
  benefits **3–4**
  evaluation and purchase **2–3**
  help **17–18, 55**
  installation **6**
  need to restart **18**
  overview **2**
  Photoshop integration **87–8**
  system requirements **5–6**
  welcome screen **13–14**
  workspace **10–16**
Dual Screen layout of workspace
    15–16
dynamic pages **31, 343**

editable attributes (templates)
    278–9
editable regions (templates)
    273–4, 276
  optional **283–4**
email links **111–12**
event-driven (behaviors) **237**
events **226, 236, 237**
  W3 Schools tutorial **237**
Expression Web (Microsoft) **4**
external links **107–8**

fade effect (Spry) **265–7**
field sets (forms) **232–3**
file fields (forms) **211, 232**
Files panel **12, 30–1**
  local/remote views **31, 328–9**
  map view **120**
  refresh icon **35**
Firefox as test browser **7, 42**
firewalls and Internet access **326**
Flash, adding **92, 93, 94**
Flash buttons as links **113–16**
Flash text as links **116–18**

Float (CSS Box property) **185**
folder structure **23–6**
font groups **64–5**
font sizing **68**
<font> tag **52**
fonts
    and visitor's computer **42,
        64–5**
    choosing **63–4**
    in Dreamweaver **51–3**
<form> tag **209**
FormMail program **220**
forms
    action on submit **220**
    content **209–11**
    creation **211–21, 229–32**
    formatting **221–2, 232–3**
    purpose **209**
    user-friendliness **233**
    validation **222–9, 295–304**
Forms toolbar **211**
frames/framesets **149**
FTP and Dreamweaver **325–6**

<head> tag **46**
heading styles **66–7**
hidden fields (forms) **210, 220–1**
hiding elements (behavior)
    245–50
History panel **96–8**
home page **24**
horizontal rule **141–2**
horizontal scrolling **20**
hotspots within images **118–19**
<hr> tag **142**
HTML **31**
    coding pages in **49–55**
    language overview **45–7**
    validator for **338**
    versus XHTML **31–2, 48–9**
    W3 Schools tutorial **8, 45**
<html> tag **46**
HyperText Markup Language
        see HTML
hyperlinks *see* links

ID rule definition (CSS) **172–3**
ID selector (CSS) **157–8**
images
    adding to page **75–9**
    editing in Dreamweaver **80,
        83–6**
    file formats **74–5**
    file size **75**
    placeholders for **90–1**
    positioning on page **81–3**
    properties **79–81**
    sourcing **26**
importing text from Word **39**
index page, significance of **35**
in-line CSS **159–60**
insert bar **10–11**
internal links **107**
Internet Explorer
    as test browser **7, 42**
    versions and CSS **193**

Javascript **222–3**
    and behaviors **236**
    for setting form focus **233**
    W3 Schools tutorial **236**
jigsaw CSS validator **338**
jump menus (forms) **210–11,
    229–32**

layers **246**
library items **284–7**
lines and paragraphs **67**
link states **106–7**
    and pseudo classes **158–9,
        173–6**
<link> tag **167, 192**
links **101**
    absolute **107–8**
    anchor **108–11**
    as menu **108**
    as navigation bar **103–5**
    attached to images **112**
    checking for broken **321**
    creating standard **101–3**
    email **111–12**

external **107–8**
internal **107**
relative **107**
using Flash buttons **113–16**
using Flash text **116–18**
liquid table sizing **124, 125**
lists
    in forms **210, 216–17, 300–2**
    in text **70–1**

menu bar (Spry) **304–6**
menus in forms *see* lists
meta tags **50**
Mozilla Firefox browser **7, 42**
Multiple IE installer **7**
multiple selections (forms) **217,
    303–4**

navigation bar creation
    with Flash buttons **113–16**
    with standard links **103–5**
navigation in Dreamweaver **8–9**
.net (magazine) **339**
notational conventions **8–9**
Nvu **4–5**

open new browser (behavior)
    262–4
Opera as test browser **7, 42**
<option> tag **221**
optional regions (templates)
    282–3
overlapping elements **250–3**

<p> tag **50–1, 67, 139**
page-level CSS **159, 160**
pages
    adding content **38–9**
    applying CSS to **173–9**
    applying template to **284**
    coding in (X)HTML **49–55**
    creating with CSS **200–6**
    creating with HTML **31–5**
    detaching from template **284**
    dynamic **31, 340**

formatting for printing **190–3**
HTML structure **46–7**
layout with tables **123, 124,
    136–42**
predefined **33, 193–6**
properties **60–3**
relevance of content **27**
static **31**
titling **38**
ways of viewing **34**
panels **12**
    in Spry **290–5**
paragraphs **50–1**
    and lines **67**
Photoshop integration **87–8**
popup message (behavior)
    239–40
Post method (forms) **212, 219**
<pre> tag **184**
predefined pages **33, 193–6**
Properties panel **14, 58–63**
pseudo class rule definition (CSS)
    173–6
pseudo classes (CSS) **158–9**

radio buttons/groups (forms) **210,
    215–16**
ready-made pages **33, 193–6**
redo **96**
reference documents **18, 55**
regions in Spry **314–16**
regions in templates
    editable **273–4, 276**
    editable optional **283–4**
    optional **282–3**
    repeating **280–1**
relative links **107**
repeating
    regions (templates) **280–1**
    tables (templates) **281–2**
replaying instructions **97**
rollover images (behavior) **240–5**
root folder **23**
rulers in Design view **19**

Safari as test browser **7**
screen resolution and page
      design **42**
select (Spry list/menu) **300–2**
<select> tag **221**
Shockwave files, adding **92**
show-hide elements (behavior)
      245–50
site
   checking **328–30**
   creation **27–31**
   folder structure **23–6**
   map **120–1**
   planning **27**
   retrieving files from **330–1**
   synchronizing local and
         remote **326, 331–5**
   uploading **327–8**
Site Definition panel **28**
sound, adding **94–6**
spacer image **145–7**
<span> tag **303**
special characters **71–2**
spelling **8**
   checking **320–1**
Split view of page **34**
Spry **265, 290**
   effects **265–7**
   menu bar **304–6**
   panels **290–5**
   regions **314–16**
   tables **315–16**
   toolbar **292, 296**
   validation **295–304**
   XML data set display **312–17**
Spry widgets **290**
Standard toolbar **35–6**
static pages **31**
static table sizing **124**
status bar message (behavior)
      264–5
Status bar of Design panel **19–20**
Style Rendering toolbar **192–3**
style sheet files (CSS) **160–1**
   and templates **274–5**

attaching to pages **167**
creating **166–7, 168**
editing **167–8**
media-specific **190–3**
synchronizing local and remote
      sites **326, 331–5**

tabbed panels (Spry) **290–4**
tables
   adding rows/columns **142–3**
   adding to page **125–30**
   deleting rows/columns **136**
   drawing in layout mode **143–7**
   for page layout **123, 124,
         136–42**
   formatting **125–6, 129–35**
   HTML tags **123, 184, 213**
   in Spry **315–16**
   nesting **135–6**
   sizing **124–5**
   terminology **124**
   versus CSS **123**
tag helper **53–4**
tag rule definition (CSS) **164–6**
tag selector (CSS) **155, 157**
tags (HTML) **45–6**
   deprecated **52, 123**
target of links **114**
<td> tag **123, 184, 213**
templates **270**
   and library items **284–7**
   attaching/detaching pages
         284
   changing **276–9**
   creating **270–5**
   using **275–6**
text fields (forms) **210, 214–15**
   adding prompts (behavior) **265**
   Spry-validated variant **296–9**
text formatting
   as image **65, 116–17**
   as list **70–1**
   using CSS **154–8, 160,
         162–6, 180–2**

using HTML **51, 58–62, 66–70, 154**
textareas (forms) **210, 217–18**
    Spry-validated variant **299–300**
TextPad (editor) **5**
<th> tag **184, 213**
timelines and animation **256–62**
<title> tag **46–7**
<tr> tag **123**

underline, usage **69–70**
undo **96**
undocked **13, 20**
uploading site **327–8**
Useit (usability guidance) **26, 338**

visual impairment *see* accessibility

W3 Schools resources **237**
web host, finding/selecting **324–5**
Web Page Design for Designers **338**

web photo album (CS3) **88–90**
web-safe colours **73–4**
web usability **26, 338**
Webmonkey **338**
website *see* site
workspace options **14–16**
World Wide Web Consortium (W3C) **32, 152**
    resources **338**

XML **306–7**
    display of data sets **308–17**
    W3 Schools tutorial **306**
XHTML **48**
    coding pages in **49–55**
    versus HTML **31–2, 48–9**
    W3 Schools tutorial **49**

Yaromat extension **228–9**

Z-index (CSS) **189**
    of AP Divs **246, 248, 250–3**